D0296525

7060004

_____ Designing for Change

To my parents
with thanks for all their support

Designing for Change

A Practical Guide to Business Transformation

Colin Bainbridge

JOHN WILEY & SONS

Chichester · New York · Brisbane · Toronto · Singapore

Other Wiley Editorial Offices

John Wiley & Sons, Inc., 605 Third Avenue,
New York, NY 10158-0012, USA

Jacaranda Wiley Ltd, 33 Park Road, Milton,
Queensland 4064, Australia

John Wiley & Sons (Canada) Ltd, 22 Worcester Road,
Rexdale, Ontario M9W 1L1, Canada

John Wiley & Sons (Asia) Pte Ltd, 2 Clementi Loop #02-01,
Jin Xing Distripark, Singapore 129809

Library of Congress Cataloging-in-Publication Data

Bainbridge, Colin.
    Designing for change : a practical guide to business
transformation / Colin Bainbridge.
        p.   cm.
    Includes bibliographical references and index.
    ISBN 0-471-96452-2 (cloth)
    1. Organizational change—Management.   2. Corporate
reorganizations—Management.   I. Title
HD58.8.B35   1996
658.4'063—dc20   96-28872
                                                                  CIP

British Library Cataloguing in Publication Data

A catalogue record for this book is available from the British Library

ISBN 0-471-96452-2

Typeset in 10/12pt Palatino by Dobbie Typesetting Ltd, Tavistock, Devon
Printed and bound in Great Britain by Biddles Ltd, Guildford and King's Lynn
This book is printed on acid-free paper responsibly manufactured from sustainable forestation,
for which at least two trees are planted for each one used for paper production.

Contents

Preface

Change is moving to the top of the corporate agenda. Our organisations and enterprises are being bombarded from every side by pressures for change, be they social or political, economic or technological. The results are manifest in various ways—new competitors enter the market-place and sweep away established customer bases, technology changes the rules about how business can be undertaken, legislation demands changes to the way in which products and services are delivered, and deregulation throws up whole new trading blocks and industry sectors. Behind it all the expectations of customers grow as they become ever more knowledgeable and demanding.

In the main, our organisations have been slow to respond, but competition is forcing a rude awakening, for in today's global shoot-out it is no longer possible to rest on the laurels of the past. Lifetime customers have suddenly become fickle, lured away by better service and lower prices. Barriers to entry have become flimsy and economies of scale can be overturned by technology, networks and outsourcing. If any one organisation does not respond to the pressures for change, then another one will.

In response, all sorts of changes are required to the way businesses and organisations are run and organised. New products have to be launched, and launched faster than ever before. Work has to be better organised and service has to be improved. New systems are required that can unlock corporate wells of data and exploit the information within them. The workforce has to be turned into a lithe, agile resource, which seizes the new opportunities of change rather than being dragged along behind them.

But it is no longer just the concept of change that is at the top of the corporate agenda. The real challenge of change is not spotting the need for it or even deciding on the direction to take. It is about making the changes happen in practice, and it is a challenge that our organisations are struggling to meet.

The problem with our organisations is that they are just not built for change. Worse still, many of them are actually built on the very premises that oppose change—bureaucracy and control, consistency and rigid functionalisation. The very structures that have served us for so long now chain us to the past. Procedures have become too complicated and the culture is one of resignation and acceptance rather than enthusiasm and innovation. People cling resolutely to what they know rather than setting out to discover what they don't know. And all too often they are accompanied by the disparate technology systems that disperse and divide our information—their threads run backwards and forwards through our organisations to act like reinforced concrete against change. Change is necessary, but we are struggling to make it happen.

In response, we have experimented with various approaches to help bring about change. In the late 1980s, it was Total Quality Management; followed by empowerment, which took place against a backdrop of downsizing and cost-cutting. More recently, we have seen an enthusiasm for Business Process Re-engineering or Business Process Redesign—call it what you will—which began to set a new tone for change. It came from the perspective that it was no use just fiddling and fixing; it was necessary to step back and take a much longer, more thoughtful, look at the whole picture—not just improvement and rationalisation, but how the whole issue of change could be addressed by looking at the underlying business processes within an enterprise. BPR focused on design, and in so doing shed a whole new light on change. It has heralded a new era of change, forcing our slumbering organisations to wake up and think afresh about what they are doing. BPR achieved some impressive results, and the concept of process is at the heart of this book.

But what all these methods failed to provide was a realistic approach to change. They were fine when it came to spotting what was wrong, and powerful when it came to looking for new ideas, but light when it came to implementation. Somehow such approaches managed to shrug off the real challenges. They failed to acknowledge the starting point from which change has to be made—the dirty, messy, complex, interrelated set of factors that our organisations are actually made up of. The prophets of BPR were silent when it came to coping with the 37 different functionally based computer systems with overlapping, inaccurate customer data. They were equally quiet when it came to the disenfranchised, weary staff who had been squeezed for every last ounce of performance in the cost-conscious late 1980s and early 1990s.

For these are the real challenges of making change happen. Change does not take place in the "greenfield" or start afresh environment. It might be possible to take a "clean sheet" during design, but few organisations are afforded the luxury of a fresh start in reality. Real change is about creating what you want from what you have, not just dreaming about what you might have one day. It is about making the changes when people, not surprisingly, are more insecure about their jobs and more cynical about what they hear than ever before. "We've heard that before," they say, and "we'll believe it when we see it".

The other problem is that change does not take place in a vacuum. All of the existing day to day activities, planned and unplanned, still go on. So the changes we are talking about have to be carried out on top of all the existing operational pressures. New products still have to be launched, competitors still have to be fought off, key people still get headhunted out of the organisation. This is the realistic face of change—and unless we face up to it, it will continue to thwart us.

The approach outlined within this book is about making change happen—not just thinking about it, talking about it and mapping it out on the boardroom walls, but making it happen. To do so, it acknowledges the realities of everyday organisational life and the fact that there is no such thing as a fresh start.

At the centre of the approach is an emphasis on processes, and process design. But it is an emphasis on processes that provides a route from start to finish, not just a design. It is concerned not with theoretical concepts but with the real capabilities that lie at the heart of our organisations—people and IT systems, procedures and management capabilities. It is by designing—and then building and implementing—these capabilities that we bring about change. But it is also about designing our organisations so that they can cope with change. Change is here to stay and we have to develop the capabilities to handle it and respond to it.

But at the same time, setting out to make such changes without a clear idea of how they affect ongoing, existing operations is like playing with fire. The holistic approach outlined in the following pages works because it acknowledges all parts of the enterprise—those that are not changing, as well as those that are. By doing so, it is able to cope with the problems that arise and control the complexities of real life.

Taking such an approach allows us to be realistic about change. It acknowledges that although it might be desirable to sweep aside the existing IT architecture, corporate policy or limited budget may prevent us from doing so. It acknowledges that during the change programme operational aspects still have to take priority, and it addresses the fact that people might be cynical about change, fed up with the hollow promises from management, which have failed to deliver any real improvement.

This book sets out an approach rather than a rigid sequence of steps for transformation. You cannot expect to open the covers, follow through from beginning to end, crank the handle and transform your organisation. Change is not like that. Just as you cannot produce a manual telling an engineer how to go out and build a new motorway, so you cannot produce a book that sets out every step required on the route of business transformation.

What this book presents is a methodology which can be adapted to individual organisations. It shows how to design what is required—and then how to specify those changes, build new components and capabilities and ultimately roll them out. But the approach can be tailored in line with different requirements. Every organisation (and every organisation's history) is different, and a holistic design, such as that provided by process-led change, ensures that each organisation can formulate a different response.

But the more structured stages that a design-led approach to change provides are inseparable from the softer issues of change. This book therefore also focuses on understanding and managing the softer, more intangible issues of change—not just what you have to produce and how you produce it, but how you change culture, manage a team, remove the roadblocks and address the resistance that surfaces along the way.

The book is divided into four parts. Part I explores the challenges of change our organisations face and, in particular, the future of change: for change is no longer something we just do once—we have to get used to doing it continually. It considers a response, in the form of a broad process-led design, which can incorporate the full range of complexities present in our organisations.

Part II addresses the concept of design. It shows how a design can be produced that not only sets out the new ways of working but is robust enough to specify the changes required across the whole business infrastructure. Because the design is holistic, it ensures that it is possible to respond to change in an integrated manner that can fully exploit the capabilities at hand. More importantly, it can cope with the realities of existing organisations, and provide a path to untangling the existing complexities and rearranging them in a new order.

Part III is concerned with the design and development of the new capability. It shows how the development of new IT systems, the modification of culture and the retraining and re-skilling of staff is carried out—but carried out to a formula rather than by bit parts. The design is used to drive the changes right from outline to completion.

In Part IV, the skills and approaches that enable process-led change to take place are examined. These include the actual deployment and roll-out of new processes and their underlying capabilities, and the competencies in programme management and communication which ensure they happen and prevent the organisation from going off the rails during the change programme.

The approach documented in the main text is also supplemented by 'Signposts for Success' which address some of the more intangible aspects of major change projects. Although the book does not present a step by step methodology, the approach is presented in a chronological manner, leading from vision to design and on to development and implementation. There are, however, many parts of such change that have to be carried out in parallel. It is as important to cover the chapters on programme management and communication as it is to cover those on design, before attempting to implement such principles in practice.

Finally, a word about buzzwords: a lot of management books pepper their pages with new concepts (holons, virtual corporations and fishnet organisations—to name but a few—have emerged in the past few years alone). Whether these buzzwords are new at all, or merely old ideas re-badged, is sometimes questionable. Either way, often they seem to confuse and obscure rather than enlighten.

This book sets out an approach to change, in both design and implementation, and in so doing also demystifies the whole notion of process. Behind it is a firm belief that we do not really need any more new ideas and concepts. We already have enough terms, models and frameworks to explain how people should be managed and IT systems developed. What we need is a better way of managing change to all of them, and a comprehensive way of bringing them all together again. Wherever possible, therefore, existing conventions and terminology are used.

Change is happening and change is necessary. But the message is that change can be achieved. We have to produce a design that maps out the face of change, and use that design to drive forward the changes that follow, building new capabilities and shaping new competencies. Because the design is holistic, it can be used to respond to existing demands and cope with change itself. Ultimately, the design is used to pull the components back together again once they have been built. The complexities are many, interruptions will occur, and there will be deviations but there is a way forward—by Designing for Change.

Acknowledgements

The completion of a book requires the contribution, support and feedback of many others. First and foremost, acknowledgement must go to Martin Webster (now at Ernst and Young) who had such a firm belief in the need for a book that talked about the realities rather than the theories of designing for and implementing change. As well as supplying the initial enthusiasm to get the project underway, he continued to provide input and ideas during the long months of writing, not to mention a very important "away-from-it-all environment" for the final few months at the keyboard.

Then there are the colleagues—both consultants and clients—with whom I have worked over the years on various assignments. With them I shared long days on projects and sometimes long sessions late into the night, working around the issues and the problems and, most importantly, the solutions. The styles were many and varied but the experience and debate were always valuable. They are Jean Althoff, Colin Bryant, Ian Faulkner, Jerry ("push the pace") Foley, Martin Heath, David Jackson, Richard Jarvis, Al Jawara, Steve Kirk, Vince Long, Faye Powell, Di Law, Darren Stephens and Nigel Vince, to name but a few, and many other colleagues past and present too numerous to mention.

During the research into various organisations which had undertaken major change programmes, many people shared the lessons—both good and bad—learned during their change and process redesign programmes. Thanks go to Peter Homa, Patricia Vaz, Andy Burton, Denise Feltham, Alan Field, Jane Goldstein, Huw Jones, Frances Ive, Sylvie Jackson, John McKenzie, John Pryor and John Richardson.

Thanks also to Martin Heath and Jon Ellis who found time to provide further feedback and suggestions during the review and revision time, and to Hermoni Edwards and Chris Preston who provided advice on the actual writing process. The finished product of course, never happens without the publisher, the team at Wiley, Geoff Farrell, Alison Mead, Claire Plimmer and Diane Taylor, who helped to bring the whole project together.

Finally there are those who offered encouragement and support in various other ways during the long days of writing and revising. Thanks are due to them for their input, their support and their ideas—or merely the light relief they provided from the late nights of toil at the keyboard—they know who they are.

Part I

Change: Problems and Responses

Chapter 1

Aspects of Change

A WORLD OF CHANGE

Change, it seems, is everywhere. In our organisations we are changing the way we produce our goods, and modifying the way we deliver our services. In our governments changes to polices and legislation alter the way society operates, removing monopolies, opening new markets and creating new opportunities. In our working life, the nature of the job itself is changing, the prospect of a long-term career replaced by short-term contracts, and demands for new skills and abilities. And beneath it all, the rapid advances in information technology change the rules about how we communicate and who we are able to communicate with.

Evidence of this change emerges around us in ever more surprising forms. What was once the norm is turned on its head, and what we once took for granted can no longer be assumed. Computer corporations merge with publishing houses and film companies in the race to capitalise on the convergence between multiple media. Entrepreneurial start-ups take on mighty established players and win. Football clubs become quoted companies on the stock market, making more profit from merchandising than from spectators. Hospitals struggle with the principles of market forces, learning to set budgets and identifying their purchasers and suppliers. Customers demand service in hours, not days; they are no longer prepared to accept poor quality goods or shoddy service. Foreign competitors sneak in over the telephone wires or the computer screens to steal market share and customers. All around us, change is happening, and happening at a relentless pace that leaves us struggling to make sense of it all. Sometimes it is hard to keep up.

In this fast moving, volatile environment our organisations are struggling to cope. Working methods are no longer appropriate, a legacy of the past 10, 20 or even 50 years rather than a competency for the present. Organisational structures have become stagnant, reflecting the days of bureaucracy and functionalisation, where information was passed from hand to hand rather than screen to screen, and turnaround was expected in weeks, not hours. Management and control structures inhibit rather than encourage, and reward structures and career paths still reflect the expectations of decades gone by. And despite our sustained and expensive efforts to the contrary, technology continues to get the better of us, and the information that is supposed to be the key to success remains inaccurate, inaccessible or inappropriate.

The good news is that within our organisations a realisation of the need for change at last seems to be aflame. We are waking up to the pressures around us and the opportunities before us. There is a recognition that out of date structures, systems and processes must be overturned if we are to move forward and stay in business. The world is changing and we are at last beginning to wake up and shake up our slumbering organisations and enterprises.

The bad news is that the attitude towards change deep within these organisations and enterprises is not always a positive one. Change has a chequered history, with previous initiatives leaving some ugly scars behind. Many people harbour a reluctance to face any more upheaval, and change is a dirty word, avoided or berated. Talk of change in the canteen or the coffee lounge draws raised eyebrows and groans of "not again". It conjures up visions of consultants and redundancies and of management making promises that are never delivered.

Against this background we have to modify our whole mindset about change. Although there is an awareness of the need for change, there is also resistance to it. There is talk of "initiative fatigue" in our organisations, which have seen Total Quality Management (TQM) followed by downsizing, and downsizing mixed up with Business Process Redesign (BPR) and Business Re-Engineering (BRE). The management may believe that they are pursuing distinct change programmes and improvement initiatives, but the feeling on the shop floor and in the customer call centre is one of constant, uncoordinated change and upheaval. In this environment we need to rethink the way the whole change equation is addressed. The biggest shift in that thinking is that we have to live with change. Change is no longer an irregular outing, an inconvenient upheaval to be undertaken once every ten years. Change is something we have to learn to live with, to structure and to manage. Change is here to stay, and the winners will be the ones who cope with it.

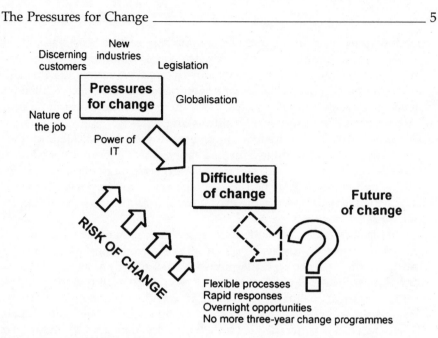

Figure 1.1 Aspects of change

The first step in developing a revised mindset is to establish a better understanding of change and the aspects of it with which we have to cope. This chapter examines four core aspects: the pressures driving change, the difficulties of managing and implementing change, the risk of change and the future of change (Figure 1.1).

THE PRESSURES FOR CHANGE

Today's organisations face an unprecedented number of challenges to the way they do business. The boundaries of traditional market-places are being dismantled and assumptions about how business is carried out are no longer valid. Cartels are swept away, and young upstarts beat the existing competition hands down at their own game. New opportunities and markets emerge overnight, and only those equipped to change can step forward to stake their claim.

The forces driving and demanding change appear in a variety of guises, but typically fall into the following categories:

- *Legislation*. New legislation has cleaved open restricted markets, allowing in newcomers from outside. This has occurred at a global as well as a national level, permitting all manner and size of overseas entrants to join the fray, often with the benefit of a significantly reduced cost base. In the private sector banks have to compete against building societies and insurance companies, while telecoms operators have to mix it with cable TV companies. In the public sector government departments are forced to develop agencies and offer their services to the outside world in a bid to become competitive and even profit making.

- *Customers.* Customers are becoming ever more sophisticated in their purchasing behaviour, more educated about what they can buy and more knowledgeable about the service they can expect. Competition has created choice, and choice has created discerning customers, no longer happy to accept the first product offered, or stay with a supplier not providing the quality of service they expect.

- *Global market-place.* The notion of a global market-place has moved relentlessly on towards reality even as we have struggled to find the metaphors to describe it. Underpinned by deregulation, an exciting new global market of trade and commerce has emerged, supported by a new world infrastructure of telecommunications and data communications. The result is an ever greater freedom of nations and individuals. Nowhere is this better demonstrated than by the rapid acceptance of the Internet into common usage and vocabulary. Although still in its early days, it throws open the doors to trade on a scale and geography hitherto undreamed of. Behind it all the significance of the global brand name proliferates, allowing multinationals to command recognition and influence across the globe as a basis from which to drive their sales.

- *Information technology.* In addition to the social, demographic, cultural and political changes taking place, the sophistication and capability of information technology continues to grow at a relentless pace. Year on year falling prices are accompanied by corresponding increases in speed and processing capability. The frantic pace of development means that innovations still in the laboratories a matter of years ago are brought to the market-place with astounding rapidity. The result is that technologies such as document imaging, incredibly powerful communications facilities and multimedia applications are brought to the market-place with a price tag and user-friendliness that make them available for almost anyone to exploit.

- *New industries.* Established industries are rapidly being supplemented or replaced by new markets and segments. Service industries replace manufacturing as technology spreads the threads of automation ever further. The industrialised world fights to develop new islands of capability based on knowledge rather than production in a bid to stay ahead of the emerging nations. In the service sector new industries in leisure, healthcare, travel and tourism, media and entertainment continue to grow.

- *Nature of the work.* The trend towards outsourcing has spread from the provision of services right down to the individual, with the rise in popularity of the contract workforce. The result is a flexible, short-term workforce for the corporation, but a feeling of insecurity and lack of loyalty among the workers. The labour market is increasingly polarising between the highly skilled, sought after individuals and the non-differentiated low-value-added capability.
- *Future uncertainty.* Beyond the factors and trends that can be measured, analysed and quantified, one of the biggest factors of change is that of uncertainty. Change occurs faster than ever before, with the result that organisations and governments can no longer set out rigid strategies stretching decades into the future. Corporate soothsayers and those claiming to understand the trends and markets of tomorrow earn huge fees providing advice to our nervous corporations. The future is neither stable nor predictable. The challenge, therefore, is to create organisations that can respond, whatever that shape emerges to be.

Stuck in the Mud

All of these factors apply immense pressure to change to our organisations. But increasingly the focus is moving on from awareness of the need for change. Enough talk and analysis has been delivered about the challenges and pressures, but what many organisations share is an inability to deal with the challenges they are facing. Businesses have been caught hopelessly off guard by these new challenges, suddenly discovering themselves paralysed by their existing infrastructures. Our organisations are stuck in the mud as the tide of global change sweeps relentlessly in—bringing with it both threats and opportunities to which they cannot respond.

In reality, the sluggishness of companies in responding to new opportunities is not a new phenomenon. For years, companies have struggled to cope with change—to get the best out of new technologies and develop new ways of doing business, to enter new markets and use the full potential of their staff. They made incremental changes, and initiatives met with varying degrees of success, but they rarely ended in a corporate life or death situation. Usually their competitors in the same segment were battling with the same challenges, and their existing infrastructures prevented them from taking any steps forward at speed.

What has upset the apple-cart this time, and in so doing created a much greater urgency for change, is the combination of pressures. New technologies are emerging at the same time as restrictive practices are being weeded out. Freer competition is being encouraged at the same time as customers are getting more choosy. The result is that new entrants are forcing the existing players to make major changes—or go out of business.

And this is happening in every industry and sector, from computers to cars, from insurance to investment and from medicine to manufacturing. While the existing players struggle to change, radical new businesses burst into the market-place and overturn the way business is done, taking advantage of those locked in the past. The economies of scale, established infrastructures and familiar brand names are no longer the guarantee of success they used to be.

The scenario is well illustrated by the changes that have occurred in the UK personal insurance market. The sector has traditionally been fragmented, although dominated by the major composite insurers with long-standing businesses and established customer "books". Direct Line entered the motor insurance market as a newcomer only a decade ago, but in a dramatic coup has seized the majority market share and shaken the very foundations of the industry. Much of Direct Line's success has been achieved by changing the very rules about the way business is done—exploiting technology and cutting out the middle man, and proving that customers will leave long-term relationships for a better service and a better price. These are the new rules for doing business. Firmly established in motor insurance, the success has provided the foothold for a leap into adjoining markets, allowing Direct Line to launch products into the household insurance and mortgages market, yet all supported by a brand name that was unknown until a very few years ago. The technique has not gone unnoticed, and the success of the "Direct" approach to doing business with the customer by cutting out the costs and delays of the middle man has been copied in every adjoining industry. In every market-place, from financial services to travel to retailing, the rush is on by companies seeking the right to use the name "Direct" as part of their branded marketing.

But another little quoted or acknowledged factor contributed greatly to Direct Line's success. This was the complacency of the existing players in the market. For years they dismissed the upstart as another niche player. They expected it to struggle to gain a foothold and perhaps take a small share of a large cake. But when they did wake up and notice the inroads Direct Line was making, it was already too late. They were unable to change quickly enough. These top-heavy, bureaucratic, stumbling organisational giants woke up to discover that the newcomer had already stolen away with a major share of their business. And, weighed down with the burdens of the past, they were not able to give chase to the upstart quickly enough.

Direct Line's impact on the insurance industry is no isolated case. It is typical of what is happening across almost every industry sector and market-place in the land, and not just in commercial and profit making organisations. The pressures to change, and the struggle to cope with and implement these changes, are occurring in state-owned institutions as well as those owned by shareholders, and in publicly owned utilities and healthcare markets as well as financial ones. Everywhere, enterprises are being challenged to rethink the way they operate, and rethink it ever more frequently; in the private sector the imperative may be to stay in business and fulfil the demands of shareholder and stakeholder; in the public and non-profit making sectors it may be to respond to public demands or to satisfy government legislation.

The Way Forward

Increasingly, though, the issue is one of capability rather than awareness. The late 1980s and early 1990s, fought out against a backdrop of recession, have seen corporate panic and confusion as the message sank home. Organisations have woken up to the need for change—they talk about change, prepare for change and set off on the route of change with a great deal of noise, expense and enthusiasm. But rarely do they achieve the expected results. Within a few months they are struggling to achieve change, weighed down by a combination of problems issuing from the burden of the past and the size of the task before them. The organisation and culture that for so long were regarded as important for control, consistency and management now inhibit the development of the flexible, responsive organisation that is required. The systems that once automated the drudgery of routine tasks have rapidly become a set of isolated silos, each holding its own secrets (or, worse still, inconsistent versions) of information about customers. And procedures and working practices that once helped to enforce consistency now engrave working methods in stone. In combination, the complexity and intricacy of the whole transformation task proves just too big to handle.

Together these legacies chain an organisation to its past. Increasingly, the management and the staff know that they desperately need to change. But there is no way that these monoliths can be dismantled overnight. Taking down what has been gradually built up, and replacing it with a newly created capability for the new ways of working, is a long, arduous task, fraught with potholes and blind alleys to trip and trap the unwary.

The Preference for Process

It was into this environment that the concepts of process redesign and business re-engineering were introduced to us in the late 1980s. When Michael Hammer started banging the drum about radical change and "quantum leaps in performance" he caught the imagination of those struggling with organisational change in a big way. His rallying cries of "don't automate, obliterate" were just what nervous CEOs were waiting to hear, and he swept the stumbling corporate world aboard. The re-engineering bandwagon was well and truly rumbling on its way.

The concept of processes, which Hammer and others in the field introduced, has changed the way we look at our organisations. They have challenged us to look again at how operations are structured, and to seek a new, more "horizontal", perspective by which to focus on the needs of the customer rather than the requirements of our organisations. Process seemed to provide a means of taking control of and exploiting IT, rather than feeling that it was leading the way. BPR and BRE seemed to offer a way out of the maze, a way of creating the new lean, lithe organisations capable of competition.

The problem with BRE and BPR was that they did not go far enough beyond the theory. The academics, the conference speakers and the consultants were all very enthusiastic about stressing a focus on processes. And they were all very good at putting forward ever more elaborate ways for redesigning businesses. But very little was said about how these new processes were then put into place. Nobody was saying much about what a new process looked like in reality once it came off the drawing board. Where BPR faltered was in showing how the radical new designs could be put into practice, given the baggage that the organisations were already carrying. How, in other words, was the existing to be transformed into the new?

The Silent BPR Prophets

Yes, a vision of the way forward is needed; and a vision that can focus on customer requirements, and design from first principles the appropriate IT systems and people skills to support the new processes is needed too. For change is about designing a new operation, appropriate for the current and future decades, and process redesign provides a way of doing all this. But change is about more than merely *designing* the new ways of working. Change is about creating the new capability—developing, shaping, testing and refining the new people, tools and IT systems that will make the new process happen.

And what the BPR prophets also seemed to overlook was the complex, tangled, embedded mess of the existing organisation. They seemed to conveniently forget the decades-old cultural system and managerial legacies. For change is also about dismantling the old capability. Few organisations are privileged enough to carry out the creation and building of their new capability in a "greenfield" situation, free from the constraints of the current customer base and the old product offerings. In the majority of cases the organisation has to create the new capability from the existing, with all the complications of conversion that this involves. Culture has to be reshaped.

People have to get used to new ways of working. Duplications on disparate systems have to be reconciled. Gaps in databases have to be identified and filled. Management have to adapt new ways of managing, both their staff and the work being undertaken. And all the time there has to be a constant reshaping of attitudes, values and beliefs as staff are encouraged to let go of the old and take hold of the new.

THE REALITIES OF THE CHANGE TASK

The second aspect of change to consider is the real size of the change task—and it is far bigger than the change masters and BPR prophets ever let on. Only when these issues are understood does the real magnitude of the change task begin to emerge. We have to design but we also have to rebuild. And we have to rebuild, but in many cases we also have to dismantle. Design-led change provides a way forward, but it needs to come with a stark realism about what the changes really mean.

The New Capability

Business processes are just a model or design—they require a new infrastructure to bring them about in practice. New organisational structures, new skills and knowledge and frequently new staff are necessary, as well as new IT systems and a fresh management perspective. A realistic understanding of what has to be conceived, created and commissioned is required if control and management of it all is ever to be achieved. The real change task consists of activity in some or all of the following areas:

- The processes themselves have to be designed and defined, then piloted, tested and refined. Fine tuning has to be made during implementation, and processes have to be adapted to specific geographical and cultural situations.
- Staff have to be trained in new ways of working, both the changes to products and the new skills and knowledge required by the new processes.
- The culture of the organisation has to be reshaped to ensure that the right skills and behaviours are in place to support the new processes. This entails reshaping values, beliefs and opinions developed over many years.
- Organisational structures have to be modified to eliminate hand-offs and wait time across the process. Job roles have to be redefined, and suitable staff recruited or allocated to the new jobs.
- Rewards systems have to be updated and new career paths drawn up. New measures and means of appraisal have to be prepared.

- New IT systems have to be built. This may require the purchase of hardware as well as the development of software, and often requires conversion of the existing systems, cleansing and capturing of missing data. A process approach seeks to exploit new uses of IT, and in turn will often require new skills within the IT department.
- Customers, suppliers and other stakeholders have to be informed about and often involved in the change programme. Often process change crosses the boundaries upstream and downstream to customers and suppliers.
- New management, measurement and control systems have to be designed and implemented, often taking a horizontal process orientation rather than a functional one.

The point is that change is neither simple nor straightforward. It is not merely a case of sketching out a few new processes on a whiteboard or a CAD package. Change is difficult. It is a dirty, messy, chaotic, upsetting undertaking, which requires immense energy and commitment to drive through. Recent years have seen many projects, often under the label of re-engineering, fail. Often this occurred as the organisation battled to implement the new design, rather than through any fault of the design itself. Successful change can only be achieved by having a realistic understanding about the size and nature of the task. It requires an understanding about how to convert and rebuild from the complexities and legacies of the old, as well as generate designs about the new.

City Facades

The complexity of the change task is well illustrated by an example from the construction trade which I encountered while working with a client in the City of London. It was in the mid-1980s, a time of immense change and upheaval in financial services. Global and national financial institutions wrestled with new legislation and deregulation, multiple takeovers, and the burgeoning impact of new technology. The client was a large multinational bank, engaged in swallowing a medium sized British stockbroker as part of a policy to develop a mighty worldwide presence in the broking, dealing and finance markets. But although many lessons of change emerged from this takeover and the struggles to align the new business which emerged, this particular revelation came not from my own client, but from the one housed in the office buildings next door.

The Square Mile, as the financial district is called, is situated in London's east end, an area crammed with buildings ancient and modern that house the national and international headquarters of many of the world's financial institutions. But despite the millions won and lost in international financial dealing each day, the whole area retains a rather grand, dignified feel.

Centuries-old buildings of fine stone and grand decor compete for space alongside the more ostentatious modern-day creations of gleaming glass and steel.

My client's offices were in a rather nondescript, grey-fronted premises of concrete and steel, a frontage that failed to stand out among the surroundings. To the rear, though, the buildings had a more attractive location, arranged in a crescent overlooking a small park. In this area at least, building restrictions were rigorously enforced and there were no signs of the polished steel or smoked glass that proliferated elsewhere. The buildings, although most of them housed powerful financial institutions carrying out business around the world, appeared from the outside as they had probably done two hundred years ago.

Or at least this was the appearance that was provided from street level. From my client's offices it was possible to view the true situation. For the owners of the neighbouring premises had embarked upon a major programme of modernisation and rebuilding. And what was remarkable about this particular renovation was that it all took place behind the original facade of the building. As I watched the progress of the work over a 12-month period, the whole building was gutted and then completely rebuilt, all the while leaving the grand, stone facade standing, unchanged at street level.

Behind the closed doors and hoardings a massive conversion exercise went on, redeveloping the shell of the old building to provide a brand-new purpose-built office. Ancient wiring and lighting runs were ripped out, and old furniture was carted away. Internal columns were removed to make space for open plan offices. Heating plant and air conditioning ducts were laid out and installed. Floors were raised to house the miles and miles of data and telecoms cables that are the lifeblood of a financial institution. Sprinkler systems were plumbed in. Eventually carpets were laid and furnishings added to make the building ready for habitation again. In just under a year the building had been completely transformed, while from the outside nothing had changed. While the image presented to the outside world had remained unchanged, the developers had ripped the very guts out of the building and transformed it into a modern office environment.

The task of transforming our businesses is just as dramatic and difficult. Like the office owners, we have to take out the old and rebuild the new to equip ourselves for the way business is done now, rather than clinging to the practices of ten or twenty years ago. It requires us to dismantle our old antiquated processes, change the way we do things, retrain our staff and equip ourselves with the sophisticated technology now at hand. But at the same time we have to set about this task with realism. The long and difficult transition has to be made while existing business is supported, just as the creation of the new offices had to support the grand old stone facade around it. All the time we are renovating and rebuilding, we have to defend our markets, attend to our customers, stay ahead of our competitors and keep on hitting our profit targets and satisfying our stakeholders.

The Unexpected Obstacles

A realistic understanding of the size of the change task helps to prepare for the journey ahead. But an understanding of what has to be created—what has to be defined, developed and deployed—still only provides a glimpse of the full picture. By their very nature, change programmes take months, and more often years, to complete. Achieving the deliverables set out in the change programme that relate to people, organisation, IT and all the associated issues is a huge task in itself.

The problem is that time does not stand still. During the months of building and rebuilding, over and above the turbulence created by the change programme, the internal and external environment moves on. Business pressures alter, markets evolve, new competitors arrive on the scene, legislation changes, new products have to be launched and staff (and sometimes whole companies) decide that they want to take on a different role.

Each of these events can have its own impact on the change programme. And to bring about change successfully, realism is needed—acknowledging that it is not possible to put our organisations on hold while they are transformed. A major change programme is like a journey, and knowing the destination is not enough. During the journey events occur that disrupt and delay—and, in the worse cases, completely derail—the change initiative. Rather than burying our heads in the sand and hoping the problems will go away, a means of coping with them and managing round them as and when they do occur is required.

Typically, over the life of a major change programme one or more of the following "obstacles" will occur:

- *Key people move on.* In every walk of life, the most able people are the ones in greatest demand. This is as true in sport (such as football, where the demand is manifest in huge transfer figures) as it is in business. It is a reflection of their worth that the best players on a major change project are the hardest ones to hold on to. A measure of their success and ability is the demand for them—either elsewhere in the organisation or beyond it. Almost every project sees a change in personnel in one of the key roles, be it sponsor, programme director or board level backer.
- *Energy fades.* The early days of change are usually carried along by a wave of enthusiasm, the energy generated helping to tackle the issues and resolve the problems that arise. Maintaining such a level of energy

through the life of the programme, often for as long as two or three years, is difficult. Change is exhausting and those tasked with delivering it have to be supported, encouraged and sometimes replaced.

- *Projects falter.* Even with excellent programme management and the tightest specification, there will always be areas of the programme that do not deliver. As well as the immediate setbacks this causes, there are ramifications if messages of "failure" reach the wider organisation unexplained.

- *Takeovers occur.* Takeovers have far-reaching effects on a change programme. At best, they create an air of uncertainty over the whole initiative, which distracts from progress while the full impact of the takeover becomes clear. At worst, they can lead to a call for the reduction or cancellation of the whole programme.

- *The curse of IT.* While the capability of IT continues to move on in leaps and bounds, development of satisfactory software and applications remains a problem. The very sophistication of IT—that it allows us to capture, move, process and analyse information so effectively—can also be its burden when it comes to specifying the computer systems themselves.

- *Operational issues take priority.* However much an organisation commits itself to a change programme, there will be times when operational issues are regarded as having a more pressing call on resources. Whether it be an increase in sales, a shortfall in staffing and the associated "call to the pumps" or a seasonal backlog, this is a reality that must be addressed.

- *Straying from the path.* At the start of a re-engineering programme, the vision of the brave new world tends to be highly visible. New objectives, process designs and ways of working are to the fore, clearly set in the minds of those involved. As time progresses, and the emphasis switches to developing the new capability and implementing the new processes, the focus can be lost. High-level visions can become obscured under the mass of detail that comes with implementation.

- *Paralysis by analysis.* A great strength of process is its ability to encompass all of the elements needed to put a new business infrastructure in place. It provides for the people as well as the systems aspects. At the same time, this breadth can also become a millstone—whereby analysis and modelling continue down to the *n*th level of detail as process designers get lost in the search for the perfect solution.

These points highlight the realistic, but not insurmountable, face of major change (see Figure 1.2). Looking at them, there are those who claim that change is unmanageable. There are so many elements involved, and so many changes to external factors, they argue, that it is impossible to manage the whole complex interconnected mass in the change melting pot. This is not

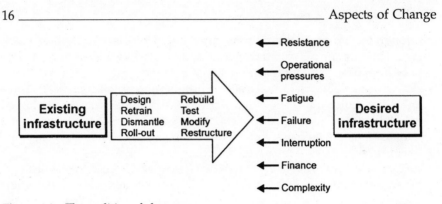

Figure 1.2 The realities of change

true. Change is unpredictable, but it is not unmanageable. When the journey begins it is not possible to determine the events that will inevitably interrupt it on the way. But it is possible to have a means of coping with them when they occur.

BETTING THE BUSINESS? THE RISK OF CHANGE

The third aspect of change is that it is risky. Change plays with the very fabric of an enterprise that operates and manages the business on a day to day basis. If those changes go wrong, there are some pretty serious risks to the business itself.

At the least, the change programme itself will fail. This carries with it all the implications of wasted budgets, resources and efforts, let alone the loss of credibility those sponsoring and managing change face from others within the organisation. The past few years have seen some spectacular failures, some public, some private, with some pretty major price tags attached.

But a far bigger risk is the risk to the existing business itself. Change is disruptive and distracting because it has to go on right alongside existing operations. It usually takes some of the best people out of the business, and, ultimately, it has to affect the customer base on which the business depends. Get it wrong and that customer base could be damaged or destroyed.

One of the most daunting issues of change, of course, is that, increasingly, it cannot be carried out in quiet isolation to minimise those risks. To get the most out of people and IT and management and other technology, they have to be designed to work together. Increasingly, this means that they have to be changed at the same time as well. Change then often demands that we play not with just one of the variables, but with many of them together. There are many balls in the air to be juggled, and there is a risk that they will all come crashing down.

Early advocates of BRE used words like "obliteration". While this might be a great word to stir the souls of eager young consultants and change managers waiting to go out and slay the next corporate monolith, the reality is that many CEOs just cannot sanction the risk associated with such obliteration. Change of any sort is risky, and change that talks about overhauling every process in the organisation overnight is often just too daunting. A more controlled, incremental approach to change is often required, which can transform the business without exposing it to ever more risks. Change is essential, but betting the whole viability of the business on it is not.

THE FUTURE OF CHANGE

The fourth and final aspect of change to consider is that of the future. Numerous change, BPR, TQM and re-engineering initiatives have taken place in the past decade or so. Not all of them have happened willingly. For years, our enterprises stumbled along making refinements, squeezing further milage out of their creaking IT architectures, struggling with unmotivated staff and inadequate middle management capabilities. Eventually the combination of open markets, deregulation and new technology brought barriers to entry crashing down and competitors rushing in. It was only then that the extent of the problem, and the size of the legacy, emerged. It was taking two, three, four, sometimes five or even six years for our stumbling corporations to find their way out of this procedural, technological and social maze to create the lean, hungry, responsive corporations ready to do business in the last decade of the 20th century and beyond.

This book sets out an approach for specifying, managing and completing such change. But change on the scale of the re-engineering and restructuring initiatives of the past few years cannot happen again. This time around companies have been able to spend years reshaping because everyone else was in the same corporate lifeboat, struggling to stay afloat and turn things around. The majority of competitors faced the same problems. But next time the response times will be much shorter, if such distinct windows for change exist at all. In the future, those who cannot change quickly and change well will go out of business. Their competitors will reach the new opportunities first. This is the final aspect of change. Change is here to stay, and our organisations must become equipped to cope with it.

The problem is that our organisations and enterprises as they currently stand are just not built to change. Change is not natural to them. They are actually built on the very premises that oppose change—stability, conformity and consistency. Instead, we have to create organisations that are actually good at changing. The organisations we create now cannot be expected to remain the same for the next twenty or fifteen or even ten years. As we tackle the long, laborious change programmes that eradicate the burdens of the past thirty years, new organisations are created. These new organisations have to come with a capability to reshape, reorientate and reorganise continuously, to respond to the opportunities and pressures and challenges—some call it chaos—that surround us. They have to be equipped to change constantly, albeit on a smaller scale in response to the new opportunities, rather than heading for one massive upheaval every five or ten years. It will be the companies that are equipped with flexible processes—and the people and IT systems that underpin them—that will capitalise on the new markets which form and seize the opportunities which emerge. The change task is, therefore, not just about transformation to cope with the current situation: it is about creating processes equipped to cope with the as yet unknown opportunities, markets, competition and legislation. The challenge is to create the "future-proofed" organisation.

Charles Handy, a respected commentator on the changing patterns of work and personal life, and the corporations where the two intersect, has long had an interest in the nature of organisations. In the 1980s he spoke of the changes that were needed, predicting the more flexible, responsive organisation of today, and looking at the impact that this would have on the careers and lives of individuals. In his latest book, *The Empty Raincoat* (Arrow, London, 1995), Handy develops these ideas further, highlighting the inadequacies of our existing organisations and career structures, offering a guide for the individual trying to make sense of it all. But a new, overriding theme emerges in Handy's book: the theme of paradox. This is an acknowledgement that there is no single correct answer—that there are always several sides to every problem. The secret to making sense of it all, says Handy, is understanding the concept of paradox.

And it is such a paradox that has to be addressed within the major overhaul now being conducted on our organisations (Figure 1.3). Yes, all that has restricted them, limited them and ultimately stopped them from being competitive has to be swept aside. And in its place a new infrastructure robust enough for the way we do business in the new customer-focused, process-orientated world has to be created. But this is the paradox. How is this change to be achieved without setting it all in stone so that the same problems arise in five years' time? How are we to unfreeze the existing and re-freeze the new without creating the same blundering corporate monoliths that currently take several years to turn around?

The optimists (and particularly those who haven't tried it) claim that it can all be achieved with a set of flexible IT systems and a clutch of empowered staff. Freed from the layers of bureaucracy and the strongholds of middle management, so the argument goes, empowered, responsible staff equipped with distributed, open systems are able to respond rapidly to whatever new

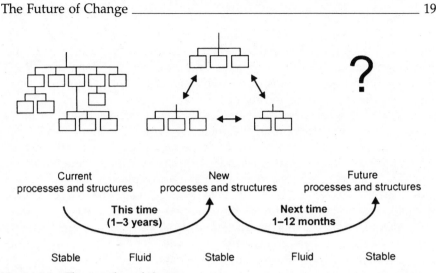

Figure 1.3 The paradox of change

opportunity comes along. Give the people the responsibility and the opportunity, so the logic goes, and they do not need to be directed or controlled.

The reality is somewhat different. Those who have tried it know that empowerment without the right training, management and guiding framework in place tends to cause even more complexity as staff tackle their working in their own individual way. "Empowerment without control", as one manager described it, "results in anarchy".

This, then, is the final aspect of change. We have to respond to the pressures for change and we have to cope with the immensity of transforming our slumbering businesses. But at the same time we have to do it with an eye fixed firmly on the future, so that we can respond readily to the opportunities as they arise.

Living on the Brink of Chaos

A real understanding of the change task—the change to the infrastructure itself, the obstacles that arise on a day to day basis and the need to leave our new enterprises equipped to respond to change in the future—is enough to scare the wits out of most organisations. Embarking on the path of a major programme of change is a long, painful undertaking. It is risky as well as expensive. It is traumatic as well as exciting.

Alongside all this, there is the challenge of just maintaining, let alone growing, a customer base in the pressures of the 1990s market-place. The very thought of jeopardising an existing customer base by changing the way it is serviced is enough to bring marketing directors running from their offices, and the budget required leaves financial directors pale and cold. And a real understanding of the problems likely to crop up along the way—however much preparation is undertaken—would blunt the enthusiasm of the most ardent programme director.

Faced with this, a very real danger of chaos exists. There are so many facets to the change programme, that there may be just too many variables in play at once. Existing processes have to remain as new ones are created. Legacy systems, with their inaccurate, duplicated data scattered across disparate platforms, still have to be maintained to support the current customer base just as new ones are developed. And staff have to be shifted gradually into a new way of thinking and equipped with a new set of skills while they support existing products and procedures. There are a mighty number of balls in the air, and a way of juggling them all—and making sure that they come down in the right order—is required.

There is, however, a means of coping with the change and the risk attached, a means of managing the crises and removing the obstacles, of communicating with the staff and managing the challenges of IT development. The next chapter looks at the importance of design within change and how design can be used to manage transformation. At the heart of those designs are the processes that underlie the way an organisation works. Process becomes a whole new concept—a framework for managing, specifying and driving the whole transformation programme, rather than merely a tool for design.

Chapter 2

Designing for Change: Making Sense of Process

DESIGNING FOR CHANGE

As the real size of the change task becomes clear, it can be a daunting prospect. To change successfully, new ways of working need to be devised—new ways that focus on the customer and make the best of people and technological capabilities in combination. To provide these new ways of working, changes have to be made to the very infrastructure of the business—the people and systems, the procedures and management. The number of variables in play, and the number of components under modification at any one time, presents a massive challenge to the organisation, and if the changes need to take place on a cross-enterprise scale, their extent may seem just too vast to tackle.

But the threat of chaos need not become a reality. Complexity can be controlled, order can be restored and the many components required to put together a new organisation can be integrated successfully.

The answer lies in design. Major transformation cannot progress without a design, a blueprint that sets out the new ways of working and how the components within it fit together to achieve strategic objectives: design that shows how customer needs are met and can identify the points of value; design of how IT is used in close integration with people, rather than as an add-on; design of processes so that they work *because* of the component parts, rather than in spite of them; design that works across the organisation to meet customer needs.

Design is fundamental to major change because it provides a means of:

- actively deciding and selecting how the enterprise will work
- documenting the requirements to make them tangible, visible and manageable rather than just a set of high-level wishlists
- specifying the actual changes that have to be carried out to make the new design a reality
- managing and controlling the multitude of changes that have to be carried out so that risk can be minimised
- understanding what the impact of the changes and proposed changes will be on the existing business operations

A design enables change to be made in a controlled manner, ensuring that the pieces of the jigsaw can be put together according to the picture on the box, rather than by struggling at random with parts that do not fit. In so doing, design and the specification that follows it help to avoid chaos and minimise risk; they make it possible to maintain control of the various parts of the enterprise being changed at any one time.

In particular, process design, because it is holistic, provides a means of managing all the balls in the air, a means of building to a specification and managing complexity rather than becoming overrun by it. A design provides a comprehensive way of determining what is *required*, but, more importantly, of determining what has to be *changed* to get there. It is, after all, one thing to determine the shape of the new organisation, but quite another to determine what has to be changed to get there. In addition, design paves the way for future change because by providing a map of how the organisation currently works, it provides a means of identifying what changes have to be made.

Not that there is anything radically new about design. The creation of most sizable products or initiatives—everything from cars to transport infrastructures to new buildings—begins with a design. The manufacturing and construction industries have applied such design-led approaches for years, and used them to architect their ideas and form a framework for all the development that follows. Contrast such discipline with our own efforts in businesses and organisations, which have dabbled with design but never embraced it fully. Such attempts always tended to focus myopically on one side of the enterprise or the other—the people aspects or the technological ones.

PROCESS: THE CURE FOR ALL ILLS?

The basis of design is the business process, and it is probably true to say that it is one of the most misunderstood concepts of the modern business world. Less than a decade ago, it wasn't even talked about. The word "process" belonged to the chemical and manufacturing industries and conjured up visions of production lines, automation and standardisation. It was an uninspiring term, reminiscent of dark factories and dull products, rather than a radical new approach with which to change and manage organisations. Then, in 1990, Michael Hammer introduced the world to business re-engineering, and the word *process* took on a new mantle. It entered the vocabulary of CEOs, managers and consultants across the land, and rapidly became the talking point in boardrooms and academia.

But process remains a misunderstood term. The concept of "redesign" has been embraced big time, and vast scrolls of new process designs have been churned out. Organisations talk boldly of their new "customer facing" processes, and new roles such as "process owner" have suddenly appeared on organisational charts. From a start point where no one had ever considered a process view of their business, suddenly everybody has one.

Process: A Quick Recap

A process in its simplest form can be thought of as a transformation, a series of steps or activities which act on inputs and convert them into outputs. In its simplest form a process can be represented as shown in Figure 2.1.

The transformation or activities of the process are undertaken by mechanisms that operate under the regulation of controls. Inputs and outputs may be physical or virtual, and include objects of all types, incorporating everything from people to information.

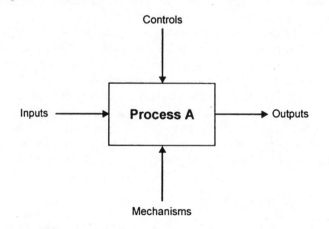

Figure 2.1 The basic process

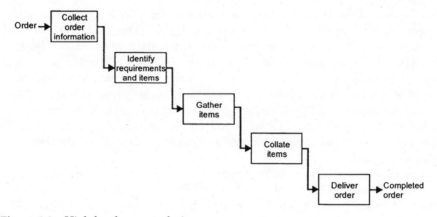

Figure 2.2 High level process design

Examples of typical processes include placing an order, paying an invoice and developing a new product. But processes are equally important in the non-profit making and public sectors, be they the visit a patient makes to a hospital, the movement of passengers or the generation and distribution of electricity.

When Hammer introduced the world to processes he forced the corporate world to start thinking about design, and in particular design around processes. The structure and organisation of most enterprises does not effectively support their existing processes. Functions disrupt the flow and departmental boundaries inhibit the speed and quality of service that is required. The essence of redesign is looking at the way these processes or transformations of the business are carried out within an enterprise and considering how they could be structured, resourced, simplified, rearranged—or designed—to be more effective (Figure 2.2).

Process redesign and BPR introduced a new way of thinking about our enterprises and organisations. They forced those in the corporate wheel-house to focus again on external requirements rather than their management structures and functions, and consider how the organisation can best be structured, equipped and managed to meet those customer needs. In doing so, process redesign appeared to promise a way out of the corporate quagmire, a means at last for organisations to shed the complex cultural, procedural and technological baggage of the past few decades and start again. It seemed to be the panacea everyone had been waiting for.

The Hollow Promise of Process

Although process has promised much and achieved some impressive results, it has often failed to live up to expectations. If we are honest, we can see that many of the dramatic claims of "process redesign" and business re-engineering have not materialised. Many organisations have struggled to turn their abstract process designs into anything operational. Process has provided some powerful new concepts, but it has not really lived up to its extravagant claims—the emperor's new clothes were rather scant when it came to actually making change happen.

The truth was that a fundamental problem with such early attempts at process change remained. The high-level design looked radical and the benefits sounded dramatic—but there was nothing there actually to drive the changes through. All of a sudden, process began to look like some sort of elaborate smoke and mirrors trick. The trap that many organisations seeking to re-engineer and redesign fell into was an inability to use their new designs to achieve change. The design had no real substance. It was still an array of boxes and arrows, concepts and wishlists. The designer or process champion who had facilitated workshops and sought feedback from the business probably had a good understanding of the workings of the process. But it was not detailed or rigorous enough to take forward as a new way of working.

An organisation that is serious about re-engineering has to put new processes in place which will actually change the way business is undertaken. This is a long, expensive and painful undertaking. But to achieve it successfully—and to get the full benefits of a top-down redesign—the new process design itself needs to drive the whole look and feel of that new organisation. The new process design needs to drive the supporting computer systems, the capabilities of its staff and the standards and procedures that govern them. Unless the new process design itself drives the creation and specification of that infrastructure, the benefits of that design will at best be diluted or at worst disappear altogether. Many designs were good and, in theory, worthy of rolling out, but where so many organisations fell down was in their ability to put the new designs in place. The void between arriving at a new process design and developing a new business was just too great for them to cross.

Delving Deeper into Process

The importance of process as a design tool is not in dispute. But to be serious about reincarnating our organisations with a "process orientation", much more than a design is required. Change of any kind is difficult and disruptive. But change that tackles both people and technology at the same time, as major change must, is especially problematic. It cannot be approached with a sheaf of process designs showing a few arrows and boxes linking inputs and outputs. To take an extreme view, process other than as a design tool is worthless. A process is nothing until it is turned into

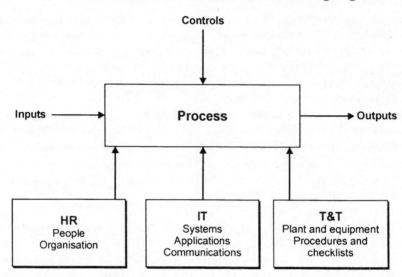

Figure 2.3 A new view of process

the components that actually make it work. To make the leap from drawing board to practice, a process design must become meaningful and must provide a way of managing the complexities that arise. Change must be driven by a comprehensive specification defining the changes that have to be made and the new capabilities that have to be designed, built, tested and rolled out.

To achieve this, a more effective means of describing new processes is required: a way of describing processes in a way that the organisation already understands, in terms of the people and computers, procedures and organisational structures that make up the very fabric of an organisation. These are the things that really "do" the process or transform the raw materials, information and physical objects that pass through an organisation, so these are the things that need to be talked about when we are attempting to produce a new design.

Returning to the basic process model, the notion of mechanisms has to be broken down into a more meaningful representation, which reflects the parts of an organisation with which we are already familiar. The real mechanisms of a process can be grouped into three areas, as shown in Figure 2.3.

Mechanisms with Meaning

This framework for process now begins to direct thinking during design into the following areas:

- *Human resources (HR)*. These are the "people" or social components of the business, such as the capability, skills and knowledge of staff and the culture required by the new ways of working. HR includes the new organisational structures and the mechanisms that regulate and reinforce behaviour, such as job roles, rewards systems, appraisal systems and career paths.
- *Information technology*. IT is any technology used to manipulate information in the new process, be it collection, processing output or transmission. As well as computers, this includes a broad range of technologies, from telecommunications and networks to printing and imaging facilities.
- *Tools and techniques (T&T)*. These are the non-human, non-IT tools or machines and manual techniques used in a process. They may be thought of as the "non-information technology" equipment or plant that carry out process steps, and are often quite specific to a particular business or industry sector. In a manufacturing organisation they include the machines and plant used to produce goods; in a hospital the equipment used in providing clinical care such as X-ray machines and instruments. Techniques also include the simple mechanisms that may be used to complete process steps, such as manual or "pen and paper" methods.

Controls

In addition, consideration must be given to the business rules or controls that operate on a process. These set out certain guiding criteria for how the process must operate; ultimately, they will impact how a process performs by setting parameters, limits and rules for different process steps or activities. Controls may be thought of as the output of management processes, which influence operational processes.

Examples include pricing rules (which define what prices must be charged for particular goods or services), authorisation rules (which define what amounts different levels of staff are allowed to sign for) and supplier rules (policy about selected suppliers). Controls may be changed without affecting the process itself, only the way in which it performs.

This is an oversimplified view of the world, but it begins to blow away the smokescreen of hype that envelops process, allowing the whole discipline of design to be made meaningful again. Instead of using concepts and ideas, it is possible to talk about new ways of working in terms of real life "mechanisms"—the things that will actually *do* the new process. The framework provides a means of thinking through (and capturing) the implications of the process design in real-world terms. So, ultimately, it can be used to guide those developing and building the new capability in the months ahead.

The New View of Process

Embracing people, system and technology issues in such a way takes the concept of process on a quantum leap. Process now takes on a much wider role, maturing from a vague design tool into a comprehensive means of designing, developing and controlling the change programme, and ultimately managing the business. This new, broader view of process is used to shape the view of the world through all the design, definition and development work that follows. There is no longer any excuse for the design to remain ethereal and conceptual. It can now become a powerful, comprehensive vehicle for change.

Process is a powerful means of designing, organising and managing a business. But making a process view of the world understandable to all those who will be tasked with developing and implementing it, and who will subsequently staff and manage it, often proves to be a major stumbling block. Although the basic concepts of process (working across functions, focusing on the customer etc.) are relatively easy to grasp, nurturing a sufficiently detailed understanding of process in the organisation so that it becomes the means of "doing and managing" is fraught with difficulty. Process is all too often vague and conceptual, and ideas encapsulated in design are in danger of being lost during implementation or proving impossible to translate into a new infrastructure. Fleshing the process design out into the three component areas of HR, IT and T&T, as outlined in Figure 2.3, puts the meaning back into process. This turns process back into a powerful tool, which becomes central to the whole change and management activity (Figure 2.4).

NEW PROCESS PERSPECTIVES

Design

A Framework for Design: Independence

The holistic nature of process now opens up the door to a radical new way of designing and implementing change. Process is a framework from which to specify the new business infrastructure. But it is now a framework for design independent of the supporting mechanisms that will actually make up that new infrastructure. Mechanisms can therefore be selected depending on process needs, rather than through any bias towards people or IT solutions.

The importance of this is reflected in the struggles that have been waged over the years to get the best from either people or IT capabilities within an organisation, but usually without taking due account of the other. One of the most frequently heard responses when explaining the concept of process is

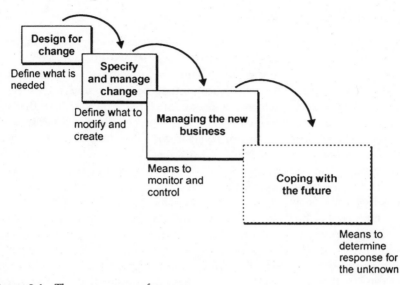

Figure 2.4 The new power of process

that such attempts to design the way an organisation works are nothing new. "But we've been trying to do that for years," is the common cry, usually from those within the personnel or IT function, and typically there is a lot of truth in such claims. Approaches exist on both sides of the technical and social fence that attempt to design and develop the most appropriate solution to meet an organisation's needs.

But the inescapable drawback with these approaches is that at the end of the day they actually belong in one 'camp' or the other. Those with their roots in HR or personnel theory focus overly on the people side or human issues, and attempt to adapt the IT infrastructure around it. Those IT methods that do take stock of the people issues tend to do so as an add on rather than as a real alternative to IT capability. The root of the problem lies in the origins—however hard those seeking to follow such methods try, they will inevitably leap towards thinking about a solution in their particular specialism or area of expertise. In so doing, they miss the opportunity actually to design the way the business should work from first principles.

Process design now provides a way of escaping the catch-22. Process now encompasses the different mechanisms needed to build a new capability—but without allowing any one of them to be the prime player. It allows the process to be designed first and the most appropriate mechanisms to be designed second. In turn, this ensures that the optimum mix of different supporting mechanisms can be designed and built. Each mechanism can be selected by virtue of the capability it provides, rather than by its preference for any methodology.

A Framework for Design: Combination

The second key aspect of this broadened process framework is that it allows the most appropriate combination of mechanisms to be considered.

In designing a new business, there will probably be some parts of the process that lend themselves fairly obviously to being undertaken by a human "solution" or mechanism, and equally there will be others that are obviously best undertaken by using IT. But in between there will be stages in the process where the choice is not so clear cut. There may be some places where a different combination of HR/IT or T&T is more appropriate. Because process can consider each mechanism from an impartial position, it can determine the optimum solution.

These two aspects of process turn it into an extremely powerful design tool. In any process, be it the application for a mortgage, the admission of a patient to a hospital or the planning and installation of a telephone line, it is possible to consider the design of the new process first. Only subsequently are the mechanisms selected. This ability to consider the *what* before the *how* helps to ensure that the overall business needs can be satisfied by design, not by any preference or whim for a particular people or IT solution.

Managing Change

Process, however, is far more than a means by which to design new ways of working. With the new, enhanced framework, process now takes on a much wider role in the whole change and transformation activity. Rather than just being a design used to envision the new way of working, process becomes the central specification and repository for change. It can then be used as the driving force for the whole change programme in the following ways.

Bridging the Void

The importance of strategy as a part of a business's *raison d'être* is now widely accepted. Most organisations attempt to analyse their own capabilities, understand their markets and the competitors within them and take a view of external factors such as legislation and the environment. As a result, most reasonably sized businesses have an understanding of their strengths and weaknesses and core competencies, and are in possession of plans for five—and often more—years into the future.

The problem with strategy is that it tends to remain rather remote from those tasked with carrying it out. While it may look fine on the boardroom table, its relevance to the man on the shop floor, the engineer attending a fault report or the customer service clerk on the telephone tends to be a bit limited. More recently, this has led to an enthusiasm for the vision or mission statement, intended to encapsulate the corporate direction in a manner that

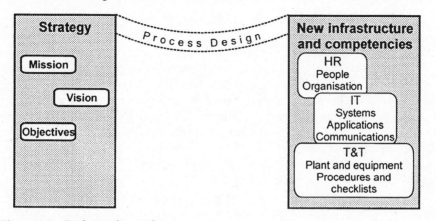

Figure 2.5 Bridging the void

everyone can relate to, and from which they can develop a shared set of values and attitudes—a common corporate mindset, as it were.

But mission statements still have a limited impact, even when they convey the right corporate direction and encapsulate the desired values. Ultimately, they fail because they provide no means of actually changing the way people work. Most employees already know that they need to provide a high speed, quality service to their customers—but just try doing it when you are weighed down with incompatible computer applications, surrounded by uncooperative colleagues or struggling with an overloaded administration system that swallows all the key pieces of information.

Process can now be used to address the gap between strategy and reality. The first role of the process design is to link the *objectives* of an enterprise to the actual *mechanisms* that will carry them out. A process design bridges the void between where the organisation wants to be (its vision, mission or strategy) and how it is actually going to perform the activities that will bring that vision to life on a day to day basis. A vision talks about vague concepts and motherhood statements—but a business is made up of people and their skills and attitudes, systems and tools, plant and equipment, and factories and offices.

The process design bridges this void and, step by step, area by area, provides a way of converting high-level, strategic requirements into the specific areas of infrastructure where changes are required (Figure 2.5).

Specification for Change

Change does not happen cleanly. Extensive change, of the size and scope now called for to shake up cultural and systems legacies, stirs up a mass of interconnected, overlapping activities. By its nature, change of this magnitude reaches into every far corner of the organisation. Ways of working have to be modified, staff have to be retrained, systems have to be recoded, and procedures have to be rewritten.

As we acknowledged in Chapter 1, the risk among all this change activity is of chaos; with so many variables in play, the change programme may lose direction. The development of process into a comprehensive framework delivers a new capability for managing change. The process moves from becoming a design tool to a specification—a detailed, documented description of what the new process will look like and how it will operate. It is used to define HR requirements and specify IT needs. It should be a comprehensive description of how the new business will look and feel, and operate. It has to provide a vision of how the new business will work. But a vision soon fades, so it also has to provide tangible, meaningful definitions and descriptions of the tasks that have to be carried out, the skills that will be required and the tools and technology that will need to be rebuilt.

The process specification becomes the roadmap for the whole change activity. It is the guiding light to return to when processes begin to lose their focus or implementation begins to get obscured in the detail.

Communication

Communication is at the hub of successful change. Communication and education have to be delivered unflaggingly during the change programme— both to those tasked with designing and building the new capability and to those who will work in the new ways once that capability is complete.

The process design acts as the basis for communication because it captures the new ways of working in understandable terms already familiar to those within an organisation. It is the starting point from which to communicate the overall vision of the new ways of working, and subsequently translate that vision down to a lower level of detail for the specific parts of the organisation affected.

Communications driven by the process design also form the basis for tackling cultural change and overcoming resistance. Because the process model represents the new ways of working, it is a key tool in answering the "what does it mean to me?" question which lies at the heart of any cultural change. In process-led change, this is more critical than ever because the shape and form of the new organisation is not visible other than through the process design. Because computer systems are built in parallel with people capability it is not always possible to demonstrate the "look and feel" of the new ways of working at an early stage. A process design, therefore, which describes and defines people requirements as well as process steps, technology needs, and inputs and outputs becomes the core of the whole

The existing   **The new**

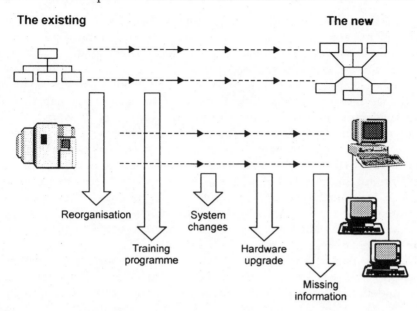

Figure 2.6 Gap analysis

communication activity. It is used to show the new ways of working before they emerge in practice.

Working out the Route

While the process design provides the blueprint for the new way of working and details the new infrastructure required in terms of people, systems, procedures and tools, this is only the first of many steps along the route to transformation. Having produced and agreed a viable process design, many organisations begin to falter at an early stage, overwhelmed by the size of the transformation task ahead. The concepts enshrined in the new process designs may look fine in theory, but how is the new capability to be achieved in practice? Somehow you need to get beyond the design documents and on to the specifics: how do you turn what you have into what you want?

The process-led approach to change provides a way of doing this by making the task manageable; rather than being overwhelmed by the size of the undertaking, it provides a way of splitting the work required into discrete, achievable parts. More importantly, because process is holistic it can be used to identify what parts of the existing infrastructure have to be changed to deliver the new ways of working—which people have to be retrained, what systems have to be recoded and what other tools and techniques modified. This is done by using the process design in a "gap analysis", to determine the work that needs to be carried out (Figure 2.6).

A comparison of the organisation's existing capabilities with the requirements of the new process is used to determine the difference or "gap". This forms the basis of the work to be carried out on the remainder of the change programme. An understanding of the shortfall or gap is then used to identify the various components that have to be delivered. Work packages, and ultimately deliverables, can then be identified across the three streams making up the process model. These will include the training programmes to be undertaken and education to be carried out; the computer hardware to be purchased, and the software and applications to be developed or purchased; the culture change to be initiated and the new measurement systems to be instigated. The emphasis is on moving from an understanding of what the new infrastructure will look like to identification of the specific deliverables that have to be produced.

The work packages identified then form the basis for those within the organisation to develop and reshape the new capability. HR specialists are used to define new job roles and career paths and to drive culture change and reorganisation; IT staff are used to define the data required and create the applications to capture, validate and process that data. Clearly, these specialists are still used to do what they do best—contribute their ability in the areas where it is needed. The difference lies in the way in which all of these individual changes are coordinated and controlled, with the process design itself being used to draw them all together. It provides the common view of the way ahead but it is also used to ensure that the changes to the various components are combined to produce the overall requirement.

This approach is core to making the whole change programme viable. Change programmes have to cope with modifying what currently exists, not just coming up with designs for the future. Because process is holistic, it can provide the tangible link between the complex, tangled mess that is the existing organisation and the brave new world that is desired. It can identify what has to be changed, but do it with an understanding of what capability that particular person or system or process step provides in the meantime. By doing so, it identifies a path between the current and the future which still allows the existing business to be maintained.

Managing Complexity

Any major change is an upheaval for the host organisation. Change that looks at processes is even more disrupting and difficult because of the multi-dimensional approach it takes to transformation. Process requires the creation of the best combination of supporting elements—the people and the systems, the manual tasks and the automated ones—and doing so demands that modification and creation of these elements is all done at once. Successfully managing this activity is a delicate tight-rope walk between control and chaos. In the past, an inability to understand and manage the multiple aspects of change necessary for success has often been one of the reasons for failure. The number of areas requiring change was just too big to comprehend and coordinate. Many balls have to be juggled at the same time. On top of this, the realities of change, the very things that threaten to trip up the change programme if they are not dealt with properly, have to be addressed. Staff leave, requirements change, budgets are cut back, operational issues take priority and people become demotivated. And in reality these are the issues that tend to inhibit successful change just as much as the design being unsuitable.

With the ability to capture and specify new levels of detail, the process design becomes a means to tackle the complexity of the whole change programme. By providing and then detailing the central vision of the new business infrastructure, it becomes the means for driving forward the rebuilding and realignment that have to take place. Process used in this way becomes a tool:

- for management—to define what has to be produced in different component areas, and as a way of identifying problem areas and risks on an ongoing basis
- for measurement—to define those key parts of the process (time, volumes, quality etc.) which have be measured to track the proposed and actual performance of the process
- to control complexity—by showing how the various component parts developed discretely fit together to provide the new infrastructure

Used in this way, the process design becomes the single source from which to carry out the multiple juggling act that process-led change demands. It becomes the picture showing how the pieces of the jigsaw fit together. In doing so it is a major means of reducing risk and maintaining control. When deliverables are vague, the process design provides the detail. When peripheral projects in the organisation threaten to interrupt or impact on the change activity, their impact can be considered and managed. When direction is lost, the process design shows the vision and requirements. When new staff are required to join the change team, the process design provides them with a picture of the new way of working and the new capabilities required. The process design, because it represents an overall view of the business, can be used to clarify and correct, to specify and manage, to communicate and to explain all that the change programme is trying to achieve.

Harnessing the Side Effects

The changes demanded by new process designs are inevitably far reaching. Changing the very nature of work—the way we service customers, apply technology and interact with colleagues—is not an event that happens at the snap of managerial fingers. The impacts of such change have to penetrate to every last corner of an organisation's infrastructure.

But what makes process-led change unique—and initially, at least, makes it seem such a massive mountain to scale—is the number of variables in play at once. To put a new process in place requires changes to the very fabric of an enterprise—jobs are changed, new skills have to be developed and measures are revised. And at the same time, IT systems are rebuilt, databases redesigned and procedures and techniques redrafted. Added to this, the pressures driving change—in particular, competition and the demands of stakeholders—demand that the change must be undertaken quickly (although even then duration is usually measured in years rather than months).

At first sight, the very size and complexity of this multi-sided change task may seem overwhelming. Indeed, who could blame the programme manager or CEO who, seeing the immensity of the task before him, feels a sneaking temptation to return the process design, and all the implications it raises, to the corporate filing cabinet. The whole undertaking begins to appear so immense that it seems there is no way that so many changes could be successfully carried out at once.

But just as the very size of process-led change task appears to imply chaos, hope is in fact at hand. The holistic nature of process itself provides the answer. The very extent of process-led change is also one of its greatest strengths when it comes to managing the myriad changes necessary for success.

To understand this, look again at the nature of process-led change. Nothing is discrete. Although changes are made to the fabric of HR and IT and management, none of them actually occurs in isolation. Each has an impact elsewhere. Reviews of computer prototypes send messages to the organisation. Adverts for new positions (and redundancies) help to change culture. The arrival of new recruits helps to change behaviour as well as inject a new skill or capability. New organisational structures change people's expectations as well as their reporting lines.

This is the reality of process-led change and, although at first sight this might suggest chaos and loss of control, it actually provides immense power to the elbow of those leading change. The very extent of process-led change actually becomes one of its biggest strengths. This is summarised by the notion of the side effect—*that each part of the change programme should be used to bring about change elsewhere* (Figure 2.7).

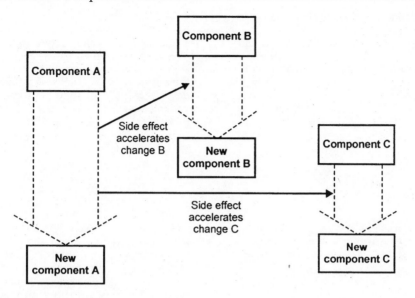

Figure 2.7 Harnessing the side effects

Underlying this principle is the fact that almost everything in a organisation's infrastructure has an influence on some other part of it. Management style affects culture, technology affects the way staff interact with customers, internal communication methods affect how people work together. Even physical office environments affect mood and behaviour. The parts of any organisation do not exist as discrete, isolated islands. In turn, this means that each element of the change programme, as well as bringing about change in its own particular area, can also be leveraged to assist change in other parts of the programme as well.

By way of further illustration, consider the packages of work that might typically be undertaken in the early stages of a process-led change programme, as shown in Table 2.1.

The responsibilities shown in the table are a high-level description of the work each team would carry out, and merely provide an overview of their scope. Within each area, a much tighter definition of tasks and deliverables would need to exist. The important point is the notion of "side effects", which arise in addition to the core piece of work or particular sub-project being carried out. Almost every change made to part of an organisation's infrastructure has an impact elsewhere. In turn, this means that almost every aspect of the change activity can be harnessed to encourage other desired changes.

Viewing change in this way turns the tables on the very complexities that threaten to swamp progress. By taking a genuinely holistic approach to

Table 2.1 The side effects of process change

Project	Responsibilities	Key activities	Side effects
Process design	Produce and document new process designs	Use people from the business to develop and validate new process designs	Provides those involved with first sight of process concepts Used to communicate the shape of the new business New ways of working within the design teams aid culture change
Information systems pilot	Develop and test computer prototypes	Develop computer screen prototypes to support new process Review with process design team and business representatives	New systems used to demonstrate "look and feel" of new process in practice Tests the viability of the new processes
Early implementation	Partially implement the new process ahead of full implementation		Further feedback into process requirements Gives those involved an understanding of what the new process is trying to achieve in practice Actual changes underpin desired culture change.

change, process allows all of the elements of a new organisation to be designed and created together. In so doing, it ensures that they can actually be used to accelerate progress and implementation in adjoining areas, increasing the speed of progress rather than overwhelming with complexity.

MANAGING WITH PROCESS

We have seen that process in its broader, multidimensional form can now be used as the whole platform for change. But it can also be used for managing the business on an ongoing basis. From being a conceptual design, process now encompasses the people, systems and technology that actually make up a business infrastructure—real objects that can be measured and monitored, and adjusted and refined accordingly. Process is now a comprehensive model for managing the business rather than just a wishlist of new, customer-orientated principles. The model is a basis for measuring performance and monitoring quality. This allows the business to become genuinely focused and managed around core processes, rather than paying lip service to the idea.

Because it takes a holistic approach, which encompasses all aspects of the underlying infrastructure, it is possible to see the effect of one variable on another, and the impact on performance of changing those variables.

Preparing for the Unknown

The final capability that process now provides is arguably the most important. This is an ability to respond to the unidentified events and changes of the future: the changes in environment and competition, and in markets, products and legislation—changes which, as they occur with ever more speed and frequency, turn the ability to react rapidly and appropriately into a key corporate weapon. Increasingly, the organisations equipped to react, and react quickly, are the ones that seize the new opportunities, businesses and customers.

Process now incorporates two key features that ensure such a readiness for change:

1. *A model of what the business does.* The process design can now be used to represent the way in which the various activities of the business are carried out at any point in time. It shows how processes interact, how inputs are transformed to outputs and ultimately how customer needs are fulfilled.
2. *A specification of how the business works.* This is a specification of the business in terms of the people, information and non-information technology, procedures, and organisational and management structures. It provides a detailed picture of how these various resources and capabilities interact to carry out the activities and process steps of the business, showing how the theory of process becomes the reality of the business.

Together these features help an organisation to ready itself for change. By providing a clear view of the starting point, they help the organisation to determine the changes necessary to arrive at a new destination.

Increasingly the issue of change in organisations is about action rather than awareness. Organisations are waking up to the new openings, new pressures, and new developments and directions. Strategic think-tanks plot the way ahead and marketing departments make undercover sorties into competitor territory. Increasingly, the new competition is about making the right changes—and making them quickly and effectively—rather than merely spotting the trends. The Process design can then be used to:

• identify the required changes to process design
• identify the specific changes that have to be made

Because it provides a picture of the way the business currently operates, the process design can be used to identify any changes in design needed to address new opportunities, threats or pressures in the market-place. Although a very basic capability, it is not one that managers have traditionally had ready access to. The real operation of a business tends to be buried deep within functions, under the control of line and functional managers. Modifications in one area have unforeseen impacts elsewhere, and improvement in one area results in problems in adjoining functions. The process template provides a way of actively designing change to process, taking full consideration of impacts on other processes, products etc. But, as with the transformation activity itself, designs are nothing if they cannot be implemented in practice. By providing a specification of the actual nuts and bolts of an enterprise's infrastructure—right down to job roles, information architecture and people skills—it can be used to identify the specific actions that have to be undertaken to achieve change. Such changes can then be planned, scheduled and undertaken in a controlled manner.

Chapter 3

Overview of the Approach

THE COMPONENTS OF CHANGE

Process has had more than its fair share of attention in recent years. The furore and fuss surrounding process, and the associated enthusiasm for BRE, have tended to hog the limelight of change to the exclusion of all else, obscuring some of the most basic aspects of change itself. Indeed, reading the books and attending the conferences, one could be forgiven for thinking that redesign was all there was to it—and that afterwards, with the wave of a magic wand, the whole promised land of new processes just appeared overnight.

The reality is that design (or redesign) is just the first element of change. Change of any sort is not achieved until new designs are put into practice, and invariably the build and implementation required to create the new capabilities demand significantly more resources and time than the design activity itself.

There are no easy answers or radical short-cuts. Implementing change is a long, exhausting exercise of working out what is required (the design), then building and creating the new capability to make that design a reality. The most basic model of change, which has to be followed for every new capability or component, is summarised by the following five stages (Figure 3.1). Driving each stage, and the growing levels of detail and development within them, is the process design itself:

1. *Design.* The design stage determines what is required. This takes place first at a process level, to determine overall requirements, and is

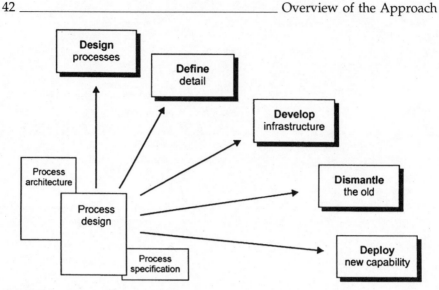

Figure 3.1 The components of change

subsequently carried out at every component level to determine how the various mechanisms fit together to meet overall requirements.

2. *Define.* Definition is concerned with the description and documentation of requirements in detail, so that they are sufficient to guide the subsequent development and build activities. Definition is a vital link between design and development, without which many projects fall over, lost between design intentions and the substance necessary to build a new capability.

3. *Develop.* The actual creation or development of new capabilities. This includes everything from running training programmes, to the coding of computer systems, to the education of management and the definition and agreement of new organisational structures.

4. *Dismantle.* The removal of existing or redundant parts of an organisation, including the conversion of existing capabilities and resources into new formats. (Note that in some environments the word *demolish* may be considered more appropriate.)

5. *Deploy.* The migration of new process capabilities into a live environment. Only when this has occurred can change really be said to have taken place.

OVERVIEW OF THE APPROACH

To be successful, change has to be driven by design. The process design itself has to take on a new role, becoming central to the whole change activity and

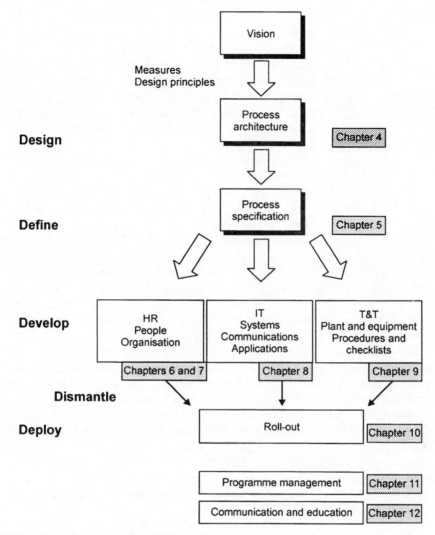

Figure 3.2 Overview of the Approach

driving implementation and roll-out just as much as initial design ambitions. It is used to determine how work will be carried out and how technology and people capabilities may be leveraged, but it is also about providing a comprehensive specification to drive the change programme forward. Figure 3.2 shows how this takes place.

At the heart of transformation is the design of a *process architecture*, which is covered in Chapter 4. This includes the definition of *design principles*, to ensure that the new processes are linked to strategic objectives, and the definition of measures that form the foundation for management and performance measurement.

Chapter 5 shows how the process architecture is developed into a rich and detailed *process specification*, which forms the basis for designing and developing the new capabilities, and managing and improving the business in the future. This concentrates on the selection and integration of the people and technology mechanisms required to bring about a new process, and the development of a rich picture, which ensures that design intentions can be turned into living realities.

Having produced the specification, the new capability itself must be created. This is addressed in three parallel streams reflecting the "mechanisms" of process introduced in Chapter 2. The development of people and organisational capability, covering both individual skills and capabilities and broader organisational, cultural and social aspects, is covered in Chapters 6 and 7. Chapter 8 addresses the IT capability required to support the new processes. This covers the extraction of IT requirements from the process design itself, integration with existing IT development methodologies and the management of the systems development. Chapter 9 tackles the remaining capability to complement HR and IT, showing how tools and techniques are developed to complete the capabilities required and produce a coherent process infrastructure.

Throughout the book there is a strong emphasis on the practicalities of process-led change and the disciplines needed to make change happen, rather than just talking about it and designing it. The development of the new capabilities is followed by the techniques and tradecraft needed to actually bring about that change and make it stick. Chapter 10 looks at the migration and roll-out of processes and their deployment into the live environment. Programme management (Chapter 11) introduces the key techniques and methods necessary to managed a change programme of such magnitude. Finally, Chapter 12 shows how the disciplines of communication and education must be established to underpin the whole change programme.

CONCEPTS FOR CHANGE

The stages outlined above show how process-led change is tackled in practice and underline the importance of process to the whole change initiative. Process is used to design the future ways of working because it focuses on the customer and can combine the most appropriate mechanisms to carry out an organisation's core activities.

But the very nature and size of the change task mean that traditional ways of working are often inappropriate. Process demands an integrated approach to change, and this in turn requires that changes are carried out in many

Early implementation
Financial returns
Create demand for new ways of working
Validation and testing

Parallelism
Enables process-led change
Faster delivery
Dependent on programme management

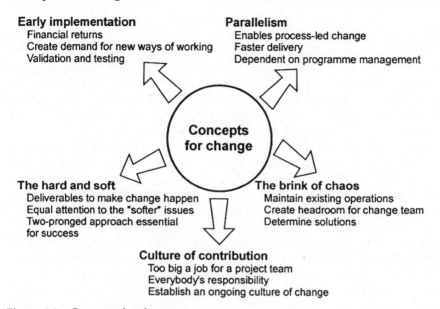

Concepts for change

The hard and soft
Deliverables to make change happen
Equal attention to the "softer" issues
Two-pronged approach essential
for success

The brink of chaos
Maintain existing operations
Create headroom for change team
Determine solutions

Culture of contribution
Too big a job for a project team
Everybody's responsibility
Establish an ongoing culture of change

Figure 3.3 Concepts for change

areas of the organisation at the same time. But process-led change is also very much a journey into the unknown. While there is an understanding of the final destination, there is no definitive route map that sets out all of the tasks that have to be completed. Process change is often about working out the way forward; there is rarely a step by step methodology. Solutions have to be found to the problems that arise on the way, and the most appropriate mechanisms have to be selected carefully—there are rarely clear, black and white answers. All of this requires a substantial shift in the way people view the world and in the way they work. Tidy, ordered environments and routine procedures with predictable outcomes are no longer the order of the day. New skills in problem solving, team working and project cultures are essential, and new concepts in the way work is allocated, produced and completed have to be adopted.

The description of such change programmes as being "on the edge of chaos" is an appropriate one. The skill is in keeping the programme on, but not over, the edge. The attitudes and approaches discussed in the following subsections are key to achieving this (Figure 3.3).

Concept 1—Parallelism

A process-led approach to change works because it provides a way of looking at all the parts of the picture—the people, the IT and the other, non-IT, elements that together make up an organisation's operational infrastructure. It then architects the integration of these components in their new form to create the new process. But making this work in practice demands that those creating the new infrastructure are able to work in parallel. This is an ability to focus on the development of many different parts of the new infrastructure at the same time. More importantly, it means doing this even if the shape of other parts is not fully clear. This represents a major shift away from traditional approaches to change, where one mechanism (say, the systems) was completed first. This component acted as the driving force around which all others were based, and only later were other elements in the equation drawn in. Towards the end of the programme, for example, a few demonstrations were run and memos circulated about the new systems or organisation. This was followed by training, and then roll-out.

Process change does away with such a serial approach. Too much change is under way for work in one area to be completed before it is started elsewhere. Information systems have to be recoded at the same time as staff are retrained. Procedures have to be rewritten at the same time as organisational structures are modified. And, of course, new processes have to be created alongside the old ones, which are still being used to serve customers. In addition, the financial imperative to deliver benefits or pay-back in a relatively short time means that a serial approach is inappropriate because it takes just too long to deliver business benefits.

Parallelism requires a major shift to the way people work, especially those unfamiliar with project based methods. Good design underpins parallelism, as it is the process which drives the requirements, rather than the development of any other parts of the infrastructure. Most people are used to working with a clear specification of the outcome; process-led change tends to mean that the final solution has to be worked out *en route*, driven by a set of guiding principles. Sometimes it is necessary to proceed on the basis of assumptions, and undergo rework if the assumptions prove to be incorrect. Parallelism requires that the people managing and driving the change are able to take the ball and run with it, solving problems as they go, rather than being provided with a full roadmap before they set out.

Concept 2—Living on the Brink of Chaos

Process-led change penetrates to the very heart of an enterprise. People, systems, procedures, processes, management and measures are all thrown into the melting pot together. Once the new design is agreed, and the changes begin in earnest, the modification and rebuilding task in all these areas gets under way. This is a hectic environment, with the constant upheaval, rework and iteration creating an air of chaos. New ways of working have to be trialled alongside the ones that have existed for years.

Reporting lines have to be changed just as job roles are being rewritten; modifications to appraisal systems are made at the same time as new staff are being recruited. And, as neither customers nor competitors will wait patiently while all this is achieved, the existing operational workload has to be serviced as usual.

During the change programme the organisation, its staff and its management have to get used to working amid this environment of upheaval. Normal operational tasks have to be carried out while new designs are trialled, old processes dismantled and the new components put in place. Working groups have to be formed rapidly to get input, feedback and review from those with the appropriate knowledge, and then disbanded, dispersing staff back into the organisation. Staff have to be removed from operational responsibilities for training and initiation into the new processes, placing demands on colleagues for cover and backup. Mistakes, inevitably, will occur, and have to be tackled rapidly before they become a threat to wider progress.

Concept 3—Early Implementation

Full implementation of a new process, with all the accompanying HR and IT support it requires, takes many months, and more often years, to complete. While the full manifestation of the process is necessary to realise all of the benefits, the new process can usually be implemented in some partial or temporary state ahead of the full version. This is achieved in a variety of ways—procedures can be used to link disparate parts of the process together, or a team approach can be used to provide a multi-skilled response.

Financial imperatives are the most common reason for seeking such "quick wins", given that the implementation of the new process, even in partial form, should start to bring in some of the benefits, but several other reasons make it important actively to seek early process implementation:

- *Visibility.* Early implementation is a tangible demonstration in the organisation that change is happening. This is particularly important in the months following a loud and enthusiastic launch event, when the change programme effectively disappears from the eyes of many staff during the design and development stages. Early implementation gives staff not actually involved in building the new processes something to "touch and feel", and keeps the change programme at the front of their minds.
- *Feedback.* Implementing a partial or interim version of the process provides an opportunity to test some of its key principles in a live environment. As well as validating the essence of the process, this provides the opportunity

to test whether it meets customer needs, that staff are able to adjust to the new format and that the expected benefits are viable.

- *Creation of demand.* Successful trial of a process in partial format can be used to stimulate demand for the complete, fully operational process. If a partial version can be shown to deliver results (improved quality, reduced costs, faster throughput etc.), even in its limited form, a demand is created for the full version. In addition, when the time comes for full implementation, those concerned are already familiar with key concepts, which, as well as minimising the likelihood of resistance, frees them to concentrate on other systems and organisational changes required.

- *Culture change.* Besides any financial benefits achieved, early implementation provides the opportunity to start changing the "hearts and minds" of an organisation. However much a change is explained, justified, sold and promoted, the most effective way to change attitudes and values is to get people doing things differently and let them see for themselves. Putting a process into practice also sends strong signals that management is genuinely committed to making the changes work, rather than hiding behind designs and waiting months for results.

Early implementation is described in more detail in Chapter 10, on deployment.

Concept 4—The Hard and the Soft

When it comes down to it, transformation is achieved by making things happen, not by writing wishlists. It is concerned with changing working methods, making appointments, building new computer systems, reorganising people, defining new job roles—rebuilding the very fabric of an enterprise.

At the centre of this transformation, there has to be an emphasis on deliverables—the specific items that have to be produced to fit into the bigger jigsaw. However huge the change task, it can always be broken down into these smaller work packages. They could be modules of code that fit into a new computer system, or strategies that map out migration options. They could be documented procedures to guide staff through the new processes, or the file of data gathered from old systems for migration to the new. Deliverables can be controlled as part of a project plan, and they ensure that the change team is always focused on producing particular outputs, rather than merely wandering along in pursuit of some activity peripheral to the core changes. Deliverables are the building blocks of change, and make even the biggest change programme achievable.

But, although a focus on deliverables is important, change is not that simple. If transformation was merely about producing deliverables, then every organisation with a reasonable project management capability would

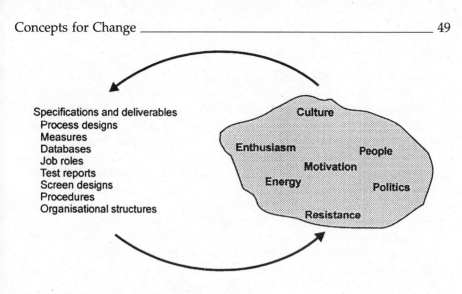

Specifications and deliverables
Process designs
Measures
Databases
Job roles
Test reports
Screen designs
Procedures
Organisational structures

Culture
Enthusiasm
People
Motivation
Energy
Politics
Resistance

Figure 3.4 Hard and soft aspects of change

be able to achieve it without half the pain and discomfort that occurs. For although many of the changes required can be achieved by specifying, managing and building deliverables, there is no way that every aspect of change can be controlled within a distinct set of deliverables. Successful transformation also requires the softer aspects of change to be addressed (Figure 3.4).

These are the nuances of an organisation, the undercurrents and sticking points that cannot be listed clearly on a project plan. They are the passions and preferences of individuals, the politics and the concerns that exist, for whatever reason, rational or not.

This is the other side of change. It cannot be specified—it must be sensed and felt rather than defined or written down, but it must take place from beginning to end of the change programme. The specification, production and validation of deliverables must be accompanied by an awareness of how people are reacting to the changes, a feeling for whether the organisation is on board or not. The responses may need to be equally informal and subtle. It may be the project manager who finds the time to talk to the individual who is an obstacle to progress, and address his or her real worries and concerns, or the project newsletter or management briefing that addresses the insecurity that staff feel about the future of their jobs, rather than merely banging on about distant messages of process change. Change can be driven solely by deliverables. But it will happen with more speed, more commitment and a more lasting effectiveness if the production of deliverables is accompanied by a sensitive and appropriate response to these "softer" aspects of an enterprise.

Concept 5—Creating a Culture of Contribution

The changes our organisations are being forced to undergo occur as a turning point in the whole nature of work is reached. Traditionally, most organisations are composed of clearly packaged jobs with routine tasks and well-defined parameters. The scope and content of the work is well known, and the job can usually be completed by following a predefined routine or set of procedures. These jobs, and the organisations in which they sit, tend to be a legacy of the rigidly controlled, specialised organisations on which bureaucracy depends. But a massive shift is taking place in the way we work and in the nature of our jobs. The requirement is no longer to work to a set routine, following the same set of tasks day in, day out. Instead, there is a demand to know the desired outcome and then work out the most appropriate route to it; for problem solving and initiative, rather than merely blindly following the steps that have always been followed.

A realisation of the need for such skills is beginning to filter through to our organisations. But major change projects require such skills now. Defining the new processes in infinite detail and handing them over to the people expected to operate them is an almost certain guarantee of failure. Not only will they object to changes imposed upon them from above, but it is unlikely that the level of detail required can be specified without their contribution. Making changes stick requires active contribution from everyone—senior management, middle management, those in support functions and those carrying out the front-line production of the organisation's product or service. Everyone has to contribute; everyone has to play their part, whether it be to provide feedback on a design or to contribute to a pilot or merely to man the pumps while other staff are drawn off into the project team.

The attitudes and skills found in many of today's organisations are not those suited to driving through major change. A new attitude of contributing and cooperating, rather than waiting to be told, has to be fostered. "If you're not part of the solution, you're part of the problem," one project manager used to intone almost continually as he struggled to get the organisation behind the changes being initiated. It is an expression that accurately reflects the new attitude required.

Part II

Designing for Change

Chapter 4

Process Redesign

Re-design lies at the very heart of major change. In many ways, it is the most exciting, dramatic stage of business transformation. It provides the opportunity to free the business from the constraints and outdated practices of the past and consider new ways of working. In so doing, it catches the imagination of staff and managers alike because it provides the opportunity actually to change the way business is done—and thus to steal a lead on the competition. Through an innovative means of creating a product or delivering a service, new business can be won, more customers attracted and better performance attained.

But the broader perspective of process, which now incorporates the mechanisms that carry out the work, ensures that the process-led approach is about far more than design. Initially the design is used to outline the new way of doing business, but it goes on to become the specification for the underlying components, and the guiding light for those involved in the development, training, piloting, decommissioning and roll-out that follow in the months ahead. And through its breadth it is also a core tool for controlling the whole change programme, and managing the ongoing business. In short, the design, and the specification it turns into, is fundamental to the whole change programme.

The design and specification of the new business processes is split into two phases:

1. The design and development of a *process architecture*, covered in this chapter, which outlines the design of the enterprise's new processes. This includes the link to strategic objectives, the definition of measures and the production of the high-level design itself.

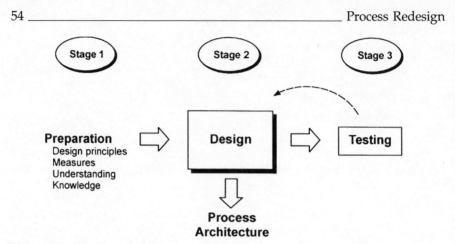

Figure 4.1   Process redesign

3. *Process specification*, covered in Chapter 5, which takes the development of the process design to a much lower level of detail. This covers more detailed design decisions about how the process will be supported, the documentation of these decisions so that they form a specification for the changes to take place in the months ahead, and the production of a rich model by which to manage and change the business.

AN ARCHITECTURE FOR CHANGE

The architecture phase is made up of three key stages (Figure 4.1):

1. *Preparation*, where the design principles that underpin the redesign of the new processes are defined in conjunction with new process measures.
2. The *design stage* itself, where the new processes are designed and documented.
3. The final stage of *validation and testing*, which leads to the sign-off and acceptance of the new process architecture.

The process architecture documents the design of the new business in the form of processes and becomes the focal point for all the change that follows.

Stage 1: Preparing for Redesign

The message about taking a design-led approach to change, and the importance of a holistic approach, which ensures that the changes made, staff trained and computer systems rebuilt reflect the real requirements of the business, has been stressed long and hard. But before giant, creative leaps are made into the realms of new designs, it is important to be sure about the real objectives. How, in other words, can those at the head of the organisation be sure that the capability being developed is what is required? How can those designing the processes be sure that they reflect the real needs of the organisation or enterprise, and how can this direction be maintained during the long months of transformation that lie ahead?

The starting point for redesign must be the strategy or vision of the organisation. But the recurring difficulty with such nebulous concepts as "strategy" is getting hold of them in a format that is meaningful. Vision statements and strategy propositions are notoriously high level and vague. "To be the preferred provider of product/service X in market Y and provide a return to shareholders" is a typical rendition. Such statements provide a feeble pointer to the future rather than any concrete indication of what an organisation should really be doing, or the capability needed to realise objectives.

The first requirement of process design is to ensure that the vision is expressed in such a way that it can be used consciously to influence the design of the process. This is undertaken using design principles.

DESIGN PRINCIPLES

Design principles are short, concise statements that guide the design and development of new processes. They are an interpretation of the vision or strategy—but an interpretation captured in a way that brings meaning and direction to an area of ambiguity. Design principles encapsulate how the new processes need to look and perform—the way they must work, behave and operate to achieve their overall objectives.

Defining design principles. Design principles are derived from strategic requirements and the constraints of existing processes. They are defined by distilling vision statements and strategy documents into short, pithy statements which reflect desired process capability and performance. Current constraints within the businesses are also reviewed, so that specific design principles can be established to ensure that particular problems (e.g. bureaucracy or excessive paperwork) can be "designed out" of new processes.

The following questions about an organisation's performance, both current and desired, help to point the way towards identifying design principles:

- Which things are key to the way business will be carried out?
- What capability will allow a lead over the competition to be established?
- What do we have to do in order to do our business well?

- What behaviour, built into processes, will ensure that performance targets are reached?
- What is the service that will really set us apart in the eyes of our customers?
- What are the biggest constraints within current business processes?
- What is the part of the process that adds the value which customers will pay for?

Examples of typical design principles include:

- minimise lead time
- capture, structure and share knowledge
- minimise number of visits
- provide accurate and binding quotes first time
- reduce bureaucracy
- use the telephone rather than post and paper
- maximise innovation
- minimise paper
- enable continuous improvement through individuals
- eliminate double handling
- minimise hand-offs

Design principles are established to influence the whole "shape" of the new design, and how, ultimately, the process will operate. They reflect both the requirements of processes related more directly to internal or operational requirements (reduce bureaucracy, minimise paper) and those of servicing the customer better (minimise the number of visits). Others, such as "maximise innovation", may embody more general strategic needs of the company. During design the principles are used to test the new processes and check that they match up with what is required. Just as a carpenter from time to time steps back to check the lie of his work with a spirit level, so those undertaking process design must constantly check that the process taking shape reflects the required strategic capability.

Applying design principles. In Chapter 2, the notion of process as a bridge was considered. Process enables organisations battling with change to span the gap between strategy and the capabilities required to make that strategy a reality. Design principles are the first strand of that bridge, establishing the first tangible link between the extremes.

Initially, design principles are used to guide the design of the processes themselves. Innovative ideas are all well and good, but unless they contribute towards the desired new strategic capabilities of an organisation, they are of little value. Design principles encapsulate how the new processes need to look and perform—the way they must work, behave and operate to achieve their goals. Consider the principle, "use the telephone rather than post and paper" listed above. On the one hand, it reflects a problem of an organisation's existing operation (that post and paper has in-built delays and the potential for many inaccuracies to arise), which must be addressed. On the other, it directly influences the way the new processes must be built—to support telephone transactions and on-line dialogue rather than forms and paperwork. Ultimately, this will have implications for everything from screen dialogues, to staff skills to the processing power required to drive IT systems.

As the work of process design moves forward, from concepts to detail and from designs to implementation, the number of decisions and tradeoffs that have to be made becomes ever greater—some departments will need to increase staff, others may be closed, one computer system may be enhanced, another may be simplified. Often, alternatives conflict. Where there is a choice between designs or mechanisms the design principles can be used to guide the decisions, ensuring that they support the overall requirements of the new processes.

Finally, design principles act as a meaningful (and documented) reminder of the real objectives of transformation. As the programme of change moves forward, a mass of other factors close in and threaten to obscure or even hijack the core objectives. IT people use it to justify new tools, kit and methods. HR people use it to roll out new personnel management methods. Marketing people harness it as a means of launching new products and services. These side issues may or may not be relevant or helpful toward the changes. Design principles are the ready litmus test that allows a decision to be made about whether a change is genuinely contributing to the overall objectives.

In reality, of course, like most good ideas, the notion of design principles is nothing new. Using a short, memorable set of principles to guide behaviour and performance is merely the invocation of a concept first used several millennia previously. The first design principles—the Ten Commandments— were established thousands of years ago!

The definition and agreement of design principles is a critical early foundation stone in the change programme. Design principles should be signed-off by senior management as a visible indication of agreement and commitment, and communicated to the wider organisation as a sign of the direction that the new processes will take. The appropriate number of design principles will vary depending on the level of detail captured in the vision, and the objectives of the host organisation, with between 6 and 10 usually appropriate. Any fewer, and it is unlikely that the vision has been sufficiently distilled; any more, and it is likely that non-core aspects of the vision are being elucidated and core detail will be lost.

Design principles are a key influence on the shape of the process during design, but are also used on an ongoing basis during the change programme to:

- *Communicate.* Although design principles are primarily a tool to guide those designing and building the new processes, they are also used to communicate the shape of "things to come" to the wider organisation. This is particularly important in the early days of the change programme during design, when there is an absence of any tangible changes for those not directly involved in the project. Design principles provide an early and simple mechanism for demonstrating progress and the "look and feel" of the new way of doing things.
- *Get agreement.* Design principles are one of the first deliverables completed for formal acceptance by the business. Acceptance, in this sense, means a physical sign-off by those responsible for the process, usually the process owner or champion. This forces those responsible for managing the process to come face to face with the changes required and the direction in which they are moving (and, while many managers readily agree to changes verbally, instigating a physical sign-off ensures a much higher level of involvement and commitment). In addition, such demonstrable management commitment can be used to start driving the change down through the organisation. Design principles are a mandate for change, a tool to chivvy and encourage people.
- *Prevent reversion.* Achieving change is a constant uphill struggle. Designing new ways of working is fine, but unless people can be made to let go of the old and embrace the new, lasting change will not be achieved. People try the new ways of working and encounter problems. Systems developers attempt to code new modules and falter. The tendency, when such difficulties are encountered, is for a gradual backward slide. Somehow it seems easier to settle back into the comfort of what we know rather than fighting to achieve what is required. Design principles are a critical tool in preventing this reversion, continually upholding the way forward by reinforcing what the changes are trying to achieve.
- *Provide a focus for early change.* Creating the organisational capability for new processes takes many months. Even after process designs are created, training, systems development and reorganisation have to be carried out before new designs can be brought to life. But in the intervening period, some degree of change must take place. Staff can move towards the new way of working, even if it cannot be completed in full. A shift towards the new process orientation can be achieved even if it is only partial. So, for example, the organisation can examine ways in which the design principle "minimise paper" can be achieved even before the new IT systems support that will help to bring it about is developed. Design principles provide the focus for these initial changes because they express requirements in a manner that people can relate to.

Although they are one of the first deliverables of a change programme, the true value of design principles usually only becomes clear much later in the change programme. The early days of change, closely aligned with vision and process designs, tend to foster a fairly clear focus on the requirements of the business. It is as the detail grows, and the distance from launch day lengthens, that the design principles become ever more valuable. Eighteen months into a change programme, as implementation teams wrestle with decisions about whether a particular field of information is required on a screen or a document, or perhaps whether customer-facing staff should be organised in one way or another, design principles help those involved to ask the question and make the tradeoff: "But how is the design really helping us to achieve the simplicity/speed/quality/customer service etc. desired?".

Objectives and Measures

The second area that requires definition in advance of design itself is that of process goals or objectives and their associated measures. These quantify what the process must achieve. They are necessary for three reasons:

1. *Monitoring.* To monitor the overall progress of the change programme in quantitative terms. Typically, this will be to track progress toward the desired performance improvement. Objectives quantify the direction and then measures form what one programme director described as the "dials on the dashboard", used to monitor the progress of change. As well as being used to track the overall progress of the change initiative, objectives are used during testing, to determine at the design stage whether the designs have the potential to provide the desired performance improvement.
2. *Relevance.* To make the change activities relevant at a local level. This is achieved by breaking down overall objectives into those that apply locally within a process step. In turn, these may become performance targets or objectives for individual teams or business units. Although design principles help to convey the desired behaviour and "shape" of new processes, there is no substitute for quantitative measures as a target for performance.
3. *Management.* To manage the business on an ongoing basis. New processes are designed and rolled out so that improvements can be made—in quality, speed, customer service, productivity etc. But to determine how well the processes work and what room there is for further improvement, measures have to be monitored on an ongoing basis. These new measures must accurately underpin the new ways of working, and are a key means of actually enforcing changes.

The craze for downsizing and cost-cutting in the late 1980s and early 1990s has left many organisations with a powerful yet short-sighted set of measures. These tend to focus overly on the quantitative aspects of performance such as throughput, volume and time. While such aspects may be easier to measure, they are unlikely to be sufficient in isolation. Measures that seek to address quality, satisfaction and service are equally important, although they are harder to establish. Often existing measurement sets prove to be completely inappropriate and have to be replaced—especially those that focus on the quantity rather than quality aspects of the process.

The exact nature of measures will depend on a number of factors, such as the characteristics of an organisation, the industry in which it operates, the extent of process change (organisation-wide or at a process level) and the requirements of stakeholders. In addition, the requirements of the organisation for a measurement system at a more detailed level will impact the detail of the measures. The use of Activity Based Costing (ABC) methods, for example, requires a correspondingly more detailed and comprehensive set of measures in place.

The following examples show both the objectives that need to be set at a high-level, cross-enterprise level and the types of measures that might be established within individual processes:

- Reduce delays in the outpatient process (healthcare)
  —100% of patients seen within 30 minutes of appointment time
  —deliver 75% of test results within one hour
- Improve customer satisfaction (generic)
  —increase transactions completed in one call to 85%
  —increase products despatched in 24 hours to 80%
- Improve the quality and reliability of the network (telecoms)
  —reduce overall fault rate by 25%
  —reduce "knock-on" faults by 20%
- Reduce new product development time (generic)
  —90% of new products developed to be completed in two months
  —reduce time to profitability to 6 months

Objectives and measures will usually refer and relate to similar aspects of the business as design principles, which can be used as a starting point to consider possible areas for measurement. Like the design principles, process objectives set a framework for the design of the new processes. By placing specific requirements on the performance that the new processes must achieve, they bring a focus to the design activity which follows.

The Balanced Scorecard. The balanced scorecard is a relatively new basis for performance measurement which attempts to overcome the restrictions of traditional measurement systems, consisting largely of financial measures. It may be used during process design as a way of developing process goals and measures.

The balanced scorecard considers goals and measures in four key areas of the business:

- customer perspective (how do customers see us?)
- internal perspective (what must we excel at?)
- financial perspective (how do we look to shareholders?)
- innovation and learning perspective (how can we continue to improve and create value?)

Because the balanced scorecard considers areas of innovation and customer satisfaction as well as internal operational and financial aspects of the business, it can be a useful tool for developing measures for process redesign. Equally important, if it is being used as a tool for measurement elsewhere within an organisation preparing for redesign, such measures can be prepared in combination with those that already exist. Again, this prevents the change programme introducing new techniques into the organisation unnecessarily.

Developing Business Understanding

The third aspect of preparation prior to design is the review of the very basics of the organisation's business or operations. This takes place in two steps.

Understand Business Basics. The objective of this stage is to develop a clear understanding of what the business enterprise does—what it produces, what it makes, what it transforms or what service it provides. In particular, the focus is on inputs and outputs, or what comes in to and goes out of the business. The understanding is achieved by reviewing the organisation's operations, looking in particular at its customers and suppliers, the goods or services produced and the market sectors and segments in which it operates. This stage provides the design team with a clear picture of what the organisation produces, and what inputs it needs to turn out a finished product.

Where external facilitators or consultants are used, this stage provides an understanding of the goods produced or the services delivered, and the form of the inputs. Where this stage is undertaken by an internal team, typically more familiar with the workings of the organisation, it helps them to distinguish what is being transformed by the business rather than how that transformation is carried out. The emphasis on this stage should be to equip those responsible for design with an understanding of the organisation's inputs, outputs, customer and suppliers—in-depth reviews should be avoided, because they foster too great an emphasis on how processes are currently carried out.

Review Transformation Fundamentals. Transformation fundamentals are the core activities that convert inputs to outputs within the current business operations. They are surfaced by asking the question, *"how* do we do what we do today?"*. The objective of this stage is to understand how business is undertaken, and through what channels—but only so that alternatives can be considered. The analysis is concerned not with *"what* business we are in" but *"how* we actually do it"—what is done to initiate, sell, produce and deliver products and services.

Typically, the following questions can be asked to prompt this understanding:

- Who do we do business with? (Individuals or organisations, personal customers or businesses?)
- How do we do business? (How are raw materials sourced, inputs transformed, products produced and services delivered, orders taken and payment received?)
- How do we interface/communicate with our customers?
- Where is the value added in our current processes?
- What middle men are involved between suppliers, core business and customers?
- What do we represent to our customers?

This stage still views the business at a high level. As well as looking at the business internally, it also looks up and down the supply chain to customers and suppliers, where changes to the nature of interaction are a key opportunity for changing the way business is done.

Bringing the very basics of the business to the surface paves the way to consider alternative means. The emphasis is on overview, rather than detail. Looking at existing processes in detail or analysing costs or constraints at a low level should be avoided because this tends to encourage the solving of existing problems, rather than the opportunity to design completely new ways of working.

Although this stage may appear to replicate the efforts of strategy or vision initiatives, it is an essential step to clarify both the business an organisation is in, and the way it currently operates. Developing this understanding at a high level puts it to the forefront of the designer's mind, but at the same time achieves this *without* getting drawn into the detail of the existing problems of the business. This approach ensures that the focus is firmly on designing the new, rather than merely fixing the old.

Table 4.1 Trends in IT

Capability/trend	Application or implication
Databases	Structured customer information and "views"
Automated call handling	Automation of telephone call handling, including sophisticated call routing, switching and logging
Laptops	Mobility and remote decision making enable "getting it right first time"
Decision support	Ability to automate complex decisions
Imaging	Storage of graphical images, reduction of paperwork
High bandwidth communications	Remote diagnostics and teleconferencing enable better use of decision makers and specialists
Multimedia	Combination of sound, graphics and text to display information
Optical discs/CD-ROM	Cheap storage, vast quantities of (reference) information available on-line
Networks	Availability of information locally, nationally and internationally; ability to capture, access and share knowledge and information
Client/server	Ability to distribute processing and availability of information, more flexible, easy to use interfaces (graphics and "windows")
Printing	Lower costs for colour and laser printing enable more bespoke documents and customisation
Home PCs, the Internet	New channels for doing business, increased familiarity with technology among customers
Falling prices	All of the above technologies are becoming more widely available as power and processing speeds increase at the same time as prices fall

Knowledge

The fourth and final preparatory area prior to design concerns knowledge and awareness of two areas that will significantly impact the new processes.

IT Awareness. This must be an awareness and understanding of the capability of IT and a vision of how it can be used to change the way business is done, rather than a desire to incorporate all of the latest gadgets and developments being pushed out by hardware and software manufacturers. It should stretch to general trends in IT, such as the increases in power and processing capability accompanied by falling costs, the emergence of new hardware technologies such as client/server and an awareness of the methods and technologies that lie beyond what is traditionally seen as computing—telecommunications, call centres, workflow, the Internet, home computing and multimedia (see Table 4.1).

These trends reflects just a subset of what IT can provide. What is important is that the understanding reflects what can be achieved technically—but also incorporates a vision of how IT can be applied within a business innovatively. It must be a state-of-the-art but feet-firmly-on the-ground understanding of the potential of IT. Bells and whistles are of no use if they do not bring business benefits.

Environment. The final area of understanding required before commencing design is that relating to an organisation's or enterprise's environment. Designing a process for the present can ultimately yield only limited improvement. A new process has to be designed with an eye on emerging trends—trends based on changes in customer behaviour, markets, competitors and products. Changes to environment occur ever faster— higher standards of service are demanded, customers are willing to do business over the telephone (or using home computers) rather than face to face, loyalty to brands is more fickle, Pacific Rim workforces can provide a lower cost base, knowledge is a new corporate capability that has to be developed. Understanding (and interpretation) of these issues is an essential input to redesigning processes. Changes may occur year on year, but an understanding of the direction in which trends are moving is needed to develop a design that can exploit them.

The definition of design principles and measures, an understanding of the business's current capabilities and operations, combined with a knowledge of IT and environment, prepares the background for change (Figure 4.2). Redesign itself can now take place.

Stage 2: Process Redesign

It is probably the very notion of "redesign" that has helped to generate so much excitement and interest about processes. Most people in large organisations today—from the CEO wrestling with bottom line costs, to the customer service clerk trying to extract coherent information from several separate databases—are aware of the need for change. But they are also aware of the problems—the legacy systems and the established cultural issues, the complexity and constraints of the existing business and the difficulty of actually making things happen differently. Change has been tried before and found wanting; all too often, change initiatives lost sight of the vision and became bogged down in politics and resistance. And gradually the corporate change enthusiasts gave up.

Redesign is exciting because it promises a way out of the organisational quagmire. It offers a more structured approach to change, a chance not only to shed current operational straitjackets, but to consciously design new

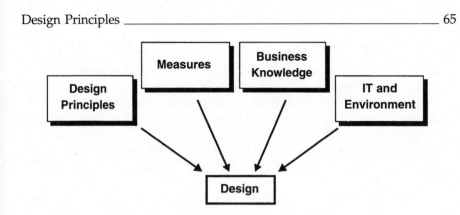

Figure 4.2 Preparation for Design

processes and establish ways of working suited to the requirements of the present and future decades, and the needs of today's discerning customers.

Designing Processes

A bewildering amount of nonsense has been spoken and written about process design. Everyone, it seems, from corporate guru to IT development manager to government standards body has had their say on processes and process design, and usually the messages have been quite different. The result is a cloud of hype and confusion which surrounds the whole area of process design, at times threatening to obscure it completely. Thankfully, the reality is a lot simpler.

The essence of redesign is about coming up with a new, more effective way of working: a way of working that focuses on the customer, takes advantage of new trends and technology and removes the bottlenecks and constraints of existing methods. There really is no miracle cure. Redesign is merely about taking a clean sheet of paper and thinking things through so that the inner workings of the business can be reconsidered and more effective alternatives designed. It's as simple as that.

This is undertaken by throwing all of the variables into the creative melting pot—a knowledge about what the business is and how it interacts with customers and suppliers, an understanding of inputs and outputs, products and services, and a grasp of the capability of IT and the trends taking place around us. From these variables, a search for a more effective way of transforming the inputs into outputs can begin. Process design has to consider how rules about doing business can be broken in pursuit of new ways of working. The phase is quite literally one of creativity, and needs to be stimulated where necessary with more formal techniques such as lateral thinking and brainstorming.

Breaking the Rules

A key part of design is to consider whether the very fundamentals of how the business and the key processes within it operate can be changed. How could business be turned on its head to steal a lead on the competition? How could it be operated differently if the biggest constraint were removed? It is the willingness to pose such ground-breaking questions that paves the way for entirely new ways of doing business. It may not be appropriate in every organisation but it provides the opportunity for transformation in the most dramatic sense.

The value of re-thinking these rules is well illustrated by the case of First Direct. First Direct, the HSBC's telephone banking operation, is now a key player among the UK's retail banking institutions. Its shareholders, staff and customers are now all quite familiar with the concept of banking by phone, and regard it as normal way of doing business. And many of First Direct's competitors are so convinced about the viability of the operation that they are now desperately trying to catch up and mimic the service. But this new business was only created because an "out of the box" idea was taken forward.

Several years ago someone had the courage to stand back and take a long, hard look at the way personal banking was conducted. They looked at the fundamentals of personal banking and they looked at the way customer needs were changing; they looked at costs, and they considered how expectations about the use of technology were moving on. In doing so, they came up with an idea which at the time probably appeared to be off the wall: "Run a bank without any branch network". The suggestion probably evoked howls of derision at the time, followed by legions of excuses. How could you run a bank without a branch network? Customers have to talk to bank staff. Customers have to get at their money. Cheques have to be deposited and payments made.

With hindsight, of course, we know that all these needs can be serviced in a different way. The radical notion started ideas flowing, and solutions could suddenly be found. Someone else's branch network can be utilised. Customers can talk to staff by phone rather than face to face. Postal transactions can be used to replace traditional banking services. But only by daring to suggest the off the wall—a bank without a branch network—was it possible to come up with a radically different means of conducting the business.

This is the first stage of redesign. It needs to be far reaching and it needs to be radical. The following questions help to point the way:

- What is the single biggest constraint and how could it be removed?
- How could technology be used to change the rules?
- What tasks could you get your customers to do?

- What tasks could you get your suppliers to do?
- What alternatives are there to the main delivery channel?

One of the oldest examples of process redesign was at Ford. They decided that they could do away with much of their accounts payable department by authorising invoices at the point at which they were delivered into the business. It was simple, different, but incredibly effective. Similar ideas, which challenge the very basis by which a process operates, are equally applicable elsewhere. In medicine it could mean using video cameras that transmit pictures over high-speed communications links to facilitate remote diagnosis and make the best use of scarce and expensive medical resources. In the travel industry it could be about service providers cutting out the travel agent and going direct to the customer.

Not every organisation will be able to undertake such a radical change to its way of doing business. Sometimes strategic decisions will already have put the scope of certain areas beyond question.

From Ideas to Designs

The next stage is concerned with designing the business processes that will be at the heart of the transformed organisation. These process designs pave the way for a new business infrastructure. Their shape and content will depend on the exact set of design principles and measures for the organisation in question but the key to a good process is one that is simple and straightforward, without delays or bottlenecks.

The essence of such design is about considering various alternatives and coming up with the most appropriate. Often there seems to be a belief, no doubt encouraged by the extravagant claims of the experts and "gurus", that there is some magical revelation about process design. Puzzled brows remain and, when faced with such a task, many people seem to be in search of some sort of Holy Grail of redesign. "But what do you actually do?" they ask.

The short answer is—*think*. Toss ideas around, look at alternatives, be creative—but *think*. What is the most appropriate way to achieve the conversion of inputs to outputs, bearing in mind the technology at your disposal and the objectives reflected by design principles?

During the design activity, certain questions help to provoke the thought processes:

- Which steps add the most/least value as far as the customer is concerned?
- Which steps have the highest costs associated with them?
- Where do the most errors occur and how can they be eliminated?
- Where do the most delays occur?
- How can we build in and ensure quality rather than check for it at the end?

- What can be done elsewhere upstream and downstream to prevent these errors arising?
- What is the simplest way?
- Is there something that could be fast-tracked or eliminated?
- Can IT be harnessed in a different way?
- Can one or more activities be combined in parallel to speed up the process?
- Where can we innovate?

These questions may help to provoke the thoughts, but the design activity itself is really one of creativity, exploring various options until a suitable one is found. In many ways redesign is an art; certainly, it is a creative exercise, because it is about coming up with new, innovative ideas about how the business could be run—whether it be to achieve higher speeds, a reduction in costs or an ability to turn out higher quality products and develop more satisfied customers. The key ingredients are brain power and a willingness to try new ideas. In addition to the key activities, and a description of how they will occur, the key controls that will regulate the process are identified.

As the creative activity progresses, the ideas and outlines raised have to be gradually distilled and refined into the new business process designs. This is represented as a high-level architecture of the new processes showing how the work will be carried out and how the key transformations will occur in the business. The emphasis is on an outline at this stage, with the production of a specification coming later, but key assumptions and major new uses of technology have to be documented.

To illustrate this further, consider how the process of fault-fixing is redesigned. It is a process that is common to many organisations which install, provide and maintain a service, in industries such as computing and telecommunications; many parts of it are also relevant in the supply of basic utilities such as water and electricity.

By way of example, take a company that manufactures, installs and services computer hardware. The organisation has to provide service on a nationwide basis, primarily into commercial premises. Customers are serviced from a number of local service centres divided into regions around the country; teams of skilled engineers carry out the fault resolution and repair. Sales and installation are also arranged through the local service centres, as are contracts, but billing is carried out nationally from a head office. Configuration information is held locally on regional systems and updated to the head-office system.

The business is plagued by inaccuracies, discrepancies and inefficiencies. These exist between the records held at head office, used for accounting purposes, and those used locally at branch offices. Contracts and installation information is held locally, but all billing is carried out from head office and

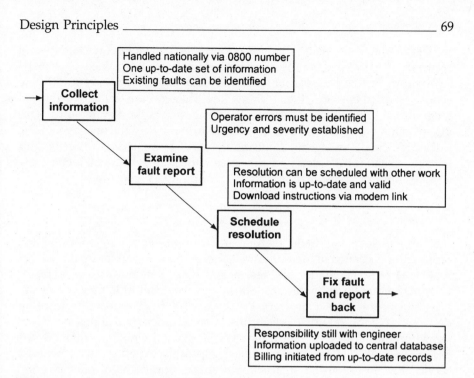

Figure 4.3 High-level design for fault-fixing

there are inefficiencies and delays in the provision of information from one system to another. In addition, due to the inability to have an up-to-date picture of a customer installation, when the fault is reported many problems turn out not to be concerned with faults at all. Frequently this results in the initiation of unnecessary and costly site visits by engineers. Maintenance and improvement work initiated by the head office to the national infrastructure is not always clearly visible to those working locally, yet only the central database can be regarded as the most up-to-date one. Finally, the dispersion of fault-fixing across several service centres makes it difficult to share information and identify the most frequent problems.

Having reviewed the way work is carried out, the major design decision is taken that all servicing will be controlled from one central location. This includes everything from the reporting and analysis of the fault through to the allocation and scheduling of work, and all records will be maintained and updated on a central database.

Having reviewed the problems inherent in existing ways of working, the high-level design shown in Figure 4.3 is arrived at.

Within this redesign, the key stages have been identified, which will both improve performance and ensure that a better service can be provided. Information has been centralised, and direct links between the engineers and the central database ensure that this information can be kept up-to-date and accurate. The actual action of reporting a fault has been refined so that the real nature of the fault can be explored, and if necessary any immediate action taken there and then. These key changes are initially captured diagrammatically as a process design which shows the key features. This design is not yet detailed, but it has started to show how the business will be carried out and the key mechanisms that will be required within it. This forms the basis for developing a process architecture, which will incorporate a more comprehensive textual description of the new processes.

Iteration of Designs

The design itself should take place in any form that encourages a rapid and far ranging exchange of ideas. Formal tools are less important than methods that allow rapid generation and rearrangement of options—scrawl on pieces of paper, move Post-it notes around on an office wall, role play the dream "customer contact", when every last little need from first desire to order delivery is completed during one transaction. The objective at this stage is to freewheel through ideas and capture the aspects of design that will allow the organisation to develop a more effective process, whether in elements of service, low cost or speed. It is as important to capture these "one-offs" and ideas as much as it is to structure or refine the model at this stage.

While the overall design itself is often best undertaken off-site, away from the demands and distractions of business, design must involve dialogue with both customers and representatives of the business. In the case of customers, the simplest means is often the most effective—getting together a group of customers and presenting to them for review and comment possible new designs for undertaking the business. In one organisation, a hospital undertaking a major process-led change initiative, the group invited for involvement were ex-complainants who were able to have their say on the proposed new designs.

In the case of internal staff, the activity of consultation is as important from a point of view of buy-in to the changes as it is for the contribution received. By consulting and actively involving people from the business at this early stage, a much greater ownership and commitment to the change is likely to be nurtured in the long term.

Throughout the design stage new designs and "straw men" have to be continually reviewed with representatives from the business, both at a management and front-line or end user level. Both of these aspects of design reflect the need for iteration, with several different versions of design usually being produced on the route to the solution ultimately agreed.

Because design is essentially a creative activity, it often helps to work within teams, or at least when designing to work in pairs. Much of the design is about making decisions, and capturing detail about those decisions, and having two heads to bounce the ideas between often speeds the design activity up.

More Guidelines for Design

Process design is more art and creative thinking than it is science. It requires a combination of "out of the box" thinking with a willingness to knuckle down and squeeze the value out of outrageous ideas so that the real gem can be found. Technology helps in capturing decisions and requirements, but ultimately it is the thought processes that count. There are, however, as always, some guidelines that help the creative process along:

- *Nurture creativity.* Coming up with new ideas that challenge the way things are done is alien to staff in many organisations. An attitude of innovation and a desire to take a new view of the world has to be fostered, and formal training in techniques such as brainstorming and lateral thinking may be appropriate. External consultants or facilitators are often a worthwhile investment in this respect. But once people get over their initial cynicism for creativity, they love it.
- *Cross fertilise.* Look around and steal other people's ideas. What have your competitors done? What has been successfully carried out in other industries? How are other organisations rebuilding their processes to exploit IT? As long as these sources are used to stimulate creative thinking, rather than as copycat material, they can be useful starting points to kick-start the creative process.
- *Encourage freewheeling.* Generate lots of ideas. Often it is not the idea itself that is valuable, but the second or third idea it sparks off may prove useful. Ninety-nine out of a hundred ideas may be useless, the hundredth little less so—but it will spawn an idea that can be developed.
- *Work at it.* Be prepared to search long and hard before something valuable is unearthed. Generating a winning process design is like panning for gold, and you have to filter through a mass of detritus before the nugget comes to light. It might take two weeks before anything of value surfaces, but then one five minute brainstorm to provide the route forward.
- *Create the environment.* Those involved in design have to feel comfortable to contribute anything, however ridiculous or "whacko" it might seem at first sight. Allowing this to happen needs the right environment, where outrageous thinking is positively encouraged and built upon rather than mocked.

In practice, it tends to be the early days of process design that are the most difficult to initiate. By their very nature, our organisations stifle creativity, innovation and imagination. Staff and management alike are used to restriction and confinement, regulation and control. Once suitably equipped, encouraged and enabled, the ideas tend to flow thick and fast.

Towards a Deliverable

The objective by the end of the design stage is to arrive at a process architecture that can pave the way for change. It therefore has to describe and document the basis of the new ways of working, and the key activities and their implications for building new capabilities. This has to be tested and reviewed within the business, and formally agreed before proceeding to the specification stage.

The most appropriate means of capturing the design is a combination of graphical and textual representation, describing the main process steps and the interfaces between them. This architecture should include:

- *Scope.* The scope of the process including any boundaries with other processes, departments or parts of the organisation.
- *Description.* A textual description of the activities or transformations that take place in each process step.
- *Measures.* The key measures that will be used to measure the performance of the process.
- *Rules and controls.* The key rules or parameters that operate on the process. These are the main business rules that control the process; the objective is to describe them and their influence on the process so that they can be defined subsequently.
- *Exclusions.* Any products or parts of the business specifically included or excluded.
- *Assumptions.* Key assumptions that have been made to allow progress to be made.

These categories help to move the design on towards the stage where it can be tested and agreed. The architecture is not yet very detailed but it provides enough information and content to move on to the next stage.

Returning to the example of the fault-fixing process outlined in Figure 4.3, the description to accompany it might take the form shown in Figure 4.4.

The key features of the new process step have thus been identified, along with associated implications for the supporting mechanisms, with both people and technology requirements beginning to emerge. For example, it can be seen that those providing the "customer support" will need the skills to investigate the nature of the fault and interrogate installation information rather than just record faults. Exceptions, which will have their own implications at the time of roll-out, are also identified. Such a description is still at a high level but it forms the basis for initial testing and sign-off and the detailed stage of specification which follows.

Process Number: 2.0

Process Title: Fault Reporting and Resolution

Scope: The reporting and investigation of faults, identification of resolution and assignment to engineering team concerned. This includes the identification of faults by internal staff as well as customers.

Measures:
- Reduction in incorrect fault report by 50%
- Incorrect work instructions reduced by 35%
- Improve customer satisfaction by 10%

2.1 Collect Information

2.2 Investigate Fault
To investigate the fault thoroughly over the telephone before it is raised for action. This involves structured steps to determine the real nature of the fault and resolve problems caused by operator error. Remote diagnostics and the analysis of information held centrally about the overall installation will be used if appropriate.

2.3 Schedule resolution

2.4 Fix fault and report back

2.5 Update information

Controls:

Geographical Regions: The areas of the country covered by each service centre.

Response Times: The minimum and maximum response times or particular service agreements.

Exceptions:

Product XYZ, which is being phased out and is only currently supported at three customer sites, is excluded.

Figure 4.4 Towards a process architecture

Stage 3: Validation

The final stage in developing a process architecture is validation and testing. This includes the testing of existing rules, assumptions and policy within the business for validity, and the formal testing of new process designs against representative business cases to ensure that they satisfy the requirements of the business and meet performance improvement targets.

Rule and Assumptions

One of the earliest obstacles to change encountered in any organisation are the business rules or "policy" that exist. These are the rules, regulations and policy—both real and assumed, written and unwritten—which specify that certain tasks be carried out or procedures be followed. Although implemented in pursuit of control, standardisation and regulation, many such rules act as constraints, adding layers of complexity to the business. Typical examples include the following:

- Physical receipt of supporting documentation is required before an order can be actioned
- Written confirmation is insisted on by authority X
- A specialist must be present to perform operation Y
- A second customer contact is required to complete the transaction
- The form must be signed before any further progress can be made
- The job must be carried out by an electrician in the presence of an engineer
- Face to face customer contact is required
- A senior partner must view every document before it is released
- Step 1 must be completed before step 4 can be commenced.

Although some policies and rules are genuinely necessary within an organisation, many assumptions and constraints exist simply because they have always been there, their validity or purpose never being called into question. "We have to do that because the back office demands it," says the sales department. "We have to record that because the sales staff supply it," maintains another.

Such constraints and controls cause delays and bottlenecks where they have not been completed or received in full. And where delays and bottlenecks occur, errors typically begin to emerge as well. The result is that organisations tend to be riddled with such procedures, forms, documents and signing authorities. Often they have been set up as temporary measures or *ad hoc* solutions; rather than being subsequently removed they become ingrained as part of the fabric of the organisation. Such constraints then become the reinforced concrete of organisations, which makes them so difficult to change, the interconnected mass of policy, procedure and bureaucracy threatening to choke new process designs before they even begin.

Having produced the ideal or "constraint-free" new ways of working during design, existing constraints have to be considered. These are the "Ah . . . but" rules in an organisation, the ones typically advanced by those opposed to or cynical about change. "Ah . . . ," they pronounce, "The process design is fine, but what about . . .". In reality, many of these existing constraints are merely historical and many can be overcome, if suitably challenged. Every rule has to be put on the table and every assumption rigorously dissected to determine the validity of its existence. Only then can its real rationale, or any alternative way of satisfying it, be determined.

The basis of this challenge is a single question: "Why?". Every control task or checking activity is linked back to a rule—written or unwritten—in the organisation. Posing the simple "why?" question uncovers a chain of dependent and often unintended events. This piece of paper has to be collected, so that this box can be ticked, so that another form can be completed, and the final transaction can be authorised. A dogged persistence and probing right down the chain of events is necessary to determine what are valid and logical requirements. Only when the real nub of the issue is reached can the questions start to be asked: Does every transaction have to have this step? Are there certain sub-categories that we can treat differently? Can the x be done away with altogether?

Like the actual design itself, this is an area where external consultants or facilitators can be used to good effect. Using staff from within an organisation tends to result in the challenges being shrugged off and the assumptions inadequately probed. The real sacred cows within an institution are just too revered for internal staff to slaughter. As well as having greater freedom to ask the questions and probe the assumptions, external consultants can be used to assist in finding alternative ways of satisfying regulations or constraints where they are found to be valid. Alternatively, staff who are unfamiliar with that particular part of the business can be used to raise the challenges, by being encouraged to pose the most basic questions. It is the naive, innocent challenges—why is it done that way? who says that piece of paper is always a prerequisite?—that tend to be the most effective ones.

The following guidelines apply when examining constraints:

- *Go right to the root.* The real reason for a particular problem or constraint is rarely obvious on first examination. Tease further at an assumption or rule and peel back the layers of a problem until the real constraint emerges. Often, one single piece of information or check required deep within the bowels of an organisation can lead to layers of procedures, cross-checks and hold-ups above it.
- *Use more than one source.* What one person or department perceives to be an immovable requirement or "absolute", another may have a quite different view on. Many people work within vertical silos, with little communication between colleagues or departments upstream and down-stream. This was graphically illustrated within an insurance company, battling to take down the procedural and regulatory walls that had arisen over the course of more than 60 years. When questioned, the managers at the front-line, customer-facing end of the business maintained that there was no way a particular change to a process could be achieved, insisting that "the underwriters would never allow it". Questioned about the same issue at a different session, the underwriters' response was that it was "a

good idea but impossible because they would never permit it operationally".

- *Be bold.* Dare to question the very "givens" that have been accepted for so long in an organisation. These fundamentals—or, more often, sacred cows—can often be at the very heart of a problem, so much an integral way of doing things that no one has ever stopped to consider an alternative. Examples include, in financial services, always expecting that the customer will fill out a proposal form, and, in healthcare, that the patient always has to visit the doctor to undergo a diagnosis. Remember, the ultimate effectiveness of the process depends on the removal of the worst constraints.
- *Don't stop at internal constraints.* Internal processes are often hampered by external as well as internal regulations or controls. This should not prevent them from being challenged; even if they cannot be removed completely, there may be an alternative, simpler way of meeting the requirement or complying with a regulation that fits the new processes better.
- *Search out the low value added.* Home in on the areas of the process where little value is being added. These are clues to steps undertaken to satisfy a requirement elsewhere, which is no longer essential, can be avoided or can be combined with a step elsewhere.
- *Make ripples.* Be prepared to upset people in authority and intrude into hallowed territory. It is often the very areas with the fiercest guardians (the established, unsmiling section head whose authority no one has ever dared question) that benefit most from such challenge. Questioning accepted rules causes the very rationale for jobs, and sometimes whole departments, to be put into question. If ripples are not being made, the questions are probably not searching enough.

Reviewing and testing constraints is necessary to establish the most effective, straightforward process. Although it follows redesign in this chapter, in practice the cycle of redesign and validation is an iterative, rather than a serial, activity. The first notions of a new design will be reviewed against the main "constraints" of business, and subsequently designs may be revised when it becomes clear which constraints are immovable.

Business Testing and Validation

The second aspect of validation is the formal testing of process designs. Although one of the less appealing tasks of a change programme, which evokes wearisome images of endless reams of data being typed into a PC, testing is a critical plank in ensuring that changes being made actually bring about the desired results. The very nature of such process-led change (which involve so many areas of an organisation in change simultaneously) makes testing a key tool to keep the project on track. This is as true in the early stages of change, to ensure that the high-level process architecture conforms to design principles and will achieve the vision, as it is in the later stages when lines of computer code and pages of procedures and people skills have to be validated.

To achieve this, the role of testing has to move from being a mundane policing role to a more positive one, ensuring that it becomes an effective part of the quality control process rather than a burden. By turning the perspective around in this way, testing becomes an activity that actually adds value by providing input, rather than merely identifying problems. Wherever possible, testing activity becomes a means of identifying potential solutions as well as identifying defects. This is the proactive approach to change which helps to speed the transformation activity forward.

The essence of testing is about checking that at any stage the process is capable of handling the full range of requirements that make up the business. During process design this is concerned with validation of the logical design itself; during the build and creation of the new capability, it is concerned with more detailed testing of computer applications, and people skills and capabilities.

Testing has to take place:

- internally—with staff who both operate and manage the existing business processes, so as to identify any major flaws or omissions in the new design.
- strategically—the design is reviewed against the design principles, to ensure that the new way of working supports the overall objectives and direction of the company. There is no point in building a high-cost, maximum hands-on service corporation if the company wants to focus on being a low-cost provider in a commodity market-place.
- externally—the new way of working should be reviewed with customers and prospective customers to identify any problems with the way in which the new designs operate.
- against objectives and measures—to ensure that the new process design meets the requirements for improved performance. This is undertaken by estimating revised costs, volumes, times etc. for the new process designs.

The testing stage should include review against formal test material that reflects typical everyday events, and interactions and scenarios with the customer and other departments within the business. These should be documented in descriptive format and cover the typical high-volume, everyday transactions as well as the one-off and exceptional occurrences, to ensure that the process can cope with both.

One of the most effective means of validation is the test script or business scenario as used by OASiS (Figure 4.5).

Document Title:	**MOTOR CLAIMS TEST SCRIPT** 📖✎	
Prepared by: Approved by: Amended by:	**Original version:** Reviewed by: Date: Date:	
Date prepared: **13/10/93**	**History of changes:** Version CL0501.1 created 13/10/93	

Scenario: Customer involved in accident at roundabout where third-party vehicle hits her vehicle in rear. Damage incurred to her vehicle, but no injury sustained by any party – the third party is liable.

Inputs/triggers (events and dates)
Customer telephones to report the accident and has full details available.

Description
Having greeted customer, the customer service clerk attempts to reassure her that everything possible will be done to rectify the situation as soon as possible, and proceeds to collect the details required to identify the customer and current policy.

Having established this, and confirmed with her that they are correct, brief details are taken of the incident, its location and the parties involved, etc. Customer has obtained the third party's name, address, details of their insurer, and the registration mark of their vehicle. She has also obtained the name and address of an independent witness who came forward at the time of the incident.

No previous notification of this claim is registered, so a new claim record is created from the known details. Cover has to be checked and appropriate action taken.

Outputs/results

•   From the information received on the initial contact the customer's records are retrieved and updated

•   The relevant claim details are recorded

•   The customer is given information on the relevant procedure, including any identified useful advice

•   A reference is provided for future correspondence

•   A partly completed claim report form is sent to the customer with an acknowledgement of the claim

Alternative actions/options

1.   The customer's father is the person to make the initial contact notifying us of the incident and not all of the required information is known.

2.   There is more than one third party involved and this leads to several negotiation attempts with each insurer before settlements are agreed.

3.   Despite being contacted and reminded about providing his account of the incident, the witness does not reply.

Business coverage
Case complexity: fairly simple   Handled by levels: 1 and 2

	1993	1994	1995
Claims volumes			
Motor	57 000	86 000	92 000
Volumes relating to this script	18 379	17 422	1565

Figure 4.5   The test script

As stressed above, testing is a continuous exercise that takes place during process design, rather than as the final stage. Design and testing is an iterative, rather than a serial, activity.

Finally, testing, as with every other aspect of the transformation programme, should not be treated in isolation. It should be regarded as a means of communicating changes and new directions to the wider organisation, which helps to build momentum and commitment toward the desired solutions, rather than as a burden on time and resources.

DESIGN OR MODELLING?

The hype that has accompanied, and sometimes threatened to obscure, BPR and process-led change has given rise to much confusion and misunderstanding. In some areas, fundamental concepts have become so blurred that their real purpose is no longer understood or pursued. This is more than just a difference in terminology and semantics, at worst resulting in months of work being wasted. The difference between process design and process modelling is a classic case in point—the two activities are fundamentally different, but are often referred to as if fulfilling a common purpose.

The difference between the two can be seen in the following definitions:

- *Process design* is the creation and description of how the business will carry out its core processes activities in future. It defines how the business will look, and helps to identify the changes to infrastructure that have to be made.
- *Process modelling* is the diagramming or mapping of the existing processes in the business, as they work currently.

The differences in definition are small, but the differences in purpose and use are vast. It is the stage of process design that provides the opportunity to shed the burden of history and create ways of working that meet the new needs of customers. Process design is creative and adds real value, when performed correctly. Process modelling, on the other hand, is concerned with looking at existing business operations.

Whether process modelling, as opposed to design, is actually used within a change initiative depends on the exact approach being followed. In particular, to avoid "paralysis by analysis", process modelling should be used sparingly, if it is not to become a distraction and a drain on resources. The most important aspect is that the difference between design and modelling is understood, and the objectives of each different technique are clarified. Design is concerned with the new, and modelling is concerned with the existing. Process models of the existing business provide the following:

- *Understanding.* A model is used to present a view of the existing business in process terms. As well as pinpointing the inadequacies of the existing infrastructure, and highlighting the need for redesign, the model can be used to familiarise both staff and management with the concepts and thinking of process.
- *Identification of bottlenecks and constraints.* Developing a process view of existing operations helps to identify the existing bottlenecks that are inhibiting performance. Because the model is captured in terms people understand, everyone is able to contribute to it.
- *Developing measures.* The importance of measures to the change programme has been highlighted previously. A model of the existing business in process terms helps in benchmarking (to identify how the organisation compares against others) and in identifying those areas where new measures should be established.
- *Identifying the gap.* Because it represents the current business, a process model can be used (by comparison with the new design) to identify the gap or shortfall between the current and desired. This forms the basis for scoping out the size of the change programme, the level of change required and, ultimately, the specific work packages to be undertaken.
- *Benchmarking.* Where an organisation wishes to benchmark existing process performance against competitor or "best in class" information, a process model can form the basis for identifying appropriate aspects of the business to measure.

Whatever use is made of process modelling, a close watch needs to be kept on the levels of detail that develop. Unmonitored, the activity can rapidly turn into a redundant intellectual challenge which attempts to squeeze every aspect of the existing enterprise into the model. The emphasis, as ever, should be on practicalities. If the modelling is not contributing directly to the progress of change, it should be set aside.

☞ SIGNPOSTS FOR SUCCESS

Be aware of, not driven by, IT

Information technology is first and last a tool. If it can be utilised to carry out core processes more effectively then so be it—but don't be blinded by it. If a pen and paper are sufficient, then use them.

Scope exactly

Careful inclusion and exclusion of particular areas of the business sets out the boundaries of the redesign work. This is particularly important when changes come to be implemented in the business, and changes at the "boundary" of the process have to be negotiated with those outside the immediate process area.

Design for the vision

Design principles, Scorecard and measures should be well known to designers and process teams, and well documented and readily available so that process designs can be checked against strategic needs. The design principles in particular should be pithy and memorable so that they act as a guiding light to the design practicalities, acting as a quick test that is always there. Pages and pages of text guarantee that no one will refer to them, but five or six bullet points on the wall help to make the vision a constant, visible goal to pursue.

Beware the corporate storyteller

When testing constraints and business rules it is important to be aware of the dangers of personal experience and anecdote (as reliable sources of business information) rather than personal investigation. It is a fact of life that people like to tell stories and sound knowledgeable—and frequently they do this even if they are not up to date.

Involve people

Bring in people from all levels of the business so that different perspectives can be incorporated and considered (and, where necessary, rejected). Those at the front-line, customer-facing point of the business often have a better understanding of real customer needs than the management and marketeers above them.

Focus on value

There is sometimes a tendency, when carried along on a powerful wave of creativity and rule breaking, to neglect the overall objectives of redesign; the innovative capabilities of IT or the opportunities to do things differently become the driving rather than the enabling factors. Ultimately, the process and the activities within it have to be subjected to a harsh test of the value they create for the enterprise itself. Where are the aspects of the process that the customers will benefit from enough to pay (and go on paying) for? What activities allow the enterprise to provide a realisable edge over the competition *which the customer needs and wants*. Slick and fancy processes are of no use if they do not create a competitive edge.

Completion of the process architecture provides the business with the blueprint for its new ways of working. This design should be signed off and accepted by both sponsors and process owners alike before proceeding. It now forms the basis of the change programme and the work that follows. The next stage is to turn it into a comprehensive specification with which to bring about change and ultimately manage the new process-led business.

Chapter 5

Process: From Design to Specification

It is usually around this stage that the black holes of change initiatives begin to open up. By this time, several months into the programme, extensive effort and resource have already been expended on conceiving and launching the change initiative, preparing staff for change, communicating new directions to the organisation and, above all, producing a process design that will take the enterprise forward. But even with all the correct foundations in place—alignment with strategy, commitment of the best people and high-level sponsorship—it is often at this point that major change programmes begin to stumble.

One reason for this lurch in progress is the dip in enthusiasm and commitment that inevitably begins to occur. Several months away from the flagwaving days of launch and initiation, energy on the change team begins to wane. The constraints and objections raised by the business begin to appear immovable; a new product has to be launched or a seasonal rise in business has operations clamouring to take their best people back off the project. People lose the energy to drive change through and make things happen. Suddenly the whole forward progress of the change effort begins to look precarious.

But the underlying problem is much more fundamental. Energy can be replenished, obstacles can be shifted and the change team can be revitalised. But the real stalling point is usually caused by the design itself. It is at this point that process designs begin to show their true colours, and usually they are found wanting. All of a sudden, change managers and implementation teams are left puzzling over how the ideals captured in design are to be translated into reality. New people skills, organisational capabilities and IT infrastructures are implied—but there is no indication of what they should actually look like, or any guide as to how they should be created.

This is the 'black hole' that has swallowed many a BRE or process-led change project in the past. The design looked good in theory, but there was no substance. The chasm between the process design and the development of a new infrastructure was just too big to cross.

In Chapter 2, the metaphor of a bridge was used to illustrate the importance of the process design at the heart of the change programme. The design acts as the essential link between the vision of the organisation and the underlying business infrastructure, which brings that vision to life by providing a formal means of designing and specifying the capability required. But the process architecture, produced in the first design phase, does not yet meet these requirements. Returning to the analogy, the design has bridged the gap but it is still only a wire rope with a hand-rail slung across the void.

The next stage is to turn the design into an enduring, integrated platform—a comprehensive specification robust enough to drive forward the two or three years of building and rebuilding that must take place as part of the change programme. The architecture must become a specification.

FROM DESIGN TO SPECIFICATION

In Chapter 1, the realities of major change were considered. They provided a stark reminder of the work that really has to be carried out to put new processes in place. Bringing about successful change is not about producing designs. It is about building new capability—of people, systems and organisations. But it is also about coping with the realities of change—staff leave, delays occur, requirements change and operational issues take priority.

Changing an organisation is a vast undertaking. Creating new processes requires the overhaul of an enterprise's infrastructure, the creation and rebuilding of whole organisational, procedural and systems components. A vast amount of modification, dismantling, rebuilding and renewal has to take place. It requires detailed specification, not high-level wishlists.

To achieve this, the following are required:

- a basis for communicating the new ways of working to the organisation
- a means of managing the change programme, and controlling changes to specification
- the business requirements from which to determine the new IS systems required
- an indication of the HR capability required
- requirements for procedural and other manual support

- a means of determining what parts of current capabilities have to be modified to create the new infrastructure required
- the starting point to determine what "quick wins" may be implemented to bring early visibility and return from the change project

In addition, if process is to become a viable means of managing the business post-implementation, and a mechanism for driving improvement, it has to incorporate the measures necessary to monitor performance and the breadth of view necessary to incorporate all mechanisms and manage change.

At this stage many organisations make the mistake of believing that the high-level design or process architecture produced is adequate to drive the change programme along. They set off down the path of implementation in the mistaken belief that this is all that is required. Not surprisingly, the programme stumbles, and invariably falls back into the abyss between strategy and the delivery of any lasting change or results. Ultimately, the initiative flounders, and becomes consigned to the list of "what might have been" projects.

A PROCESS SPECIFICATION: FROM CONCEPTS TO REALITY

To move forward from a high-level design to a specification that can support the creation and roll-out of a whole new business infrastructure, the design must be developed and "fleshed out" until it is substantial enough to act as a genuine specification for change. The key actions within this stage are to continue the design of the processes outlined in the process architecture down to a lower level of detail (Figure 5.1).

Producing this specification is essentially concerned with further design activity and adding levels of detail. In short, it is about determining and documenting how it is going to work and who or what is going to do it. This involves making tradeoffs between alternatives, and describing and documenting the outcomes so that a specification can be produced. This is achieved by working through each process step identified in the process architecture and:

- defining what transactions and transformations are carried out
- describing (but not yet defining) the information required
- outlining the role of people (the human element) within the process step
- describing the types of skills and attitudes required
- identifying common exceptions and likely pitfalls that may occur
- defining interfaces and boundaries with customers, suppliers etc.
- specifying the main measures of performance

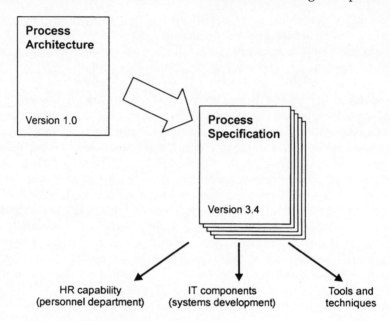

Figure 5.1 From Architecture to Specification

- identifying and describing the rules and controls on how the process operates

Process design is about coming up with a new, streamlined, possibly radical way of doing business. But the really hard part of this 'redesign' is converting the design into reality: transforming the bold new ideas into the new infrastructure. The real secret of good design, once the innovative ideas have been thrashed out, is capturing it in a format that can be used to implement the new ideas. The real secret of design is producing a good specification.

A Word about Format

The process specification has to be captured in such a way that it can act as the guide for all those involved in making the change. IT developers, HR specialists, trainers and Process Owners all take their cue from the new design, with inherent demands on how it is captured. The most effective means is a combination of graphical and textual descriptions, which states in words and diagrams or pictures how particular "things"—be they physical entities (such as raw materials, goods or people) or information entities (such as requests or orders)—pass through the organisation and are transformed.

The actual means by which the design is captured is not critical. The main criteria is that a sufficient level of detail can be captured to produce a specification, in the areas described above. There are numerous software packages on the market claiming to automate process design but many tend to force structures or conventions onto a process design which are unnecessary; others, with too much of a systems background, tend to concentrate overly on the information aspects.

One of the unique points of the process-led approach is the opportunity it provides to capture detail about the "soft" as well as the "hard" requirements of the new ways of working. So, for example, it is possible to capture requirements about the nature of the interaction with the customer, rather than just specifying the fields of information required at point of sale. The ability to capture such "free text" and descriptive qualities is as important as any automated diagramming and updating facilities. Ultimately, some degree of IT support is likely to be necessary in view of the iterative nature of design and the large numbers of versions and revisions that have to be made, but an elaborate process design tool is not essential. Indeed, many organisations still display a preference for the simplest of all, the "brown paper" approach, where scrolls of brown parcel paper are bedecked with Post-it notes to map out process steps.

ESSENTIALS OF DESIGN

During this stage, the substance of processes has to be fleshed out: the way outputs are converted into inputs; the way a customer query becomes an order; the way an order becomes a paid for product; the way controls influence performance; the way staff talk to customers and requirements are conveyed to suppliers. The specification must capture the 'soft' requirements as well as the hard—the attitudes and behaviours required as well as the information and operations. These are aspects that process is unique in being able to specify, and pave the way for a comprehensive, rather than a one-sided business model.

The process specification must capture the requirements of the new processes in enough depth and detail so that those responsible for the building and rebuilding understand what they have to produce. To this end, there are three essentials of a good specification (Figure 5.2):

1. Searching for the optimum mechanism
2. Style and manner: designing the nuances
3. Making the decisions

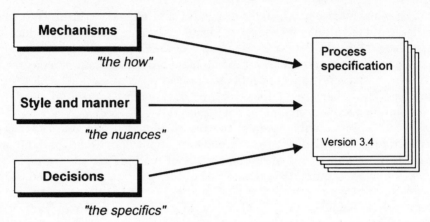

Figure 5.2 Essentials of specification

Essential 1: Searching for the Optimum Mechanism

The first quality in turning a design into a specification is the description of the mechanisms (the people, IT, organisational and manual capabilities) responsible for each process step. This paves the way for development teams to create the new capability required, whether it be the training of the customer service clerk or the coding of a new computer application. The objective at this stage is to describe the mechanisms that will be used; further analysis then takes place at a later stage about the specifics required.

Because the process approach is holistic, it can encompass all mechanisms, rather than any one in isolation. This has two implications for design. The first is that it ensures that any appropriate mechanism can be considered as a means of actually supporting the process. This avoids bias towards a particular "people" or "systems" solution, which tends to occur when a people-focused or IT-orientated method is used.

The second is that it provides a framework for designing and specifying how different mechanisms work *together*. For each process step or activity it is possible to specify how the appropriate mechanisms are combined with others. The process step can therefore be described in terms of how staff with particular skills use a particular subset of computer systems, or how procedures link together different process steps.

Although such a structured, top-down approach to design may appear novel in designing businesses and organisations, it is one that has been successfully adopted in other industries for many years. When an engineering and design team sets out to create a new car, they do so with an understanding of the capabilities of many different materials and components. As well as the overall 'shape' and concept of the vehicle, the design also considers what components would be most suitable in combination. For an off-road vehicle, certain suspension and tyre combinations will be selected; for a low-cost, urban run-around, components of lower strength and durability might be selected, but still chosen in combination.

Applied to business design, it can be seen that this holistic approach is a far more appropriate means of designing how organisations work than traditional methods have provided. The specification can therefore capture how processes and process steps may use a *combination* of skills, capabilities and technologies rather than any one in isolation. This is a part of design hitherto missing in organisational change.

Designing and specifying these combinations during design paves the way for the new process to be realised by a truly integrated set of capabilities. In telesales it could entail designing how human "selling" skills are combined with a particular set of information provided by an IT system. In product development it could encompass how representatives from marketing, design and production in the early stages complete the pro-formas that shape the framework for a new product and subsequently share designs over interactive communications links.

Essential 2: Style and Manner—Designing the Nuances

Process is a vision for the future. But a process is not limited to an inanimate sequence of activities or list of possible mechanisms. If process is to be the route map for transforming the way that work is done, it has to be far more. A process has to address the living, breathing way in which we service customers and design products. A good enterprise—one that produces quality products, wins new orders, retains its customers and develops new ones—is not just about staff following procedures by rote, computer systems crunching data and machines churning out products. It is also about the attitudes and policies that permeate the organisation—the nature of the interaction with the customer at specific points in the process, how particular problems are resolved and where staff go the 'extra mile'. In short, the 'softer', less tangible aspects of the organisation are as important as those that can be touched or reprogrammed.

Traditionally, these are not aspects of an organisation's fabric that have been subject to design—they emerged as a result of management or procedures or history, rather than through any conscious decision. But the process-led approach changes all that. Process offers a means of actively designing the very idiosyncrasies and defining touches that make an organisation unique. The design can capture how the staff in an organisation talk to customers in specific parts of the process, rather than just trying to embody them in far away strategy or vague mission statements. "Customer care counts" can become "confirm the order with the customer and then cross check the previous delivery to make sure it was satisfactory". It becomes as important to design the 'look and feel' of personal interactions as it is to design information systems or manufacturing plant.

For in the brave new world design is as relevant to dialogue as it is to databases. If a member of staff has to perform a particular task, ask a particular question or offer reassurance to improve the performance of the process then this must be captured. If it is decided that a particular image or message is to be conveyed to the customer, then it must be captured during design as a requirement. And design, as part of the wider process-led change methodology, ensures that the requirement, once captured, can be turned into a reality. Glibly recited corporate motherhood statements can be translated into specific requirements, and specific requirements can be translated into training programmes, and systems and procedures which ensure that the desired capability to make such activities happen is actually created. By providing this perspective the process approach ensures that the activities required to create an edge on service can be designed in.

Taking the insurance industry as an example, consider how differentiation could be achieved by focusing on particular aspects of the process. Most insurance requires customers to contact their insurer at various times over the lifetime of a policy. Typically the transaction is routine and straightforward—it is an administrative issue involving a change of address, an increase in cover, or a request for an additional person to be included on the policy. Many organisations have invested millions of pounds in ensuring that the service provided in these areas is slick and effective.

But the opportunity to differentiate is no longer here. The routine servicing of customers is important, but the opportunity to shine comes elsewhere. Crunch time occurs when a claim is being made—the customer is potentially in a state of shock, panic or upset. This is the point at which an organisation can really differentiate its service—by designing a process that can capture information to put the wheels of rapid settlement in order, but combine it with reassurance, assistance and comfort to the customer, which only another human being can provide. These are the edges in service which ensure that a customer recommends a product or service to colleagues, or relates anecdotes in the bar that pitch the organisation in a positive light.

The design of such "nuances" is not limited to the financial sector. They are equally important in telecommunications or in healthcare. Consider the point at which a patient is discharged from hospital after a successful operation. This is a key time for education and advice. Building into the process enough time for a few words of counselling or after treatment may be a far more effective contribution towards prevention than at any other time.

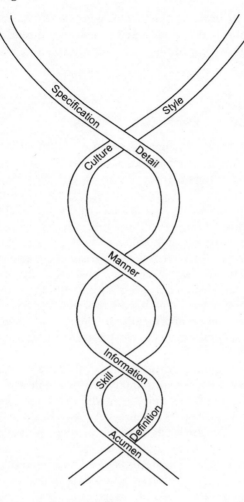

Figure 5.3 The woven strands of design

The inclusion of these 'softer', more intangible aspects into an organisation's processes is an essential of process specification. Because process-led change is not limited to specific categories or rigid information structures, the capture of *ad hoc* requirements and the "things that don't fit" becomes possible. As the differences between information systems and technologies are eroded further, these are the capabilities that provide a competitive edge. Change is an ever more pervasive influence around us; the opportunities are vast and the range of responses required immensely varied. But it is the ability to shape a response—to the 'softer', unpredictable aspects—which will provide a means of genuine differentiation. These are the aspects of design which ensure that a customer is made to feel part of a caring organisation with a human face rather than just a cog in a machine (Figure 5.3).

Essential 3: Making the Decisions

The third essential quality of a good process specification is that of decisions. Earlier, we said that a specification is concerned with describing how a process works and who or what carries it out. Change creates choices, myriad choices, and much of process design is about making the difficult tradeoffs between options. Process design requires changing existing processes—collecting different information, doing steps in a different order, adding a completely new step to the process or combining several stages into one. And for each change there are knock-on effects up and down the organisation, into different functions and adjoining departments. The early stages of process design may seem radical and ground-breaking, but as the detail is gathered, the exercise becomes one of tradeoffs and decisions as much as one of innovation and creativity—high-level requirements have to be turned into the specifics that staff can operate on and information systems can process.

The very power of the process model is its breadth and flexibility; its ability to define and capture requirements about people and attitudes as well as about the systems and technology. At the same time, this very breadth becomes a gaping void if decisions are not made to tie the various options down. The process design is the bridge between the vision and the new business infrastructure, but between the two lie a thousand and one decisions, which ensure that the design can be translated into the new reality of computer applications and hardware, motivated staff and retrained managers, and new measurement systems.

In the example of the fault-fixing process outlined earlier, decisions have to be made about information. What information has to be retrieved to deal with the customer? How is the severity of a fault determined? At what point does escalation occur to initiate the call-out of an engineer? Equally, decisions have to be made when process design results in the empowerment of staff with wider responsibilities and capabilities, to enable greater freedom to complete work without management involvement. This might include the signing limit for a cheque or the ability to authorise a credit limit on a loan. But should the signing limit be £250 or £500 or £1000 and who should have it? Should it exist across every product and service or just a subset? And what are the cross-checks and audits required to make sure such limits are not abused.

The decisions to be made are manifold. They arise over jobs (the boundary between multi-skilling and the specialist), products (to what degree are products amended to fit a simpler framework that enables multi-skilling?), information (what information should be captured and displayed if it has to support many rather than single customer needs?). Typically, these decisions which have to be made emerge in the course of documenting the process design. The questions that arise, or changes that are proposed, gradually flesh out the specifics around which decisions need making. There are, however, four aspects that are particularly significant:

- *Design principles.* The importance of design principles as the guiding lights of process design has been constantly stressed, but they do inevitably come into conflict. A design principle about speed, for example, may appear to be in opposition to one about quality. Similarly, a design principle that sets out an expectation of 'customer service' might appear to be in conflict with one that refers to 'maximum productivity'. Alternatively, there may be a cultural design principle attesting to "providing interesting and stimulating work", while parts of the process require extensive periods of mundane data entry. The important emphasis is that of "principle"—it embodies how the process should work, if possible. Where there are other factors to take into account, the process designer has to make the tradeoff and determine the most appropriate solution using the process specification to capture the design decision clearly.
- *People.* Process, by its nature, cuts across functions, departments, territories and fiefdoms. Decisions about how a process will work typically impact more people than changes contained within a vertical function. The process designer has to make these decisions and propagate them up and down the process—forcing the tradeoffs that no one wants to make. These are the tradeoffs that have strangled efforts to change and improve in the past because so many other people and departments appear to have a vested interest in the way tasks are carried out. Giving more staff access to a database ensures that more customer queries can be answered, but it also means there are many more ways of that information becoming corrupt. Devolving responsibility to empowered staff may allow them to solve a problem or meet a customer requirement—but it also opens up questions of how standardisation and consistency are to be maintained.
- *Maintainability.* Tradeoffs have to be made between current and future concerns, or the maintainability of processes. Although the initial viability of a process is the first concern, the ability to modify or update that process, or the people structures or IT systems which support it, is also important. Design decisions have to be made with an eye on the future and some compromise on the "perfect" solution is often necessary to build in maintainability and modularity. There is little point in creating an

all-singing, all-dancing computer system if the maintenance and enhancement costs are prohibitive.

- *Revision.* Finally, it is important to revise decisions rapidly when they are wrong. The free reign that process design provides creates an immense number of choices and decisions to be made. Almost inevitably, this means that some decisions will be wrong. Wrong decisions are not a problem in themselves—only wrong decisions that are not corrected at a later date or decisions that are never made at all.

Returning to the example used in the process architecture stage and taking the process step "Investigate fault" as a case in point, the original definition was as follows (see Figure 4.4):

"To investigate the fault thoroughly over the telephone before it is raised for action. This involves structured steps to determine the real nature of the fault and resolve problems caused by operator error. Remote diagnostics and the analysis of information held centrally about the overall installation will be used if appropriate."

The definition now has to be expanded to provide a more detailed view of both the activities within it and the mechanisms that will be used. Consider Figure 5.4.

2.2 Investigate Fault

Information about the customer (name, location, size of installation, size of account) will be retrieved automatically where call routing has been used. Using information provided by the customer and from on-line records about the customer's installation, the severity and size of the problem is investigated (eg, the number of people affected, the number of machines down) to determine a priority. The nature and type of the fault is also identified. The customer is taken through a basic set of questions (simple decision tree) to determine the likely source of the fault. Depending on the nature of this source:

- Carry out further actions with customer in attempt to resolve fault
- Undergo remote diagnostics to determine problems
- Evaluate rest of infrastructure and network
- Instruct engineer to visit site and issue work instruction

Key Features: Potential customers must be closely involved with the diagnosis and analysis work going on, to provide reassurance and avoid a feeling of isolation in line with enforcing the corporate image of responsiveness and service.

Scope: Includes checking whether the fault has been reported before.

Note: where the call has been answered and routed automatically this step will provide the first point of human customer contact.

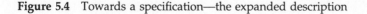

Figure 5.4 Towards a specification—the expanded description

The description is now expanded so that implications for mechanisms to be used are included (the use of ACD technology to retrieve customer information and its associated implications for linking telecommunications and computer technology, the need for remote diagnostics and interrogation of other databases holding configuration information). The emphasis at this stage is still on description. The information required is still outlined at a high level, rather than at the level of entities and possible values at this point.

The mechanisms are not, however, limited to IT mechanisms; there are implications for people skills (staff answering phones will need the ability to conduct or access remote diagnostics and interrogate databases) and the use of a decision tree (whether implemented manually or electronically), and even for the part the customer plays in the process.

BEWARE THE ONE-LEGGED CHINAMAN: APPLYING THE 80:20 RULE

The final consideration in the design and development of effective processes is the application of the 80:20 rule. This is based on the premise that within any business or operational environment, the vast majority of cases or objects that are transformed (whether information, people, goods or raw materials) show a fair degree of commonality and standardisation. They fit within a certain set of parameters, even if some lie at the extremes of those parameters. These inputs, or throughputs, can therefore be transformed by a set of processes governed by a particular set of rules or controls, and a relatively basic set of knowledge or capability.

But beyond these more straightforward instances lurk the more complex cases. It may be the customer who is a one-off case, and has special requirements to be met, it may be the client whose completely obscure set of demands lies beyond the normal service offered, or it may be the patient seeking treatment whose condition is complicated by a secondary illness. By implication, these exceptions often demand a different, usually more complex, response, along with the application of a more sophisticated set of rules. The process that handles them is broadly similar, but it requires an additional shell of expertise or knowledge, and more cross-checks and rules, to carry it out.

Given that a key objective of redesign is simpler, more straightforward processes, often serviced by multi-staff, these exceptions or "one-legged chinamen" can rapidly become a massive burden on an otherwise slick process. Suddenly, all manner of additional complexities—demands for rules, systems and more specialised human capabilities—creep back in right across the process. Very quickly they choke up the rest of the process once more.

The response is to subdivide the handling of the core process. A good process design may have to cope with all eventualities—but it does not have to cope with them all in exactly the same way. Complex, exceptional or 'one-off' cases can be routed out for handling in a slightly different way so that they do not clog the arteries of the process for every straightforward case.

Getting the balance right is key: too many cases routed out, and the 'special-case' route rapidly becomes too great a demand on resources; too few, and the performance of the mainstream process is compromised. This is the skill in designing good processes. To get the balance right during design, the question "but how often does this occur?" has to be to the forefront of the designer's armoury, to determine how often particular idiosyncrasies or exceptions occur. Does the mainstream process have to be designed to cope with this particular case, or is it a one-off, rarely encountered example? If the answer is the latter, then it is often more appropriate to route the case out from the mainstream process.

Although a further layer of rules, expertise and specialist skills has to be brought to bear to handle these 'special-cases', it can at least now take place without clogging the arteries of the main process. Often this 'peripheral' process may be less sophisticated than the mainstream process, and make more use of manual, procedural and human resources rather than system solutions. Again, this is a strength of the holistic approach— that the most appropriate solution (mechanism), rather than the most sophisticated one, can be chosen. If it is more appropriate to use human expertise than an on-line rule set to handle the exceptional cases, then this method can be chosen.

The alternative response to such exceptions, of course, is to eliminate such cases altogether from the business. By defining the business it wishes to be in, and the customers it wishes to take on, very tightly, an organisation can select against certain, more complicated, cases and eliminate them from the market segment it wishes to operate in. This is an approach that has been effectively adopted by some insurance companies, cutting out the complexities and costs of servicing certain driving groups.

CAPTURING THE DESIGN

The wider role of process as a blueprint for capturing new ways of working, controlling and managing change, and managing processes on an ongoing basis, now begins to emerge. Decision making, rich descriptions and the definition of mechanisms are all essentials for turning a design into a specification that can drive the whole change programme. Inherent in this role are demands on the clarity with which requirements are documented. It is the depth, breadth and richness of the specification that ultimately ensures that design decisions and requirements are translated into a new working reality.

Since process design emerged as a discipline in its own right, whole legions have been written about the pros and cons of various design tools, and the value of IT support in capturing process designs. Ultimately, the tool is of less importance than the requirements captured and the capability developed from them. The following aspects are important guidelines in capturing the design:

- *Avoid data myopia.* Avoid tools that focus solely on data—one of the key benefits of the process model is its ability to capture the "soft" requirements. An extreme emphasis on data (and the intellectual wrangles it spawns in attempts to squeeze every last entity into its correct place in the model) tends to detract from other aspects of the design. Data modelling should follow process design, not drive it.
- *Language.* Clear language and unambiguous terminology is essential, given the range of audiences dependent on the design. Words such as "system", which can be interpreted in a specific context (computer systems) in addition to their literal sense, should be avoided. A glossary should be implemented from day one on the project, its use made mandatory and regular updating carried out.
- *End to end view.* Several tools incorporate a hierarchical design facility. While this is useful to aid a "top-down" perspective during design and hide levels of detail, it can also make it incredibly difficult to understand the end to end 'flow' of the process.
- *Develop the design as you go.* Be prepared to document requirements and move on, adding more detail later as it becomes clear. Describing, rather than defining, requirements helps to set the context of a particular process step without slowing down progress unnecessarily. Hence, "information about the customer" can be used, and in due course can be expanded. Avoid at all cost becoming involved with detailed data analysis at this stage. As well as being incredibly time consuming, it also places an overly strong emphasis on IT too soon. The purpose of this stage is to describe the new way of working, so that those skilled in developing the supporting components are able to understand the new requirement.
- *Avoid excessive levels of detail.* Or, as one project director put it, "it is better to be approximately right, than precisely wrong". While the object of the process specification is to define the requirements for change, this does not imply that every last word needs spelling out to HR, IT and training staff. Process designers (or owners) stay with the design during implementation to assist in its interpretation. As with process modelling, there is a risk that

endless hours are spent dotting the *is* and crossing the *t*s of material produced in a locked room, when time could be better spent in getting new designs in front of those who will actually be doing the work.

- *Remember the audience.* The process specification is a blueprint for change with many different readers. IT staff, the training department, line and board level management, design teams, sponsors and external stakeholders may all need to review parts of it. The quality of the written word is key and it needs to be comprehensive, yet concise and tight.

- *Scope clearly.* Scope clearly and carefully inclusions and exclusions to particular process areas or designs. The actual location of particular areas of the business is less important than the fact that they are clearly included or excluded. This avoids particular aspects slipping through the gaps.

- *Avoid ambiguity.* Be specific and unambiguous in the specification, while stopping short of capturing every single attribute of information, which is a job for IT analysts. The specification needs to describe rather than define data: for example, "Capture customer information (name, address, personal details and occupation) details". The objective at this stage is to describe the information required, not define it down to every last field name or validation check.

THE TASK BREAKDOWN

The final activity within the specification stage, and indeed in the overall design of new processes, is to break down the processes into their key tasks and confirm the mechanisms used to carry out each of these tasks. This forms the basis for controlling and coordinating the development of the new business components, covered in the chapters that follow.

So far, the design of the new business or enterprise has concentrated on the design of new processes. In so doing, the focus has been on producing a design that describes how the new process works—and, in particular, how the various people and technological capabilities within it are combined to produce the desired ways of working. The design has to be rich and comprehensive enough to describe the various components within it, so that they can be identified for construction.

The process design has been used to embrace any or all of the mechanisms that may be required to carry that process out. This is a key part of the process approach, but for the purposes of development, the requirements for these capabilities now need to be split up into their component areas. So, for example, all of the tasks that require IT support have to be identified so that the required support can be specified in more depth and developed. Similarly, all of the tasks within the process that require procedural support or the definition of other manual mechanisms can be identified.

Process: 2.0 Fault Reporting and Resolution		
Process Step: 2.2 Investigate Fault		
Main tasks	**Primary mechanism**	**Secondary mechanism**
2.2.1 Identify site	System (via call routing identifier)	Manual
2.2.2 Identify location	System (from existing records)	Manual
2.2.3 Determine nature of fault	Procedures and guidelines	Manual
2.2.4 Diagnosis	On-line system	Manual interpretation of results

Figure 5.5 Task breakdown

This is achieved using a task breakdown, which maps each of the tasks or activities within a process to the actual mechanisms that will be used to carry it out. Using the example of the fault report process used earlier, the task breakdown might take the shape shown in Figure 5.5.

The format shown in the figure lists tasks independently of each other, but the information can also be presented graphically to show the link between one task and another. As well as mapping key tasks to the mechanisms that will carry them out, the task breakdown identifies secondary mechanisms which may be required. The development of requirements in individual component areas can now be established. The system requirements point the way toward the functions and screens (and ultimately the applications) that have to be developed. The manual requirements point the way towards the people capability required, both in terms of the job roles and organisational structures and later as an input to the training required.

The task breakdown is a key deliverable to ensure the overall integrity and completeness of the new components that have to be built. It is the link between the actual design of the new business (the process specification) and the development work that needs to be carried out to put that design in place. Ultimately, it helps to ensure that whatever capabilities are required to put the new processes in place can be assigned to a development area.

☞ SIGNPOSTS FOR SUCCESS

Business requirements, not user requirements

The power of the top-down process approach is that it can be used to derive a supporting infrastructure directly from strategic requirements. Although staff involvement is critical to the design phase, it is not intended to respond to the whim of everyone consulted or to satisfy personal wishlists. Staff who have spent years buried within the lower levels of detail in an organisation often have rather narrow-minded and unrealistic expectations of particular features required based on a purely local perspective. The end to end process view has to be maintained.

Seek out early implementation

The opportunity for early implementation and "quick wins" should be sought from day one. Besides showing that change is happening and sending messages about the commitment to the change, it also provides feedback on the viability of new designs. The criteria for early implementation should not be driven solely by financial pay-back.

Don't get hung up on design

Despite the importance of the design stage, it is important not to become obsessed by the design itself. The process design is a means to an end—the route map to the new business and the means to drive the changes necessary. Ultimately, the new ways of working are achieved by trailing the process designs in anger, and refining them if they are not 100% correct—a process design does not on its own deliver any improvement.

Avoid perfectionism

Although this may be anathema to the quality school, it is an important rider. Quality can be achieved without perfectionism and an obsession for dotting *i*s and crossing *t*s can drastically inhibit progress. The emphasis should be firmly on fitness for purpose: once the design/specification is detailed enough to drive the next stage, it should go forward. Take the design and run with it.

Validate sources

A journalist validates a story from three sources. Process design, when rooting out information or testing constraints, should do the same. The information provided by single individuals is not always up to date or correct. It is a truism that people like to tell stories and anecdotes, and like to sound knowledgeable even if they aren't. This "double testing" is particularly important where constraints are being stretched—what one source perceives as 'immovable', another may have a more flexible view on.

Maintain visibility

Don't wait too long before putting something before the people—in front of senior management (which probably means board level) and the people who actually "do" the business. Letting a major project slip back beneath the surface after a loud and enthusiastic launch allows the "just another initiative" feeling to fester in the workforce. If the board are not being asked to sign off resources and sign up to changes in the way of working, and business people are not involved in design input and review, then something is wrong.

_____ Part III

Building for Change

The preceding section has shown how to produce a rich and detailed specification for change, based on the process designs of the enterprise. The next step is to move forward to make the real changes to the underlying infrastructure. This section therefore addresses the very crux of change—showing how to determine the changes to organisational structures and the shape of new IT systems; how to identify (and create) the new people skills required and determine the modifications needed of procedures.

As ever, it is the design which is central to the changes made. The conversion of the process designs into new capabilities is tackled in three areas (reflecting the mechanisms of process introduced in Chapter 2): Human Resources (Chapters 6 and 7), Information Technology (Chapter 8) and Tools and Techniques (Chapter 9).

Chapter 6

Human Resources

This chapter is concerned with the development of the human resource capability to support the new processes (Figure 6.1). This includes people capabilities (such as the definition of job roles, and the development of the skills, knowledge and capability required to carry them out), the organisational or structural issues (how employees are organised and arranged to carry out particular roles and responsibilities) and the reinforcing mechanisms (such as measures, remuneration and benefits). The successful deployment of new HR capability is inseparably tied to issues of culture, which are covered in Chapter 7.

ORGANISATIONS IN TURMOIL

Major change arrives at a time when the human or 'social' side of our organisations is in a state of turmoil. We are, make no mistake about it, at a watershed for the role of people in organisations and the relationship they have with their corporate parents. On the one hand, organisations claim to pay more attention to HR policy and people needs, making reassuring noises about job design and concern for their human 'assets'. On the other, the relentless waves of downsizing and cost cutting of the past few years have squeezed the very last drops of productivity from staff and management alike, leaving many people disenfranchised, tired and demotivated. Many organisations, as a result, have seen a drop off in commitment and loyalty, and a reduction in the willingness to go the "extra mile" for the organisation.

These events take place against the backdrop of change to the very nature of work. The "job for life" is no more, and in its place there is an increasing tendency towards (short-term) contracts, flexible working hours and

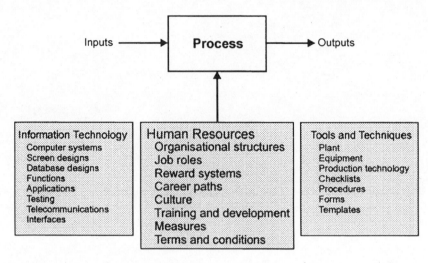

Figure 6.1   The HR components of process

outsourcing. The skills required in the workplace are changing rapidly, too rapidly for many to keep up with. Not surprisingly, a widespread feeling of insecurity is emerging among the workforce. Coupled with this, communications and computing technology remove any constraints about location of staff to carry out jobs that are heavily reliant on processing information. It is as viable to consider locating a computer-based customer call centre in low-cost Asia as in London or Manchester. The result is that people in every organisation are left trying to make sense of the changes going on around them and working out the implications for them as individuals.

In the main, the arrival of process-led change into these turbulent surroundings is good news. It offers the opportunity to sweep away the worst legacies of our human resource policies—rigid bureaucracies, over-specialisation and poorly designed jobs that constrain rather than stretch the potential of the individual. Process opens up the organisation, freeing the individual to work across functions and serve the customer rather than being locked into a particular field of expertise. The new ways of working require new skills and capabilities and in return offer opportunities for more interesting work, and a level of involvement that can genuinely influence the end result. There is an opportunity to actively design jobs, with an eye on the content and interest for the individual as well as the requirements of the enterprise. Command and control can be replaced by creativity and responsibility, and prescriptive instruction can be replaced by problem solving and empowerment. In career and development terms, progress and promotion can become aligned more closely to skills and achievements rather than length of service and previous grades held.

THE PECULIARITIES OF PEOPLE

Throughout this book there has been an emphasis on bringing the vision of a new process to life—turning the design into a specification and creating the capabilities that will actually carry out the process. The essence of this transformation is the "Five Ds": Design, Define, Develop, Dismantle and Deploy as introduced in Chapter 3. Within the IT arena this is a relatively structured exercise, with specific boundaries. It is clear when a particular application has been tested or programmed, or new hardware installed and made operationally live. Providing the inherent challenges of IT can be overcome—specifying requirements correctly and ensuring that they are delivered within time and budgets—the task is a relatively distinct one. Once requirements have been specified, modules can be coded, applications constructed and ultimately new systems created. The challenges of IT development are immense, make no mistake about it. But with the right disciplines in place they can be surmounted, and, once built, such systems will continue to perform in the consistent, predictable, regular manner in which they are instructed

People, unfortunately, are not like that. Changing behaviour, and reshaping capabilities and organisations is an altogether more nebulous task. People do not conform rigorously and reliably to norms and expectations. They have preferences and idiosyncrasies, personal motivations and emotions; sometimes they just have bad days when they don't feel like cooperating. They stray from procedures, modify the way work is carried out and amend their own jobs according to particular preferences or capabilities. And this is reality, reality which will always be true. So, although the HR components can (and must) be consciously designed (just as an IT system is designed) as a direct derivation of process requirements, the task of then creating these components is a different one entirely. Consequently, although the development of the HR component still requires the same stages of change—design, define, develop, dismantle and deploy—the distinction between stages is much more blurred. Sometimes it is not even possible to distinguish the completion of one stage from the beginning of another.

THE HARD AND SOFT ASPECTS OF HR CAPABILITY

To address these challenges with any hope of success, the creation and deployment of the new HR capability has to be tackled from two quite distinct angles (Figure 6.2).

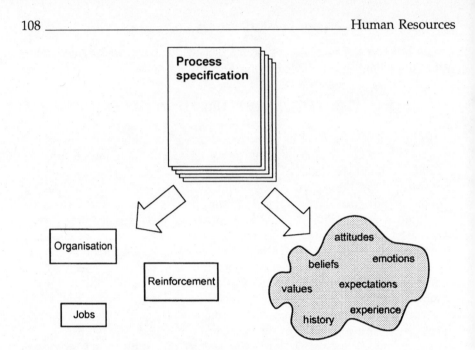

Figure 6.2 The hard and soft aspects of people change

The first consists of the tangible outputs that have to be produced to support the new process infrastructure. Jobs have to be designed, organisational structures drawn up, reinforcing mechanisms (such as contracts and remuneration) put in place and training programmes conducted. These are the physical deliverables, which can be specified, managed from a project plan and tested for conformance with certain quality standards. The second area covers the "soft" aspects of change, often referred to as culture—the realignment of the attitudes and values of the organisation to fit the new process. This embraces a myriad of more indistinct, almost ethereal aspects, which underlie change to organisations, including the management of resistance and the building of commitment— techniques that require sensitivity to the nuances and undercurrents running within organisations, backed up by constant monitoring and feedback activities.

Although these areas are separated for the purposes of explanation, they are inextricably linked in practice. With the people issues, more than any other part of change, this multidimensional approach is acutely important. Process-led change may be about specifying and then producing new capability, but that is only the first step. Successful change is not achieved by working out a set of deliverables to train and reorganise staff and then sitting back to tick off progress on a project plan. There is a need to listen and to monitor, to watch and to sense, and then to fine-tune the approach accordingly. The 'soft' aspects of change are the ones that are unique to each and every organisation, and the responses, too, have to be unique. There is no right or wrong answer. Individual responses have to be crafted depending on the nature of the organisation in question.

Process, by providing a holistic approach to change, ensures that such a two-pronged approach can be taken. From the process specification, the requirements can be determined for both the hard and the soft aspects of HR capability—by doing so, the change required to put those capabilities in place can be managed in a coordinated manner.

Taking a hard and a soft perspective is the basis for making HR change happen. But being able to meld the two approaches together is the real key to success. There is a requirement to nurture the 'soft' aspects of commitment and buy in at the same time as hammering home the "hard" lessons of new appointments and even redundancies. Successful change demands that you pull from the front and push from the back, but also that you cajole, encourage and support from the sides. Modifying the human resource capability of an enterprise is both an art and a science, and the winners are those who can successfully bring both disciplines to bear at once.

THE "HARD" SIDE OF HR

This chapter covers the design and development of the "hard", or more tangible, deliverable-based side of HR capability. The 'softer', cultural issues are covered in Chapter 7.

The design and development of HR capability can be split into three areas:

1. *(Physical) organisation.* This is the physical organisation of people—how staff are grouped and arranged, who they report to and where interfaces to other departments occur. Traditionally, this is seen merely as the organisational chart, but within process-led changes it underlies the very way in which particular pieces of work are allocated across the organisation. This is obviously a key part of implementing a process organisation because it ensures the process orientation becomes the new way of working, and that hand-offs and delays are minimised.
2. *Jobs.* These are the individual jobs or job roles within the overall organisation. They are the lowest units or building blocks of organisational capability. A job role gathers a set of tasks to be performed within one job role along with the skills and knowledge required to carry them out. Job roles drive training and development needs and help to shape organisational structures.
3. *Reinforcers.* These are the mechanisms that reinforce the jobs and their place and performance within the organisation. They include

remuneration (financial and otherwise), career paths, performance measures and terms and conditions of employment. Reinforcers may be seen as the skeleton of human resources, helping to keep the desired shape of the organisation in place.

Before considering the redevelopment of HR capability, a word of reassurance should be offered about the process-led approach.

Immense amounts have been written and spoken about process in recent years, much of it immersed in so much hype and extravagant language that one could be forgiven for thinking everything it describes is radically new. How, the organisation faced with the challenge of transformation may wonder, are such radical new concepts ever to be brought about in practice?

The truth is that although the process approach provides a new way of looking at the business, it does not necessitate a complete departure from traditional disciplines and techniques within HR. People still need to be organised, trained and managed. They still need to be rewarded, and to understand their work within the context of future opportunities and promotions. A key emphasis throughout this chapter is therefore on showing how the organisational infrastructure can be built by those who are already equipped with HR development skills. A different approach is needed, but it is an approach that still utilises many of the core components of HR management to make things happen. The existing personnel department staff, not an army of external consultants, are the ones who need to help reshape the enterprise's people capabilities.

The development of HR capability consists of five stages, which, although tackled sequentially, require some iteration, especially between stages 1 to 4.

Step 1: Generate Organisation Options

The first stage is the design of possible organisational structures to support the new processes. This is the "who does what" overview of the new process-led enterprise, showing how work is allocated across different job roles and departments. Like the original process design work, this is very much a creative exercise, seeking to develop the most appropriate organisation on a "clean sheet".

Various options need to be considered, with the process specification and the design principles serving as the key drivers of requirements. Reviewing the various process steps provides the detail of the skills and capabilities required, and the design principles indicate the way in which the process should be supported. These demands are reviewed together to consider appropriate arrangements for combining or separating process steps, with skills combined within the same job role to reduce hand-offs and multiple handling.

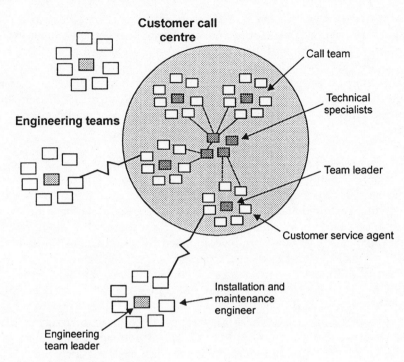

Figure 6.3 Organisational design

One of the prime objectives of a process approach is to focus on the customer, and to do so by minimising the delays, hand-offs and double handling which detract from speed and quality. This tends to imply that as much of the process as possible is carried out at one point rather than passed from role to role. In turn, this tends to mean that process change often results in the provision of either multi-skilled individuals or teams.

The objective of this stage is to establish an outline of the new organisational structure, showing the main organisational groupings and capabilities. Consider the case of the computing services firm introduced earlier, which is redesigning its fault reporting and maintenance process (Figure 6.3).

In this example, one of the main shifts has been to centralise expertise in the call centre, where it can be used to greatest effect, rather than have it dispersed around the regions, where it may rarely be used. In addition, the design sketches out the likely makeup of teams, but without establishing exact numbers at this stage; this will not be possible until the job roles have been defined. This exercise has to be carried out with an eye on what can be achieved, rather than what is carried out at the moment. Having product or technical knowledge isolated in different departments may be a legacy of existing organisational structures, and should not be regarded as a necessary constraint. With appropriate training and some product simplification, it is possible to equip individual staff to service many more products.

Generation of organisational options is an iterative, creative exercise where the various option for organisations are played out. The following prompts should be considered in seeking the most appropriate design:

- *The mix of specialist versus general skills.* Although an overriding objective may be to handle all aspects of the process at one point, this is rarely possible. The work within most organisations requires a variety of skills, some highly skilled and specialist, others less so. Reaching the appropriate design is, therefore, a task of tradeoff and compromise. It is often the case that the majority of work can be completed by a multi-skilled individual, with a small percentage of cases requiring specialist knowledge. In this situation the most important design consideration may be a means of applying this 80:20 rule to route out more complex cases to those appropriately skilled to deal with them.
- *Teams versus individuals.* Where it is not possible or practical to accumulate the required knowledge in one individual to perform several parts of a process, a team approach may be appropriate instead. Each part of the team provides one or more skills or capabilities, and a process step or customer requirement can still be satisfied as a one-off under the control of the team, rather than being handed around the organisation.
- *The nature of the industry.* The nature of the industry will dictate certain aspects of the organisation. Telecommunications and computer servicing will tend to imply a (typically centralised) customer service centre and engineers operating in the field. Healthcare is characterised by multiple specialists typically separated from the patient by long delays and the transfer of information (patient records etc).
- *Legal constraints.* Legal constraints and legislation may limit the over-lapping roles that can be handled by one person or team, for security or confidentiality reasons. In some financial services industries, account (and particularly credit) information can only be handled by appropriately qualified staff. This has implications where, for example, a financial services firm is seeking to sell and service multiple financial services products.
- *Geography or physical location.* Where the main role of the process is to handle physical rather than informational objects, the location of different process steps in the same place may be important. Where information is the key throughput it may be possible to create a virtual team via the use of IT, even though physical separation prevents the combination of staff

with appropriate knowledge and capabilities in one place (e.g. field service engineers and customer service staff).

- *The role of IT.* IT enables new ways of work and organisation, by providing multiple access to the same data and information. Historically, much of our work has been designed around a serial workflow, because only one view or copy of a particular customer existed. Typically this was manifest as a file, which had to be passed, and was frequently delayed, between departments. Instead, the potential of IT to enable new arrangements of working, for example through multiple views, should be considered. (This overlap into the area of IT reinforces the need for iteration during design; if a particular application of IT is felt to be beneficial to the organisation aspects, the overall process can be realigned accordingly. Process-led change provides a framework to consider how different capabilities can be used together. In doing so, the optimum combination of supporting elements can be designed together, rather than in isolation, to ensure the best overall result.)

To make the right decisions about organisational structures, a thorough understanding of the business in terms of the nature and numbers of transactions is required. Some businesses are made up of large volumes of very similar transactions, which a similar level of knowledge and abilities can handle. Others are made up of smaller volumes of more complex specialist tasks. In between, there are likely to be enterprises where the majority of tasks are straightforward and consistent, but intermittently complex, specialists tasks are encountered. This latter case may suggest a routing of specific cases to a more specialist level of skills.

The design of organisational structures is carried out by a joint team led by the process designers and owners, and including representatives of senior management. IT staff should be included to advise on the feasibility of certain options (e.g. how shared access to databases can be used to allow multiple access to the same information by different people). The generation of organisational designs is highly iterative, taking place in conjunction with the definition of job roles, as defined below.

Step 2: Decide and Define Job Roles

Having completed the first-cut organisational design, the job roles on which the design is based have to be firmed up. A job role is the logical grouping of a particular set of tasks, along with the capabilities required to do those tasks; essentially, it is the "package" of work that one individual will do. As well as being a key step in defining the detail of the new organisational structure, job roles help to identify training, recruitment and development needs.

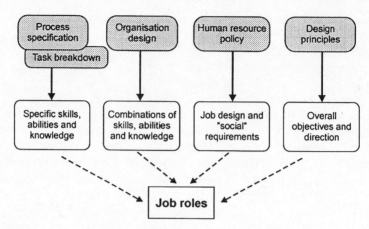

Figure 6.4   Requirements for job roles

Process-led change tends to overturn many of the concepts of specialism that have existed for so long in our organisations, many of them a relic of the long-established division of labour theories propagated by organisational theorists many decades ago. Often, this results in the combination of elements of several different jobs within a new, composite job role because this reduces the need for hand-offs and the associated opportunities for delays and errors to creep in. At the same time, there is always a balance to be struck—it rarely makes sense for highly skilled (and correspondingly expensive) specialists (such as underwriters or doctors) to spend time performing simple administration and data collection activities.

The content of individual job roles is derived from reference to four different sources of requirements, with the process design taking priority, as shown in Figure 6.4.

The detail of job roles is driven from the process design itself. The specific skills, capabilities and knowledge required are elicited from the task breakdown produced as part of the process specification (see Chapter 5). This provides information about the types of steps and activities to be carried out, and hence the skills, knowledge and capabilities required. This underpins the importance of developing a rich and detailed specification during the earlier design stage.

The organisational design outlined in stage 1 indicates the likely combination of skills and capabilities necessary to bring about a process orientation. Definition of job roles firms up on the assumptions made within the organisational design so that each individual role can now be agreed. Many of the skills, capabilities and knowledge required are unlikely to be new, but it is the exact use of them within new job roles to facilitate a process way of working that is important.

Job Role: Customer Service Agent

Job Role Reference: HR/004/v2

Main Activities:
- To respond to fault reports and maintenance requests
- To investigate and categorise faults and determine likely cause
- To initiate corrective action

Abilities and Knowledge:
- Customer orientation
- Basic product and product type knowledge
- Ability to interpret basic technical information and identify solutions
- Attention to detail
- Decision making

Skills:
- Keyboard and interpersonal
- Simple problem solving and diagnosis

Responsibilities:
- Determine when further diagnosis in conjunction with Diagnosing Engineer is required
- Determine when engineer call-out to site is required
- Maintain flow of information to customer

Experience:
Engineering role or customer services role

Figure 6.5   Defining job roles

Thirdly, HR strategy must be considered for specific aspects that impinge on job design or content. For example, there may be a requirement for every job to contain a minimum level of variety or have a certain element of organisational learning.

Finally, the detailed requirements derived from actual process specification need to be balanced against design principles to ensure that the new job roles are helping to meet the overall objectives of the new processes. Design principles such as "minimise hand-offs" or "everyone contributes to learning" obviously have a bearing on the arrangement and content of individual jobs.

Job roles are prepared by reviewing the four areas above and detailing the content of particular jobs. The output should be a documented job role, in a format such as that detailed in Figure 6.5.

The example given in Figure 6.5 illustrates the job role for the customer service clerk. A similar one would be produced for the two levels of specialist working with the call centre, and the engineers themselves working from the regional centres. The job role helps to firm up the decisions made in the high-level design about how work will be carried out into more specific job roles, which form the basis of both recruitment and training. Gradually, the overall requirements of the process are being distilled into the components that can actually rebuild the organisation with its process orientation.

Typically, the focus on processes and the needs of the customer means that jobs become enlarged in scope and content. Individual job roles become more extensive, with an associated increase in the range of skills and abilities required in one job role or individual, so that more steps in a process (or across several processes) can be carried out. The definition of job roles is a key building block for developing HR capability. As well as confirming organisational structures, it forms the basis of recruiting new staff, retraining existing staff and ultimately moving both new and existing staff into their new roles to create the new organisation.

Management Roles

The preparation and definition of all new or revised job roles within the organisation is important. There is a tendency to concentrate overly on operational and staff roles, whereas in reality the changes to management roles are often more dramatic.

The drive to equip staff with wider ranging skills and more responsibilities, which process demands, tends to alter fundamentally the role of managers. In many organisations managers have been specialists and experts in carrying rather than managers in the true sense of the word. Roles have to be redefined to establish the new management capability required to support the process organisation, with managers becoming genuine coaches and facilitators rather than technical experts and controllers. A key aspect of new management roles is the responsibility for personal development and career progression of staff. The "what does it mean to me?" question which is so important to commitment and motivation can initially be a lot harder to find an answer to in the process-led organisation. The ability of management to guide staff through the answers is a key step towards maintaining direction and building commitment to change.

The importance of management skills can be seen by the detrimental impact that a lack of new management skills has on the introduction of new processes. Core staff may adapt to the new ways of working, but managers fail to provide the support they need. Defining management roles helps to identify the real gaps in managerial capability in the new organisation and plan recruitment and training accordingly so that the new capability is put in place. This avoids the temptation to leave existing managers in their place, on the basis of history rather than merit.

Finally, it should be noted that job roles are the building blocks for developing and implementing the new organisational capability, rather than detailed procedural descriptions of any job on a task by task basis. Job roles are used to define the types of task and activity involved in a particular job, not the individual steps. Where a detailed, step by step guide to completing tasks is required (for example, to conform to quality standards) this is produced as part of procedure specification (see Chapter 9).

Step 3: Specify Organisational Structures

Completion and definition of job roles provides the necessary detail to firm up on the design of the organisational structure produced in step 1. The key difference in this stage is in the level of detail and coverage. The structure is now developed to include the whole organisation, and the specific job roles identified in step 2 are used. This stage should show both the processes and functions in the new organisation, and actual numbers of staff rather than merely groupings. The key parts to include are:

- *Job roles.* The allocation of specific job roles as identified in step 2 within particular functions.
- *Team structures.* The number of people within each team and the combination of job roles. This includes the span of control.
- *Functions.* Although functions tend to imply disconnection between process steps, they will still be required in some form. Functions provide room for the development of common capabilities and knowledge by grouping similar skills together and for the management of corporate knowledge such as organisational learning.
- *Reporting lines.* The links between staff and managers, and the links up and down and across the organisation.
- *Staffing/numbers.* The actual numbers of staff required to carry out the new processes. This needs to be based on an understanding of the volumes of work, including weekly and seasonal peaks and troughs. Due consideration has to be given to any changes in working hours, and efficiencies achieved from the new ways of working. Temporary and part-time staff can be used to smooth peaks and troughs.
- *Physical locations.* Where the organisation is dispersed across more than one site, actual physical locations need to be decided. This is important given that team structures can still be achieved virtually, using technology, even if they are not physically located together. Hence, if a particular process step requires expert capability for certain complex process steps, this can be provided by those with the appropriate capability located remotely but accessing the same information on-line.

The reshaping of an organisation inevitably causes a considerable amount of upheaval and distress. Jobs and positions provide status and identity as well as employment and income, and all sorts of accepted norms, privileges and assumptions are called into question by the changes to organisational structures. Power structures and political smallholdings exist in every organisation, and cutting through them unearths resistance and obstruction, both implicit and explicit. Approaches to tackling such issues are considered in more detail in the following chapter, but one rule should be followed rigorously to ensure that the required changes can be made to stick: *organisational design should be agreed at a logical level, independently of any specific names or individuals.*

This ensures that the most appropriate organisational design and the alignment of roles within it can be agreed first, in isolation from the emotive issues of deciding who will occupy particular roles. The allocating of "names to boxes" can then be considered as a separate step. This is a key application of job roles, ensuring that the shape of the organisation can be established with roles, rather than names, in the boxes on the organisational chart. It is critical that this design is then agreed and signed off by higher management at this point. This design subsequently forms the basis for allocating individuals into positions in the new organisation. Getting commitment and agreement to the new design in advance helps to minimise the resistance and political manoeuvring that subsequently take place, especially when particular individuals realise that they may not occupy their existing role.

Step 4: Design and Define Supporting Mechanisms

Supporting mechanisms reinforce the desired characteristics of the new organisation. They help to maintain the shape of the new organisational structures and encourage the behaviour on which the performance of the process is dependent. Both the more visible elements, such as financial rewards, and the softer aspects that affect performance, such as motivation and career opportunities, have to be considered.

Reward Structures

Reward structures are the various elements of a remuneration or benefits package that employees receive. As well as financial remuneration (the basic pay or salary earned), they include non-monetary elements such as healthcare and pension provision, and other fringe benefits or 'perks' such as subsidies and free or reduced goods or services.

Existing reward structures usually need significant modification to support process change. Rewards have to be more tightly allied to process performance so that the appropriate focus on processes is maintained, and, when successful, rewarded. This is achieved by selecting measures in the process that reflect the desired performance, typically more closely aligned to quality than to quantity. Some part of the overall remuneration package (typically a percentage) is then aligned to the measures. Such changes to reward structures have to be made at both staff and management levels to demonstrate the commitment to the new ways of working. In particular, the process owner or manager should have an element of his or her remuneration tightly linked to the overall process performance.

Changes to remuneration packages tend to be one of the most closely watched (and often strongly opposed) areas of change. Although monetary reward is just one of several influences on performance (besides status, recognition, career progress, job satisfaction and so on), it is the single most sensitive issue to adjust within an organisation. Communication of intended changes has to be made frequently and unambiguously so that the reasons for the changes are clear. Similarly, senior management must be clearly seen to embrace the changes made to their remuneration packages. This is one of the real practical tests of management commitment to change.

While revising remuneration packages will undoubtedly cause some initial upset and resentment within the organisation, in the long term most people can be made to see the rationale for such change. Many organisations have become so locked into an incremental system of remuneration that rewards no longer bear any close relation to performance. Hierarchy, rewards and promotion have become the result of length of service or grading rather than a direct reflection of an individual's contribution to the organisation. Aligning reward systems to processes restores a much closer link, and although there will inevitably be those who fight such changes, usually they are the ones with the most to lose. As elsewhere, the importance of a firm, fair hand in dealing with such issues is the key to moving forward. The harsh reality is that there is rarely an easy, comfortable solution if an organisation has been rewarding people out of proportion to their contribution for a number of years. There is no longer any hiding place for such anomalies, and the inconsistencies have to be ironed out.

Measures

Measures are a key part of reinforcement because they provide the necessary information about how individuals or teams are performing. People are motivated by "success", and feedback on the results being achieved is needed for motivational reasons, as well as aligning financial rewards as outlined above.

The framework of measures is established during process design (see Chapter 4) and these measures can now be rolled out in practice, and at a lower level of detail.

New measures need to be selected with care. Typically, they need to focus on those aspects of the business that reflect the overall performance of the process, end to end, rather than just particular points of it. This helps to maintain the end to end perspective, rather than the "bit part" that any one

Table 6.1 New and old measures compared

New	Old
Number of faults recurring	Number of faults fixed
Number of sales closed	Number of quotes issued
Number of cases completed with NFA	Number of transactions handled
Number of patients treated in full in one visit	Number of patients treated per day

process step may be playing. Besides operational measures, new measures should reflect the requirements of the customer, rather than the throughput of different stages of the process. As a rule of thumb, a good starting point is to consider "What is the customer bothered about?", and then to establish a suitable measure to track it. New measures usually reflect a shift away from quantity and throughput to quality and the overall performance of the process, as illustrated in Table 6.1.

As well as being set out operationally, the validity and importance of new measures needs to be enforced elsewhere, such as in the organisation's support functions. Accounting and budgeting processes may need to be refined to incorporate the new measures, and management reports generated by IT may need to be revised or rewritten.

Moving to such a quality rather than a quantity perspective is a difficult exercise. It requires new points of measurement as well as new measures, and some trial and error may be necessary before the appropriate measures can be established. Once new processes are implemented, it is important to hold fast to the new measures even if the results are not initially as expected. The impact of the new ways of working inevitably takes some time to become visible in the figures as the existing ways of working are gradually phased out, and the new, process-orientated ones bed in.

Career Paths

Career routes through an organisation have traditionally been both stable and clearly visible. For most employees, a clearly marked upward route existed, which tended to go hand in hand with promotion and a pay rise. In the office new starters could rise from clerk to supervisor and typically on to a middle management position such as section manager. On the shop floor a route stretched from the simpler, low-skilled jobs through to a more technical role and on to production supervisor or controller, reporting to middle management positions above them. This was the way hierarchical organisations worked, offering a natural upward progression to employees, often based as much on longevity of service as ability or potential. Over the years it was possible to work your way from one end of the organisation to the other. Indeed, in one company the deputy chairman himself had trodden just this route, having worked his way right up through the ranks from post-room to board-room during the course of more than 25 years.

The drawback of this traditional route is that the skills required at various stages tend to be quite different. The person working at the top of his or her field as a technician or specialist tends to have quite different skills from the manager above, where the skills are concerned with making decisions, determining and controlling budgets and (traditionally, at least) conveying information up and down the organisation. Nevertheless, this model has been the bedrock of organisations for decades, and shapes the career expectations of most people within them.

Process-led change overturns much of this. Firstly, a number of jobs within the traditional hierarchy tend to disappear altogether, thus knocking out several steps in the career ladder. Indeed, the "ladder", which has been used as a metaphor for career progress, is no longer valid, and the notion of career path, which includes sideways moves in the organisation, is much more appropriate. Secondly, the new arrangement and nature of jobs, with more responsibility and decision making further down, tend to result in fewer positions higher up the organisation and thus less opportunity for an individual to move up the organisation.

Career paths are an important part of reinforcement because they are a key motivational force, and help answer the "what does it mean for me?" question. Four steps need to be carried out to establish new career paths:

- *Map out new career paths.* The career path shows suitable links between jobs and possible transitions for an individual through the organisation. The definition of new job roles acts as a pointer to this, the qualification of skills, attributes and knowledge helping to identify other job roles that act as suitable preparation grounds. It has to be stressed, however, that the emphasis in the new organisation is on having the right abilities, rather than merely having held a particular job.
- *Establish new credibility and status.* Traditionally, it was the level of a position within the organisation that reflected status and ability. In turn, this contributed to the attraction of a particular role as a career objective. Within the new organisation there tend to be jobs requiring specialist skills that do not fit well within the hierarchy. These include those with skills core to the actual work (such as doctors, underwriters and designers) as well as those having support skills, such as project managers. The importance and standing of the new roles have to be established both by the attached salary and by credibility, through involvement in decision making etc.

- *Communicate to staff.* As ever, communication is the linchpin, with failure so often occurring because no one has taken the time to tell staff of the changes (again and again) until they are aware of the new opportunities and routes available to them. Given that few people can now expect a "job for life" within one organisation, this may include encouraging staff to think about their career in the wider sense. One organisation we encountered which was gradually reducing staff numbers as a result of competition and new technology took the bold step of encouraging its employees to view their careers in a much wider context, regardless of the organisation in which it might be pursued. This encouraged them to consider the skills and capabilities they needed to develop to follow their career path wherever it occurred—rather than merely looking at what was in store for them within the employ of their own organisation.
- *Build into the appraisal process.* Career paths and opportunities have to be built into the appraisal process on a regular basis rather than as a one-off review initiated by a change project. This enables managers to review with staff their capabilities, performance and potential, and work out development requirements and the most appropriate route forward.

As noted in Chapter 2, the holistic nature of process-led change should be harnessed wherever possible to speed changes along. Thus, the various aspects of organisational change should be reinforced by changes happening elsewhere.

Terms and Conditions of Employment

The final "reinforcer" is the definition and acceptance of any new or amended terms and conditions necessary to underpin the new ways of working. Contracts of employment may have to be amended to reflect new measures of performance. Changes to working hours may need to be incorporated to provide the increased opening and availability required to meet customer needs, such as 8 a.m. to 8 p.m. opening, weekend availability or, in some cases, round the clock 24 hour provision. Changes to working hours usually raises the emotional issue of overtime, given that hours outside 9 a.m. and 6 p.m. on weekdays have traditionally been seen as overtime, and subject to an additional payment. Similarly, the concept of a "job for life" is now fading, with the implementation of shorter, typically two-year, contracts for employees. After two years an individual's contract is reviewed, and renewed providing the employee is deemed to be still fulfilling his or her role. Many organisations are now attempting to change such 'norms', although often this can only be achieved during the course of staff natural turnover, as new staff are taken on, rather than as wholesale change. Negotiations with unions or staff representative bodies also have to be considered.

While changes to both overtime and short-term contracts contribute to the flexibility and responsiveness that many organisations seek, such actions need to be considered in the light of the ultimate impact on the workforce. Implementing such steps leaves the power and control firmly in the hand of employer rather than employee and tends to contribute further to the disenfranchised, demoralised workforce; as such, the benefits brought by such changes should be balanced against the impacts on employee loyalty and commitment.

Step 5: Develop Capability

The fifth, and perhaps the largest, stage within human resources is the development of the actual capability required. This includes the recruitment of personnel from outside the organisation as well as the development of staff internally through training, education and experience.

The key determinant of the capability required is the difference between current capability and that needed by the new, process-led organisation. This "gap analysis", as it is called, forms the basis for determining recruitment, training and development requirements at both an individual and an overall level, as shown in Figure 6.6.

Having confirmed the capability required, the development is a two-stage process consisting of the selection and allocation of the appropriate staff and the completion of any training and development required to bring them up to the desired level of capability.

Selection and Allocation of Staff

Using the job roles identified earlier, staff with the skills (or the potential to develop the skills) necessary to fill them are selected. Depending on the extent of early implementation and the migration strategy being pursued, positions may be advertised and filled gradually or it may be necessary to "convert" many roles en masse.

Many early re-engineering and process-led change initiatives have, of course, been associated with redundancies (or tagged with the more euphemistic "downsizing" label) and ultimately, of course, this option has to be considered if fewer staff are required to support the new processes or existing staff prove unable to make the transition. Such a course of action has to be balanced against the impact on staff morale and the knowledge and expertise that may be lost, and wherever possible this usually makes the re-skilling and retraining of existing staff preferable.

The skills and capabilities within existing job roles should provide a good idea of likely conversion routes, but potential as well as actual capabilities should be considered. The past few decades of command and control in our

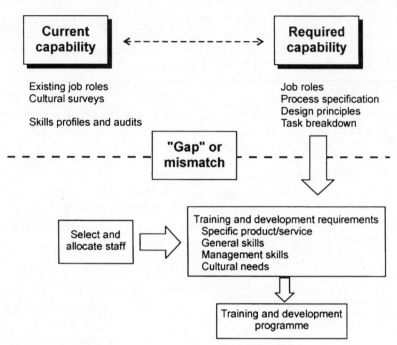

Figure 6.6 Gap analysis

organisations have tended to stifle rather than nurture the abilities of staff, and existing competence is not always a good indication of future capability.

Where capabilities internally are insufficient, the recruitment of personnel from outside the organisation has to be considered. This often proves necessary to fulfil some management positions, especially where a much more genuine management role replaces a supervisory one. Recruiting externally where skills are not available serves as an important cultural lever as well as a practical one, sending messages that those managing and sponsoring the programme are serious about getting the right staff in place, rather then merely making do with inappropriate skills because they are available internally. Where staff are recruited externally, a strong and comprehensive induction process needs to be in place to ensure rapid uptake into the organisation.

Training and Development

The second part of capability development is the actual training, development and education of staff. Such development needs have to be considered in the broadest sense, rather than limited to particular product or production skills.

Table 6.2 Training and development requirements

Existing role	Key existing product skills	Existing capabilities	New job/role	Skills required	Training required
Role A	Product A sales	Customer facing	Generic customer support	Products A, B and C sales and admin	Products B and C sales; products A, B and C admin
Role B	Product B sales	Customer facing	Generic customer support	Products A, B and C sales and admin	Products A and C sales; products A, B and C admin
Role C	Product C sales	Customer facing	Generic customer support	Products A, B and C sales and admin	Products A and B sales; products A, B and C admin
Role D	Products A, B and C servicing	Administration	Generic customer support	Products A, B and C sales and admin; products	A, B and C sales and customer relations skills

Although requirements for training and development can be undertaken at an individual level, it is generally more practical to establish them for the transition between particular roles that exist in the current and new organisations, as shown in Table 6.2.

Plotting out the transitions between roles in such a way quickly begins to reveal an overall picture of training and development needs. From this information it is possible to develop a schedule for an overall training and development programme.

The second stage of training is to produce the actual training programmes themselves, which will ensure the development of new capabilities as outlined above. As ever, the process itself has to drive the requirements. Training needs have to be determined by reviewing the process specification itself and the various components that have been developed from it (job roles, computer systems, procedures etc.). As with the eliciting of IT requirements from process specifications, this is an act of interpretation as well as analysis, determining what skills are required if processes are to be carried out in a particular manner. Invariably, process-led change demands a more highly skilled workforce, able to think on their feet and solve problems rather than just complete tasks by rote. Training needs are therefore likely to be far ranging and may encompass:

- *Product skills*: concerning the core products or services of the organisation, the features within them

- *Process skills*: how the processes themselves work, including the use of IT systems, procedures and other tools and techniques
- *Production skills*: basic supplementary skills (e.g. telephone and keyboard skills)
- *Enabling skills*: problem solving, brainstorming, sales techniques

The extent of training needs may at first seem extreme, but this is the cost of developing a set of effective processes. It is no use expecting people to work differently if they are not equipped with the skills to do so—no use empowering people to find solutions if they are not trained to solve problems. Training, therefore, needs to go far beyond the traditional realms of product knowledge and systems training. It will inevitably be an expensive exercise in both time and resources, but much of this training is an investment in the future as well. It is the cost of equipping an organisation with the skills needed to compete, rather than to struggle on in the present.

Having established needs, training programmes are designed in whatever format is most appropriate. Depending on the skills and capabilities required, everything from role playing to formal computer based training may be used. Where appropriate, external rather than in-house training services should be utilised.

As always, the emphasis is on a practical rather than a perfectionist approach. Some individuals may undergo some training and development that is surplus to their individual requirements, and, similarly, others may be left short in particular areas, but to define specific training needs for every individual in the organisation is usually impractical. The normal course of management will identify any further gaps in capability once the new processes are in place.

In the case of management capability, more specific training and development requirements may need to be mapped out for each individual role. In the case of a process owner role, for example, a wide range of skills and capabilities is required, ranging from an understanding of process through to an ability to facilitate and lead cross-functional working. The exact training needs will depend on the background and experience of the individual selected.

COMMUNICATION . . . AGAIN

This chapter has covered the specification and development of the more tangible or "hard" aspects of HR change. It includes changes to the very way in which people work, and the way in which they interact, communicate and are managed—as well as the way in which they are rewarded and paid. The response to these changes can potentially lead to some of the most profound and chronic resistance to progress. The following chapter deals with the softer aspects of change—culture and commitment—but communication is still one of the most important techniques for success. People need to understand why changes are being made—they need to understand the market pressures, the cost structures, the competition, the role of technology, the possible responses, and the costs of new technology. To foster such understanding takes communication: constant communication, over and over again. Senior managers and change architects, by default, understand the pressures. They are faced daily with the reminders of competition, the challenges of cost and the threat of superior competition. But the 'workforce' are not so close to the figures. They are buried in the detail of their day to day job rather than the comparison of benchmarks and performance measures. Throughout this book, the importance of a holistic approach is stressed, and nowhere is this more so than around the development of HR capability. Communication is essential. It must be constant, comprehensive and coherent.

Every time a deliverable is produced and rolled out, its purpose and rationale have to be explained and put in context.

☞ SIGNPOSTS FOR SUCCESS

Involve people

Ultimately, change never happens unless the people in an organisation drive it. People have to be involved—in building the new capability as well as being a part of it once developed. While those driving the change programme can provide the framework within which the changes take place, the people themselves have to breathe life into the new ways of working and supply the detail about specifics. Finished solutions from the change team should be avoided, even if they can be achieved, because they leave no room for involvement, and without involvement there is no commitment.

Reinforce

When change throws up obstacles and staff become disillusioned, the natural route tends to be backwards. Appropriately defined jobs and clear organisational structures, underpinned by new measurement and reward systems, help to reinforce the process way of working. In turn, this ensures that the 'new' gradually becomes the 'norm'. Management performance must be clearly linked to the success of process as well as that of operational staff.

Communicate constantly and continuously

Make no mistake about it—adopting a process view of the world is a difficult, demanding undertaking. Process itself is a perfectly logical concept—a way of viewing the world, and structuring an organisation, which makes obvious sense when viewed in isolation. The problem arises in making this new view of the world clear to all who will see and do it. For years, people have worked in their regulated, straitjacket organisations, with layer upon layer of management above them and wall after wall of functions between them. Process asks them to take a new view of the world, to adapt a new framework for all that they see and do. This requires constant, regular communication—of ideas and concepts in the initial stages and of specifics and details as implementation progresses.

Be firm, be sensitive, be honest

Changing the human side of an organisation can ultimately change the lives of the individuals who work there. A person's job (and the status, salary and position which accompany that job) is a significant part of his or her life, and making fundamental changes to the way people work, interact and manage can creates major personal upheaval for those involved. While the onward progress of society, competition and globalisation forces us to change, this change should not be undertaken without due consideration of those involved, and the impact it will have on their lives.

Chapter 7

Culture Change

CHANGING CULTURE

Culture tends to be one of the most misunderstood areas of change, with as many different opinions offered as there are organisations where cultural change has been attempted. On the one hand, there are those who talk rather glibly about it, as if it is a distinct task that can be outlined, specified, planned and then carried through until a particular end point is reached. Such approaches talk about reshaping values and attitudes as if these characteristics can be taken down off the organisational shelf, given a slight tweak and then slotted back in to exert their new influence. At the other extreme, there are those who believe that all that is required is a slight change in thinking by employees, which can be brought about by the adoption of a few new slogans or corporate 'values'. Such "key rings and coffee mats" approaches tend to be underpinned by the appearance of a plethora of posters, pens, newsletters—and the inevitable key rings and coffee mats—all proclaiming a new corporate slogan in bright, bold letters.

Culture can be changed—but like the rest of the change programme, it has to be changed by design. Although it may be the least tangible of any of the components that underpin new organisational and process capability, it still has to be consciously designed, shaped and amended in line with a set of requirements. Process-led change works because it provides an integrated way of defining new ways of working—but that design must be used to shape the attitudes, values and behaviours of staff just as much as it is used to define new computer systems.

With culture, possibly more than any other aspect of change, the holistic aspects of the process-led approach need to be exploited. There are all sorts of horror stories about why culture change programmes have failed—but usually failure relates back to the inability to put into practice the new behaviours that are desired. Process-led change positively enables culture change. At the same time as setting out the very attitudes and behaviour that need to underpin that work, process can also change the very way work is done—by doing so the actions will speak louder than the words.

CULTURE IN THEORY

The textbook models of culture refer to the values, assumptions and beliefs of individuals, which shape the behaviour in an organisation. But these theories tend to remain rather dry and academic compared to the everyday aspects of culture that influence an organisation from day to day. Don't forget what the real nub of culture is: culture is the real, living organisation as you see, perceive, experience and feel it. It is the cynicism or the enthusiasm for what management say. It is the buzz emanating from one team meeting, or the dumb silence that pervades another. It is what strikes you when you walk into an office for the first time, and the impressions that you form when you talk to six or seven people from the company; it is the way staff talk to customers and whether employees stay past their clocking off times when overtime is not being paid.

CULTURE IN PRACTICE

The underlying culture in an organisation is manifest in numerous ways. Merely walking around an organisation and experiencing the decor, the office layout, the level of noise and the type of work being carried out often provides telling insight. Every aspect, right down to the way staff dress and the average age of employees, provides clues to the organisation's culture. Even within the same industry, such as financial services, vast differences, which permeate to the very heart of the way work is done, are experienced. The City dealing room of a multinational bank exists as a vast, open-plan arena of an office, crammed full of all the latest information technology, with VDU screens and monitors banked one upon the other to provide dealers and traders with five or six different information sources and applications. People shout into phones or call each other across the office. There is an atmosphere of energy and urgency, of business being transacted before opportunities slip away.

Contrast this with the offices of an old, established family insurance firm based in the provinces. Here most of the staff are long-standing employees with many years' service, transacting business almost unchanged, in the way they have done for the previous five, ten or even fifteen years. Technology is minimal, perhaps a terminal and a keyboard on the desk, but few personal computers in evidence; in some departments the most advanced technology remains a dictating machine.

The cultural differences within such environments are vast. In one, staff have grown with the developments in technology and moved rapidly with changes to the way business is conducted, embracing modern state-of-the-art technology and new ways of working. In the other, the staff remain rooted to their established practices, with attempts at improvement either shunned by management or tripped by the first obstacle that arises.

But culture is more than a vague concept shaped by past events and current surroundings. Culture is a powerful force, and different aspects of it exert a strong influence on the way people work and interact on a day to day basis. Culture can have a dramatic effect on the way an organisation behaves and develops, on how customers are looked after, staff are treated and new ideas considered. Worse, many organisations exhibit cultures, which, as a legacy of past events, exert a less than positive effect. Some of the worst aspects of culture are manifest in the following ways:

- *Negativity.* Everyone has experienced the manager who casts a shadow of doom, gloom and pessimism around him. And an attitude of obstruction and disapproval emanating from management gradually seeps out to subordinate staff. Worse still, this can become manifest in dealing with colleagues and even with customers. A feeling of "that's the way it is, there's no way it can be changed" becomes established and people give up making suggestions or trying to make things better.
- *Focus on quantity.* The drive for efficiency and cost cutting in the late 1980s has left many organisations with a fanaticism for quantity and throughput. The result is a blinkered focus on volumes and numbers, often to the exclusion of all else, especially quality. Hence, staff servicing the customer are measured (and rewarded) on the number of calls they complete, rather than the number of satisfied customers that result. Engineers are measured on the number of faults they fix, rather than the number of faults that do not reappear. The emphasis on speed and throughput fails to deal fully with the customer requirement because staff are focused on completing one task so that the next one can be started. Because such measures fail to pay attention to the real drivers of performance, such as customer satisfaction, quality suffers.
- *Not my job.* The rigid functionalisation that has prevailed in our organisations for the past few decades has fostered a "hand-off" mentality, which discourages ownership or responsibility for results. Frequently this is manifest in the passing of a task or job from one

department to another, and the associated delays, losses and confusion that result. The hand-offs tend to occur more frequently with complex or difficult pieces of work, as a feeling prevails that it is easier to shift the work into someone else's in-tray than deal with it personally. The result is a lack of accountability and ownership for getting tasks completed.

- *Why bother?* A further legacy of functionalisation is the inability of individual staff to influence the final outcome of a task or activity. This is as much a result of the complexity of organisations as it is of the distance many employees are from the customer. It leaves staff disinterested and isolated, with a feeling that they have no control over the other parts of the process needed to complete the work satisfactorily. In turn, this impacts the motivation for completion of individual responsibilities, especially when problems arise, and leads to a feeling of "why bother?".

CULTURE CHANGE: THE NATURE OF THE BEAST

Work is one of the foundations of society. During employable years, it typically occupies around half of an individual's waking life. But the job is more than just a wage earner: it provides status and identity to the individual as well as resources to the corporation. Little wonder, then, that attempts to change the "hearts and minds", let alone the jobs and salaries, of our workforce send reverberations up and down the length of the corporation. It might make sense to the board to "reorganise jobs in line with process requirements" but all that staff see is a drop in overtime payments that were going to pay for the new car. So, although culture change is sometimes referred to rather glibly in terms of 'freezing and re-freezing', the reality is that it is an extremely difficult area of change to get right. The real extent of the culture change task is reflected by the following:

- *It is a massive task.* Culture is made up of the values, attitudes and beliefs of people. It is held in the hearts and minds of individuals, not in some corporate pigeon-hole where it can be unlocked and realigned overnight. Individuals harbour their own idiosyncrasies, agendas, abilities and preferences, and some also have the desire and ability to wield power and influence over those around them. Add to this the fact that many organisations have cultures developed over several decades with constantly reinforced norms and behaviours, and the true size of the task begins to emerge. An organisation's culture is made up of hundreds of thousands of different elements, and dozens more interconnected subcultures and informal networks.
- *There's no such thing as a fresh start.* In most organisations the waters have already been muddied by previous change initiatives. The past few years alone have brought TQM, BRE, customer care and downsizing, usually

accompanied by more specific local initiatives in search of cost cutting or as demanded by particular product, sector or divisional requirements. In the background, IT projects have carried on apace as computers and technology have expanded beyond their initial scope of automation to telecommunications, printing, imaging and multimedia. Each project, whether integrated or discrete, has its own particular impact on the existing organisation. As change projects forge on, staff tend to have a much more realistic (and usually cynical) view of such initiatives than their managers or directors. They remember the problems as well as the successes, the staff who were made redundant as well as the ones who were given new opportunities and the bugs that remain in the new systems rather than the ones that were removed from the old. No culture change initiative can start without the burdens of what has gone on previously.

- *Volatility.* Attempting to modify culture is like playing with a test-tube full of unknown chemicals—just when the mixture appears to be stabilising and progressing towards the desired output, it blows up in your face. Culture change is as much about emotions as it is about rationale or logic—it is about how people think, feel and react, not just what they should say or do in the cold, clear light of day. Add to this the fact that during change the rumour mill or organisational grapevine works overtime, and the slightest signal of change can be exaggerated or misrepresented in the wrong direction. More often than not, the facts become distorted as part of this informal communication process and rumours fly about all manner of subjects. In this environment the smallest, even indirect, changes can send ripples right across the organisation. One organisation undergoing process-led change designed new jobs as part of their HR redevelopment and then advertised them internally, as was the norm. The new position came with a new title, and outlined new roles and responsibilities to meet process requirements. But although the job description was about the new job, it was the terms and conditions that got noticed—the more flexible working hours were immediately construed by the organisation as a means of cutting overtime payment, and the new process designs were regarded as a means of de-skilling the workforce; before long rumours were widespread about short-term contracts, redundancies and how the company was trying to "show the staff the door".

- *Culture change is exhausting.* The origins of culture seep down to the very roots of an organisation—its history and its incremental development over many years, which have set certain expectations in stone and created behaviours that are now the established norm. Changing culture requires immense energy and commitment—for as fast as one aspect of culture has been hammered home, another seems to rebound or take a backward step.

IT systems development may be exhausting and demanding—but systems do not at the last minute perform an abrupt *volte face* and reject everything that they have been programmed to do. Finally, culture change by its nature is never complete—it is a constant reshaping and realigning exercise.

- *The spoon feeding legacy*. It is a burden of our bureaucratic, command and control pasts that the staff of organisations are used to spoon feeding, accustomed to being told what to do and blaming the management if it doesn't work out. Working to establish a culture of empowerment and responsibility, which process-led change tends to demand, after years of rigorous control and direction is like freeing a bird that has been confined to a cage for all of its life. Given the freedom to spread its wings and make its own way, there is a tendency to take a few uncertain paces forward and then stop, unsure of what to do next. Similarly, people have to be nurtured in their new freedoms and opportunities. After years of predefined tasks and inviolable procedures, they have to be encouraged to take the reins and do things for themselves.

From Problems to Solutions

It is easy to be put off by such a daunting, yet realistic, picture. Culture is a volatile and unpredictable component of an organisation. It is a powerful, elusive force, which exerts a major influence on the way a whole enterprise performs. Worst of all, it can go off in completely unexpected directions. But culture, like every aspect of an organisation, can be modified. It is difficult, and it is indistinct and sometimes it is very frustrating, but it can be analysed, understood and designed—and ultimately changed.

WHAT SORT OF CULTURE?

Many organisations are trying to change their culture. Recognising that the values, behaviours and norms that exist are not appropriate for the way an enterprise must be structured and managed at the turn of the 20th century, they have set out to create a new culture. But probe beneath the surface of such claims and few organisations seem to have a real grasp of the culture they are trying to create, and why. Their culture is changing, but the roadmap is rather vague.

For, unlike some aspects of an enterprise, culture is not something that has traditionally been consciously designed or chosen. Over the years experiments have been made with organisational structures of all shapes and sizes, and the notion of job design has been rolled out as a means of selecting the most appropriate combination of activities within a job. But culture itself was never chosen or designed. It was just something that emerged as result of other factors—the jobs people did, relationships with colleagues and managers, the way staff were treated by employers and the values and beliefs individuals brought with them from beyond the workplace.

The only exceptions to this were some of the small, fast-growing start-up enterprises, which have flourished under the new rules of competition in the past decade or so. Typically, these are service organisations and small entrepreneurial outfits, the offspring of the computer industry in hardware and software development or high-tech manufacturing outfits. They were able to actively determine the culture required to support their businesses. (Typically, this was one of team working, flat management structures, an energetic workforce with an ethos of "work hard, play hard" and a focus on solutions and results, with long, demanding working hours rewarded by high salaries.) The advantage that these companies held as they set out consciously to define and establish the culture needed to support their business was their lack of cultural baggage. They had no legacy. They were able to select a new culture to suit the new company rather than trying to change the one they had, just as they selected office premises and a computer infrastructure.

Most organisations undergoing major change are less fortunate, and carry the legacy of the past as well as the infrastructure of the present. As with other aspects of change, it is the holistic nature of the process approach that provides the power necessary to achieve the change. Culture can be tackled as an integral part of the whole change programme, and, built to a design rather than in isolation, real change can be achieved.

The first step to changing culture is to design and define the shape or requirements of the new culture. As ever, this is driven from high-level requirements, namely the design principles, the process specification and the Balanced Scorecard, if used. Like the determination of the organisational and people requirements, this is an exercise of filtration and extraction, working through process designs and design principles to determine the most appropriate culture required. By looking at designs for how work is to be carried out and customers serviced, and the environment in which an organisation operates, it is possible to determine the culture required. Often this also needs to incorporate the changes that need to be made to break the stranglehold of existing cultures, many of which are based on command and control.

Consider the scenarios in Figure 7.1, and the new culture that the organisations within them might seek to create.

These two examples illustrate different ends of the spectrum, but other cultures demand equally drastic changes. Many organisations, with their staff buried behind layers of bureaucracy and procedures, are unable to understand the real costs and values of customers, so the requirement may

Example 1: A major financial services company with a long history of command and control is organised around rigid functional and product boundaries. Existing operations are characterised by numerous delays and hand-offs, and the work is plagued by inaccuracies. In pursuit of change, the company is moving from a primarily paper-based operation to a set of processes that aim to allow 90% of products to be sold and serviced by one multidisciplined team. A legacy of the 1980s cost-cutting is a set of measures that focus on throughput of cases, rather than completion of work to customer satisfaction. Staff are very traditional and do not like change.

The requirement is for a culture that:
- places a much greater emphasis on speed, service and accuracy
- focuses on completing what the customer wants, rather than completing the task to get the file and paperwork off the desk
- encourages team-working to bring together the most appropriate set of capabilities
- will be able to respond to change much more quickly in the future

Example 2: A professional computing services firm providing outsourcing and consultancy services has a reputation for high fees and average service. They are implementing a set of processes that focus on delivering value to clients with whom they are aiming to develop and sustain long-term relationships. This is to be underpinned by a global "learning and improvement" process in an attempt to make better use of the company's worldwide knowledge and experience gathered from clients.

The requirement is for a culture that:
- ensures that staff go out of their way to give the client high value added service in every part of the process and relationship
- seeks to identify, capture and pass on knowledge at every point in the process

Figure 7.1 Requirements for culture

be to foster a much more commercial mindset. Others exhibit the "we get paid whatever" attitude, and there is a need to restore a much closer link to results and the performance of the process; this is particularly important to underpin most process-led change.

Only when the requirements have been clearly defined is it appropriate to set about attempting to change the culture (Figure 7.2).

CULTURE: THE LEVERS FOR CHANGE

Educate

The first and most basic stage, which many organisations nevertheless omit, is to explain *why* change is necessary. While an awareness of the overall

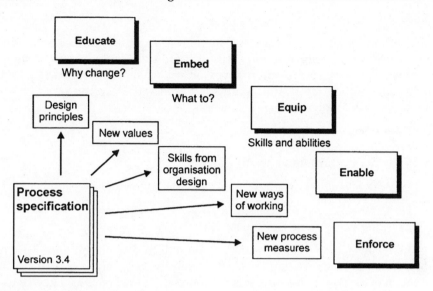

Figure 7.2 Process-led culture change

change programme should provide the main context, tailored messages specific to the cultural impacts need to be provided.

Firstly, information about the general pressures for change, such as the increasing demands of the customer and the new challenges of the marketplace, has to be provided. This has to be accompanied with more specific education, relating to the organisation's own industry sector and competitors. In telecommunications it might mean explaining the need for services to be improved and attitudes to be changed in the light of deregulation. In the NHS it might mean explaining the need for new attitudes and values demanded by budget holding and trust status. The overriding objective is to make staff understand the need for change to their ways of working—to raise the perspective beyond the limitation of internal processes to the external pressures being faced. Management tend to assume that their staff are already aware of the forces driving change, but often this is not the case. Undertaking this first very basic step to explain why change has to be made, rather than foisting it on staff from above, can significantly reduce resistance in subsequent stages.

The other side of education is to communicate the desired new culture to the organisation. This has to be reinforced by showing *how* the new culture will help to achieve the process objectives as set out in design principles or measures.

Embed

The second stage is to ensure that the new cultural requirements become embedded in the organisation. This is best done as a series of value statements, which encapsulate the new attitudes and behaviours required. Returning to the example in Figure 7.1, the financial services organisation might use the following value statements:

- "Do it once, do it right"
- "Provide the one-stop shop"
- "Individual contribution, team results"

The professional services firm might use the following:

- "Underpromise and overdeliver"
- "Learning is everyone's responsibility"

These values then have to be embedded into the organisation, an activity that cultural change initiatives have usually been strong on, often to the oblivion of all else. In essence, this remains the "coffee mats and key-rings" aspect of cultural change. Posters, slogans, pens, videos, newsletters, logos—and even coffee mats and key rings—are used to hammer the message home. The objective is to make the new values become the first thought of staff in how they approach their work, their contact with customers and their relations with each other. Previous experience of change initiatives has left many staff cynical about such statements, so the practical and direct should be used in preference to the clever and the trite.

Equip

It is no use expecting people to change their behaviour in line with new processes if they are not equipped to do so. Cultural change has to be supported by any new skills, knowledge and capabilities required to work and behave differently. This may include training to provide specific product skills, for example to ensure that staff really can "Do it once, do it right", and more general education and development, about the theory of process, the importance of organisational learning or the tools for continuous improvement.

Enable

This is the missing cornerstone without which efforts to change culture usually fizzle out. It is also the reason why culture change can be achieved most successfully under the umbrella of process-led change. It is about providing the means for people to change the way they work, and freeing them to put into practice the values they have been struggling to believe in.

The main mechanism is the new processes. Changes to ways of working should support and enable the changes in culture. Cross-functional processes should give staff the power to meet the customer needs. New systems should allow them to enter data and get it "right first time". This stage is the turning point for cultural change. If people begin to see for themselves that they can change the way they work, and that it will help them to achieve the desired results, commitment to the new ways of working begins to take root.

It is this behaviour change that allows culture to be reshaped. Culture is not changed by telling the staff in an organisation how you want them to behave, showing them promotional videos or launching a new corporate logo. These tactics go skin deep, at best. Culture is changed by getting staff to do things differently and getting managers to manage differently. Allowing staff to take the reins and do things differently is probably the single most important point of culture change.

Enforce

The final aspect of culture change is to enforce the desired behaviours. Performance against the new values and ways of working has to be measured, and rewarded or penalised accordingly. This needs to take place on an informal basis as much as a formal one, by monitoring staff performance and providing appropriate feedback and, if necessary, further training and education. Behaviour as such is difficult to quantify or measure, so a more qualitative assessment and appropriate action may be necessary. This reflects the new role of management in a process-led environment, with the emphasis on nurturing and coaching skills in preference to command and control.

HARNESSING THE SIDE EFFECTS

The message of this section is that culture change is difficult and, in particular, that it cannot be achieved without *enabling* people to do things differently (Figure 7.3).

The single most important aspect of successful culture change is that it needs to be tackled from every angle. The task is so large that every tool in the toolkit needs to be brought to bear, and every trick of the trade applied. More importantly, every other aspect of the process-led change programme needs to be brought to bear to make the change happen. Process change, as has continually been emphasised, is a holistic, multidimensional approach to transforming an organisation. It throws all of the elements of people, IT and organisation into the melting pot in one go. While the complexity, breadth and depth of the task is sometimes overawing and intimidating in its extent, it also provides tremendous power to the elbow of those leading the change.

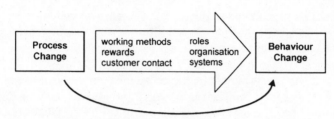

Figure 7.3 Using process change to modify culture

The diversity of the approach actually becomes its strength. For, rather than battling on in isolation, every other aspect of the change programme can be harnessed to change culture. Rather than planning out an isolated programme of culture change to tackle attitudes and values, other aspects of the change programme itself have to be harnessed to make headway.

So prototypes of IT systems should be used to demonstrate rather than talk about the new processes, the establishment of non-hierarchical project teams should be used to reinforce messages about jobs being allocated on merit and ability. The definition of new terms of reference can be used to demonstrate the size of the change. The strategic requirements can be reflected in measures that are relevant and understandable at a local level. Staff should be actively involved in the design and review of process designs. This is the key to cultural change—work out what has to be achieved and tackle it from every single angle.

CULTURAL CHANGE: ATTENDING TO THE RAGGED EDGES

The stages described above outline the approach to changing culture. They show what must be defined and communicated to tap away the chocks of history and set cultural change moving. More importantly, they show how cultural change is utterly dependent on changes to underlying mechanisms, and must be tightly coordinated with other aspects of process-led change. The development of new information systems capability must be seized on as a lever for culture change; pilot implementations must be held up as paradigms of the new ways of working.

But cultural change is not just a mechanistic, prescriptive undertaking. People are rational as well as irrational, and, in addition to the formal stages outlined above, a number of actions are likely to be necessary to address the more ragged edges of cultural change:

- *Remove the roadblocks.* Ultimately, every organisation tends to harbour a number of individuals who resist change and new ideas. Left to fester, they eventually become a roadblock to the progress of the whole programme. For a variety of reasons—for example, a vested interest in the current, a fear of change or just a stubborn refusal to move on—some people just do not want to change. Such individuals have to be removed, either to a different position in the organisation where they cannot interfere with the changes being made, or altogether.

- *Don't forget the customers.* Culture change is not limited to the internal organisation. Process change is about designing more effective ways to work, and often that means installing simpler, more straightforward processes. New ways of ordering, delivering and paying for products and services will arise. Customers are just as susceptible to being locked into long-established ways of doing things as employees, and many need encouragement and education to change the way they interact with the organisation. There may be a need to shift from paper to telephone, or for bigger customers there may be a need to shift from telephone to on-line links. Finally, changing the customers' perception of the company, and perhaps the whole product or service they are buying, may be important to the way in which products are sold or services are delivered. Like the changes required internally, such changes need to be backed up by communicating the benefits of changing to the customers, and reinforcing the messages sent.

- *Target opinion leaders.* Within any organisations, opinion leaders exist. By nature of their standing, reputation or personal charisma, they influence those around them by words or actions. Much of culture change is an issue of critical mass, the change in behaviour of colleagues and peer groups a strong inducement to change. Spending a disproportionate amount of time in identifying opinion leaders and nurturing their behaviour change will ultimately speed the culture change process by virtue of the people they in turn influence.

- *Underpin words with actions.* It is a problem that much of the early days of major change programmes appear (from the front-line sales force or shop floor, at least) to be filled only with words, or at best, with words and designs. Great promises are made about new, customer focused ways of working, a process orientation for the business, more opportunity for staff to take responsibility for tasks and see them through from start to finish, and promotion based on merit rather than longevity. While such messages may not quite fall on deaf ears, they will almost certainly fall on cynical ones. Staff in most organisations have longer memories than their superiors, and without substance such promises will soon be consigned to the "we've heard it all before" category. Only when the promises are underpinned by action do the new ways of doing things actually begin to have an impact on culture itself. The new roles of process owner have to be drawn up, recruited and deployed, the withdrawal of key people from the day to day running of the business shows that senior management are committed to the changes. New measurement systems have to be implemented, and appraisals and bonuses based upon them.

- *Inject new blood.* Sometimes the potential of existing staff is such that they are not able to provide all of the skills and capabilities required for the new processes. This may be true at both staff and management levels, leading to a requirement to supplement the existing capability with new recruits from elsewhere or from outside the organisation. As well as bringing in new ideas and encouraging a less parochial, more receptive attitude to change and new ideas, such a move again sends signals from the change team and their sponsors about the seriousness of their intentions and the commitment to the whole change programme.

MULTIPLE PROBLEMS, MULTIPLE SOLUTIONS

We close the chapter with a repeat of the warning issued at the beginning— that culture change is not a distinct task. It is like a river in flood, about to burst its banks, and it requires constant monitoring and constant action; just as the desired form is established in one area, culture spills over elsewhere in a different form. Changing culture demands a portfolio of different approaches, backed up by different measures, and constant reinforcement, sometimes established as temporary or *ad hoc* solutions on the fly.

As such, culture change is not for the CEO or programme manager who is only comfortable when all of the steps required to complete a task result are mapped out clearly on a project plan, with clearly visible milestones along the route. It is about testing the temperature as well as laying down new cultural edicts; it is about continually raising the perspective from the detail of everyday modifications to see what new changes in direction are required. It needs regular consultation with the crew, as well as a firm hand on the tiller.

Finally, remember that it is not deciding to change culture, or even designing the new culture, that is difficult. What is difficult is carrying through the things that change culture, and standing by those things. It is making board members take a pay cut if they do not meet targets, or moving people out of a position if they no longer have the capabilities to do the job that will change the culture.

☞ SIGNPOSTS FOR SUCCESS

Excite and energise

Ultimately, most people do want to break out of the straitjacket of today's organisations and seize something more challenging, stimulating and satisfying. The problem is that they have seen so many half-baked attempts in the past that they are reluctant to try again. Staff have to be encouraged and excited to take up the ball and run with it, to help solve the problems that inevitably arise, and contribute to the change programme as their own responsibility rather than waiting for it to be handed down to them.

Ask for help

Process-led change is too big to be undertaken without the help of the organisation's staff. By its nature, process-led change is multidimensional and the changes required are too extensive merely to be left with a change team for implementation. In addition, change driven solely from the top tends to be resented, with staff regarding it as another management initiative imposed from above. By emphasising early on that the undertaking is a joint one, which cannot be achieved by management and the change team alone, a culture of contribution rather than indifference and avoidance is fostered. It has to be made clear that the management and the project team do not have all the answers—to some extent, process change is a journey into the unknown—and everyone has to help to create the solution.

Make it relevant

Process change works because it provides a way of focusing the organisation on the customer's requirements and needs. But although such a perspective may be clear from a management or process owner viewpoint, it may be of little relevance to those buried in the detail of the organisation, carrying out a particular process step. The "what does it mean to me?" question has to be answered, ultimately, for every individual in the organisation. Messages have to be tailored, design principles have to be interpreted, new ways of working have to be explained, so that individuals can see why and what they have to adapt to.

Create headroom

Change places massive demands on the staff within an organisation—both those tasked with creating the new capability and those left with running the existing operations. Freeing up the best people to create and implement new process designs cannot be achieved without plugging the gaps they leave behind. This frequently requires a budget commitment as well as a verbal one, because temporary staff may be required to supplement the existing workforce to cope with operational workloads. As the programme progresses, further headroom has to be created to free up staff so that they can contribute to testing and validating new process designs and undergo training and development in the new ways of working.

Tackle it from every side

Cultural and organisational change is an indistinct, endless, amorphous task. Unlike the creation and development of new IT capability, it is not possible to define all of the steps involved and specify predictable outcomes. Cultural change is about dealing with a thousand and one preferences, politics, personalities and motivations. However well a programme of organisational and cultural change is conceived and managed, it is unlikely that it will ever be comprehensive. People issues are living: new problems will emerge, and old issues will arise from the ashes. Progress on organisational change has to be monitored, measured and tackled from every angle to ensure the required level of success.

Chapter 8

Information Technology

Information technology is the second of the three capabilities that have to be developed to put a new process infrastructure in place. This chapter describes how the new IT capability is developed from the process design. It covers the key stage of requirements definition, through to the subsequent stages, which address the design, construction, testing and implementation of the new IT capability. Ultimately, the product of this stage is the new IT infrastructure required to support a process, such as new computer system and applications, hardware and software, networks and communications.

The choice of the term "information technology", rather than "computing", is deliberate; process change relies on leveraging the power of IT and, as such, this could include any technologies that capture, process, store and output information (imaging, multimedia, telecommunications etc.) rather than just computer systems.

The IT components of process are shown in Figure 8.1.

A NEW AGENDA FOR IT?

Traditionally, the starting point for IT, and in particular for computer systems development, has been to automate existing processes or methods of work in an organisation. Established tasks and manual systems were analysed and modelled, and computer systems were then designed and constructed to automate the steps involved.

Process-led change marks a fundamental shift away from this approach, with the process design itself becoming the source of requirements for the new IT capability. This ensures that the IT capability developed fully reflects the needs of the business as captured in the process design. By developing IT

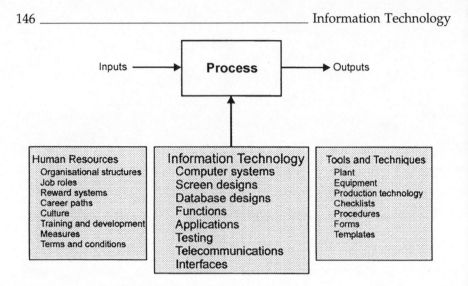

Figure 8.1 The IT components of process

that supports a process design, rather than merely automating an existing set of tasks, it allows the organisation actually to change the way business is done. This opportunity for a fundamental rethink about the way work is done is at the heart of process-led change, and provides the opportunity for real competitive advantage to be achieved. At the same time, it presents significant challenges to getting the development right. Rebuilding computer applications and IT systems under the umbrella of process has proved to be one of the most troublesome areas of process-led change.

Amid the self-appointed gurus and experts on process-led change, opinions differ when it comes to addressing IT. There are those who imply that process is such a radically different way of thinking that existing development methods become extinct. Others seem to ignore the issue altogether, as if somehow expecting the new process to appear, with or without a new supporting IT infrastructure.

Process-led change does not replace existing methods of IT development; it merely modifies some of the early stages of development, in particular the derivation of IT and systems requirements. This chapter is concerned with showing how existing development methods are adapted so that the appropriate IT support can be developed and other needs of the process can be taken into account. It does not attempt to cover the "traditional" steps of an IT development, which are not affected by process led change, merely to show how such methods need to be adapted.

Finally, before embarking on the path of IT development, a word about iteration: although IT development is treated within a separate chapter, this does not imply that the development occurs in isolation. Process is about creating a new way of working—a new way of working that combines the appropriate mix of IT, people and other capabilities in the optimum way. IT development must therefore iterate with other areas of development, in particular HR, and vice versa. IT staff need to understand the capabilities of the people who will be using the new systems and applications, just as HR staff, trainers and managers must understand the nature of the new IT systems. This demands a new level of cooperation and dialogue between areas of the business that have traditionally been isolated.

THE IT MINEFIELD

Exploiting the full potential of IT is a long-standing corporate headache. Since the early days of computerisation, when technology was used to automate the simpler functions in an organisation, through to the more ambitious applications to which it is put today, there has been a constant struggle to make the machines deliver what the people wanted. Over the years, despite the falling costs of hardware and processing power, the overall costs of IT development have continued to rise, and problems have proliferated. In the background, high-pressure salespeople have continued to press ever more powerful machines brimming with sophisticated features upon beleaguered organisations, insisting that each particular generation of IT represents the real panacea.

In reality, the issue remains not one of technology, but the *application* of technology to meet business needs. But, with their tunnel vision firmly established, organisations have continued with the struggle to try to make computers work in isolation, without looking at the other parts of the equation, such as the people elements or the way in which work is carried out.

The problems encountered in IT development were many and varied, but typically the following issues were encountered:

- Computer systems delivered failed to meet the needs and requirements of those using them. Usually this arose through a misunderstanding of requirements between those who specified new systems and those who built them.
- Computerisation occurred incrementally, resulting in a large number of disparate systems with areas of overlap and duplication. This in turn led to inaccurate information and errors, and the requirement for multiple updates and extensive cross-checking and double entry.
- Applications were difficult to operate in use, and inflexible when it came to making modifications and changes.

- The large number of disparate systems varied widely in design, screen layout and naming conventions. As a result, user interfaces came to vary widely, and it was difficult for users to switch between different systems.
- Costs continued to rise, especially those associated with maintenance and enhancement of the existing IT infrastructure.
- The extensive suite of existing applications meant that corporate data was dispersed across many disparate systems. This issue of legacy systems became an increasing burden, from which forward progress was increasingly difficult, even when the desired direction was understood.
- The prevalence of new IT applications—the non-stop arrival of new and more advanced technologies and platforms (client/server, portable and desktop PCs requiring networking, remote access and telecommunications capabilities) raised ever more challenges of integration, compatibility and access.

Over the years, various efforts have been made to address these issues, including the creation of a number of sophisticated methodologies for computer systems development. These aimed to bring rigour and discipline to the whole development life cycle, in some cases from the definition of strategic objectives right through to the production of individual lines of computer code. But, despite sterling efforts to apply these methods, two limitations remained. The first was an inability to address the people issues with any great success or reliability. Although some of the better methods included stages to look at the human and organisational issues, their incorporation was peripheral rather than core to the development. Fundamentally, the methods had their roots firmly in computer systems development, making it impossible to get the best out of people capabilities. Any acknowledgement of the human factor was an add-on rather than an incorporation of the people issues from first principles. Secondly, computer systems development tended to be myopic, focusing almost exclusively on the existing business. IT was wrapped up in looking at what went on within an organisation and how it could be computerised and automated. There was little or no effort to use IT actually to change the way the work was carried out and free an organisation from the burden of the past. The result was that inappropriate work methods rapidly became inappropriate computer programmes—albeit undertaken more quickly and with less resources.

The process-led approach introduces a new way of looking at the world. It is used to take a much broader view of the whole enterprise by designing the processes first. Only subsequently does it consider how these processes can best be supported—using a combination of people, IT and any other mechanism, rather than concentrating blindly on one or the other. This in turn has major implications for the way IT capability is both designed and defined, and subsequently developed during process-led change. It becomes closely integrated with people issues and the development of HR capability, rather than looking at them as an afterthought.

THE SEARCH FOR REQUIREMENTS

The enthusiasm of the past few years for Business Re-engineering and Business Process Redesign have met with varying degrees of success in the IT departments of major corporations. Typically, the baptism of the managers and staff of IT departments into the notion of process occurred in some variation of the following manner. From out of nowhere, it seemed, the concept of process appeared. It was rapidly seized upon by managing directors, CEOs and internal and external consultants as the solution to all organisational ills. This was the solution everyone had been waiting for. Working groups and process teams were established, targets were set and there was exciting talk of radical new designs. Eventually, after several months of process analysis and design, a new "process design" was produced and trumpeted as the new way forward, the brave new world that would cure the organisation's ills. The IT department were then handed a document purporting to represent the new processes, and asked to assist in developing new processes.

Not surprisingly, some pretty major confusion resulted in the area of IT development. Process designs had been produced that looked perfectly sensible in theory, showing flattened, cross-functional operations focusing on the customer. But typically they offered no clue about how this new view of the world was to be translated into a new IT infrastructure. There was no specification of the information that had to be captured, and little indication of the transactions that had to take place. And, worst of all, there was no existing manifestation of the process. Unlike previous developments, there were no existing manual systems to model or users to talk to.

As a result, the IT function often struggled to deliver the new capability required to bring about a process orientation. They looked in vain at the process models, designs and flowcharts, and failed to find any detailed indication of the information required, or any clues as to how that information should be processed. Eventually, they returned to what they knew, resorting to the existing business as a source of requirements. Not surprisingly, the new systems reflected only limited improvements and the changes encapsulated in the new process designs were either absent or a poor shadow of the original design. The quantum leap that process had promised had become a minor shuffle forward.

In retrospect, IT staff can be forgiven for struggling to get the development right. In most organisations the gap between a process design and a specification that could be used to drive forward a new IT system was big enough to swallow the best intentions and new ideas. Process designs showed high-level processes, not detailed information requirements.

In practice, the maze is not as bewildering as it first seems. One fundamental principle is key above all others in IT development, and must be followed religiously: *the process design drives the IT requirements*. The process design is about new ways of working and, as such, it is the only representation of these new ways. There is no existing manifestation of it for the business analysts and data modellers to go and copy, analyse and pore over. There are no "users" already working that way, who can be interviewed. So the process design itself must be the sole source of IT requirements.

This in turn demands some change to the way in which IT is developed. But it does not replace the IS development life cycle—it merely changes where the requirements come from. The information requirements of the new process, rather than the existing business, drive the IT life cycle. Instead of looking at current operations and automating them, IT analysts and designers take their cue from the process design itself. This represents a major shift in the way requirements are obtained—but not in the way systems themselves are produced. The differences in the traditional cycle, from user requirements through to test and roll out, are shown in Figure 8.2.

CULTURE CHANGE FOR THE IT DIVISION

Process-led change marks a significant shift in the role of IT. Rather than being the overriding driver behind change, as it usually is during major systems development, it becomes just one of several components within the change programme. IT no longer leads; it plays a bit part. More so, a design itself leads, and the IS development team have to look to this, not a set of users or existing methods, for their requirements.

This has a major impact on the IT division itself, and on the way in which design and development have to be carried out. Achieving it requires significant changes in culture, which are not easy to bring about. Often there is cynicism and resistance to methods that do not have their roots within the IT world. Nevertheless, a culture change has to be made, which ensures that the emphasis is on IT as one part of the overall process, in combination with people and other mechanisms, rather than the sole overriding tool.

Historically, the IT department has never had a particularly rosy relationship with the rest of the organisation. In the early days, a struggle to deliver the requirements that the business needed and the staff within it really wanted strained a partnership that always struggled to bridge the gap opened up by terminology and technology. Latterly, the response has been

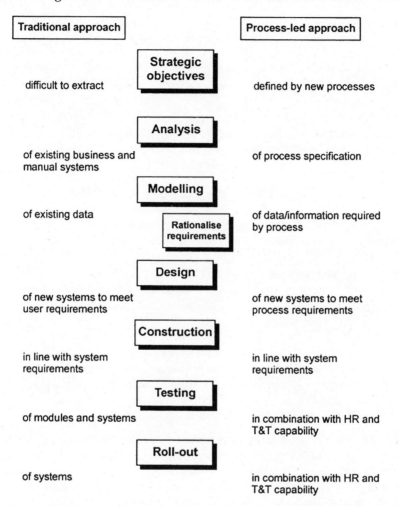

Traditional approach		Process-led approach
difficult to extract	**Strategic objectives**	defined by new processes
of existing business and manual systems	**Analysis**	of process specification
of existing data	**Modelling**	of data/information required by process
	Rationalise requirements	
of new systems to meet user requirements	**Design**	of new systems to meet process requirements
in line with system requirements	**Construction**	in line with system requirements
of modules and systems	**Testing**	in combination with HR and T&T capability
of systems	**Roll-out**	in combination with HR and T&T capability

Figure 8.2 The development life cycle: traditional and process-led methods compared

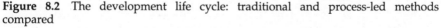

for a set of requirements to be produced, defining to the nth level of detail a vision of the systems to be developed. This hefty tome was then signed off by both parties as the specification for all of the development work that followed. Once documented, these requirements became set in stone, an exorbitant price and convoluted change control procedure usually being attached to any request for modifications. While this gave the IT department something to point to and say "you got what you asked for", it still rarely ensured that the most appropriate solution was delivered.

Taking the process design rather than the existing business as the source of requirements calls for new ways of working. But it is the only way in which a new process can be developed that fully escapes the baggage of old ways. A good process design will ensure that many of the old constraints have been designed out. This is a fundamental starting point. IT systems, therefore, have to be built to support the new process, not to solve the problems of the old one, and this often proves to be a problem for IT departments whose methods are based around modelling an existing operation, rather than working afresh from a paper or conceptual design.

DEVELOPING THE NEW IT CAPABILITY

In developing the IT capability to support the new processes, the objective is to identify the information needed by the process and to define how that information is captured, transmitted, processed and stored. Underlying this, there is a requirement for the new systems to be built to a specification, and to be developed in close conjunction with other parts of the process to ensure that the benefits of a holistic solution, which makes appropriate use of people and IT capabilities, can be realised.

From this it should be clear that process-led IT development is not radically different from traditional methods. It is still concerned with eliciting the IT requirements so that those with the expertise to do so can build the necessary programs, applications, databases and interfaces.

The development of new IT capability reflects the five stages adopted throughout process-led change as outlined in Chapter 3:

- *Design* of the overall IT architecture and applications required.
- *Definition* of detailed requirements for information processing and the associated applications and databases.
- *Development* of new capability as a suite of programs, databases, screens and applications.
- *Dismantling* of old systems, including the capture of any new data required and merging and migration of data to new systems.
- *Deployment* of new IT systems into a live environment as part of the new process capability.

Design of the IT Framework

This stage confirms the overall information technology requirements for the new processes. It describes the technologies that will be required for collecting, validating, storing, processing and communicating information, and how they fit together. It may be considered as the IT architecture or framework, and will be closely allied to the organisation's IT strategy. As well as setting out the various technologies required to support the new processes, it helps to identify the individual development areas needed to build the new IT capability.

As elsewhere, the process design serves as the prime means of determining requirements. The preceding process design stages will have identified the main uses of IT, especially where it is being applied in a new or innovative way. However, as the process design is concerned with all mechanisms, those specific to IT must now be elicited. This is achieved by working through each process specification to confirm the most appropriate use of IT to support the new process. The task is undertaken jointly by the process designer/team and IT staff such as chief analysts and designers. The exercise requires cooperation and iteration, with the process team clarifying the requirements of the process design and the IT staff advising on the most appropriate technology. Most "appropriate" depends on many peripheral issues, such as the cost of maintenance and compatibility with other parts of the organisation. Given that some significant decisions may have to be made (such as the implications of re-skilling an existing IT development workforce if a switch from technology platforms is considered), this stage needs to be overseen by senior IT managers able to make decisions about existing and future IT strategy. The other key influence on the IT architecture may be any design principles that relate specifically to IT.

By the end of this stage, a clear understanding of the following should have been reached:

- *Key technologies.* The main technologies to be used. This includes both those that will be used to support the mainstream computing applications (e.g. client/server or mainframe, office-based PCs or remote laptops) and additional technologies required to support peripheral activities such as telecommunications (within a customer service centre this may include call routing, distribution and identification), networks, printing (laser or continuous feed, black and white or colour), imaging and the like.
- *Communications.* The communications requirements, both between staff within the organisation and between customers and staff. This needs to address voice and data communications, and to consider any links required between telecommunications systems and computers (such as automatic call dialling), and whether hardwired or mobile access is required.
- *Interfaces.* Where the component parts interface to exchange, upload and download information and how the various elements of IT identified above fit together.
- *Design principles.* Any specific principles to which the organisation wishes to adhere during development (e.g. UNIX conformance or a "windowed" environment). Such principles may be established specifically for the

change initiative or may already be in place as part of wider organisational IT strategy.

- *Principal applications.* The core applications that will be required to support the new processes. The main databases and applications that will be required in each area are identified and form the basis for detailed specification and development. The actual applications required will depend on the industry in question, and the processes being redesigned. Typically they will include a central customer information database, usually complemented by a pricing or quoting package and accounting and administration applications by way of support. Beyond these, each industry will require its own packages, reflecting the nature of the business. In telecommunications, this could include network configuration; within manufacturing it could include order picking, packing and dispatch. In healthcare, it may be the sharing of patient records between different players in the healthcare process, or the capture, structuring and dissemination of knowledge for education and research purposes.

The example shown in Figure 8.3 is an illustrative one, but it shows how the key requirements for IT within the new processes are identified. Of particular importance is that it incorporates all aspects of IT, rather than just computer systems. This is a key part of the process approach, given that it is IT, and the integration of IT with people capabilities, that is important to a good process, rather than just isolated computer applications. Identifying the key technologies at such a level also ensures that the presence of other, peripheral projects in progress can be identified and "plugged in" to the architecture, so that any impact can be identified. Thus, for example, if the organisation in question is already involved in overhauling its billing and invoicing system, it is possible to identify early on where this will have an impact and what that impact will be. It is essential that this "broad brush" view, which process provides, is exploited to the full if the realities of change are to be properly addressed. It is not possible to prevent other projects taking place but it is possible to understand and manage their impact within the context of the overall change programme; the breadth of the process approach facilitates this.

The definition of the IT framework is an iterative exercise, which involves revisiting both process requirements and the organisation's existing IT strategy before final decisions are reached. Where the process change is organisation-wide, and a major change to the existing IT architecture is envisaged, the company's IT strategy may have to be revised, and board level agreement and sign-off is likely to be required. Alternatively, if the change is taking place within the context of a wider organisation, such as a multinational with an established IT strategy already in place, some constraints may exist. So, for example, even if a client/server platform was

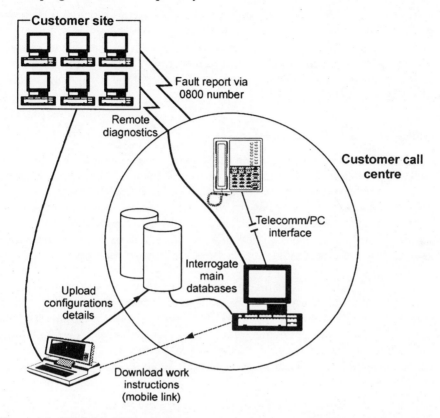

Figure 8.3 High level IT architecture

envisaged as the most appropriate support for the processes, a compromise may be necessary if there is a higher level commitment to mainframe systems. Either way, this stage sets out the IT required for the new processes, either in its own right or within the context of existing organisational prerogatives. In the latter case it helps to identify where interfaces to existing systems will have to be built.

The IT framework needs to be confirmed at an early stage so that the necessary project areas for development can be established. Separate initiatives incorporating the sizing, sourcing, tendering and procurement of the necessary equipment can then be started. It may be necessary to evaluate options from several different suppliers. So, for example, where a new call centre capability is required, services may have to be trialled from several different third-party suppliers where the capability cannot be built in-house.

Finally, the design of the IT framework is essential to identify the impact of any existing IT development initiatives or projects. It is exceptional for an organisation not to have any such projects in progress; usually, they are numerous—one organisation reported having over 70 under way at one time. Once the overall IT framework is established, it is possible to identify such projects and then assess their impact and relevance. Decisions can then be made about whether they are integrated as part of the change programme or managed discretely.

Define Detailed IT Requirements

This stage defines in detail the information requirements of the new processes. This includes both the information (data) and its associated values, and the operations and transactions that will be performed upon it. This is a long and detailed phase of work, taking many weeks, and probably months, to complete. It is a critical stage in the development of the new IT capability and requires the highest quality individuals assigned to it, be they IT staff, process design teams or those co-opted from the business as required.

As with the IT architecture, the process design drives the requirements. The detailed requirements are elicited by a joint team of process designers and IT analysts working through the process specifications and task breakdowns to determine the information required and the transactions that will be performed on it. The difference to the design of the IT framework is one of detail. The objective is to determine what must be done to support the process with IT, namely:

- What is the most appropriate information (information about what, and in what form)
- What has to be done to that information
- How that information is accessed, transferred and stored
- What validation is required

Ultimately, every single item of information required to support the new processes has to be defined, along with the associated values, validation, format and operations that will be performed on it. This includes the business rules that operate on processes, and their format or values.

Returning to the example of the fault report and maintenance process, requirements are provided by the task breakdown and the description of the process step within the process specification. The first stage of the analysis might produce the results shown in Figure 8.4.

This analysis has to determine not only the sequence of events and the data used, but also the preferred way of performing a particular process step (using the call routing mechanism), and also the alternative method when the preferred method fails (the customer site still has to be identifiable via a lookup routine, which searches on customer address). The information or

---

Process: 2.0 Fault Reporting and Resolution

Version: 3.4

Task or Function: 2.2.1 Identify Site

Data items	Description
Site name	Name of site
Site code	Code of customer site
Customer name	Customer corporate name
Site address	Address of customer site
Configuration overview	Overview of machines installed at customer site (number, types, networks, numbers of users)
Last contact	Details of last contact with this customer regarding maintenance or repair

Controls and Rules:
Response times: response times define the time within which a first response must be provided to the customer, and the maximum time within which the fault must be resolved or an upgrade provided (customer, initial response time, maximum fault time, maximum upgrade time).

Functionality:
Retrieve site details of customer site using site identifier. Site identifier is either entered by the customer as part of the automated call-routing system or provided by the customer during the dialogue with the service centre agent. The site code can be derived from the customer site address where it is not provided by the customer or not known. Detail to be displayed includes customer name, site address, configuration overview, summary of customer service agreement and details of last contact. Any recent or ongoing network maintenance or intervention for this site must be displayed.

Figure 8.4   Towards Detailed IT Requirements

data required is still in a format easily understandable to business people; the data analysis stage, outlined below, will break this down further to validation, values and attributes required. By defining the information that needs to be displayed (and the context within which it is used) this stage also forms the basis for screen designs to be drawn up, which can then be used during prototyping to confirm the user interface. The controls or business rules that act on a process also form a significant part of IT requirements given that many of them lend themselves to being implemented automatically.

The example given is drawn from the computer servicing organisation, but it could equally well apply to processing an order or accessing patient records in a hospital. The emphasis at this stage has to be purely on the information required to support the process, and how it is captured, validated and evaluated. Consideration of solutions at this point should be avoided because this immediately draws the debate into more specific matters of systems design. The exact format of the IT requirements depends on the methodology being used, but this stage should gradually draw out the information required, how it will be displayed and the processing (or functions) that will operate on it.

The important point is that the information required is extracted from the overall context of the process design. Because the process specification describes the new ways of working in generic terms (rather than purely informational ones) it is possible to determine the information required to support these new ways of working. So, for example, a process step can contain the requirement "Use the information from past transactions to check the customer's satisfaction with previous work carried out", and this analysis stage can then consider the most appropriate information to support such an action. This is one of the key strengths of the holistic approach that process provides—the ways of working that will provide a competitive edge can be designed first in the processes, and subsequently the information needs to support them can be consciously driven out.

The definition of detailed information requirements often proves to be a major stumbling block to progress. Problems that develop here can in the worst cases bring a project to its knees, and even in less critical situations cause major delays to the information systems and technology development. The whole stage should be regarded as high risk and watched and managed with care.

This stage encapsulates much of what is new about process-led design and development. Firstly, IT staff have to use the process specification as their source of requirements rather than analysing and modelling the existing business operations. Secondly, they have to work closely with the process designers and owners, working out the most appropriate solution where it is not yet clear. Thus, the activity is a recursive, discursive one, rather than merely a case of looking at the existing *modus operandi* and computerising it. Finally, it has to be made clear that the process model does not equate to the set of user requirements traditionally produced. It represents a total business requirement for a set of new processes, which has to be further analysed to determine the most appropriate information needs. The process specification is a guiding light, not an IT specification or a statement of requirements. Although it represents a picture of the new ways of working, it still requires interpretation by the process designer and analysis by the IT team. A simple message has to be driven home to IT staff. It is a process design, not a data model.

Driving out the Data

Definition of the detailed IT requirements is a key stage in IT development. It has to be driven by the process designers (given that they understand the desired shape of the new process and the design principles it has to fulfil), working in close cooperation with IT analysts and designers. At the same time, the process designers are unlikely to have the depth of knowledge required to specify every single item of information, the value it might take and the rules that need to be applied to it. Additional staff have to be co-opted from existing business operations to supply more detail as required under the management of the process designers. While these staff provide the detailed knowledge in particular areas, it is critical that the whole activity is still driven by the process designers, given that staff drawn from within the existing operational environment understand information as it is collected, used and processed within current operations.

While the structure, format and values of some of the existing information and rules is a good starting point and source of detail, it cannot be used without any refinement. It is up to the process designers to keep their eye firmly on the ball and ensure that this information is reviewed, adapted and designed to ensure its suitability in the new process environment. In many organisations the legacy of quick fixes and *ad hoc* solutions has become embedded in an organisation, with ever more complex procedures and validations around them. Information requirements have to be driven from the top down, and redundant data items need to be removed if they are no longer required. Similarly, new information items may have to be created and ultimately collected if the process demands it.

THE ROLE OF PROTOTYPING

Prototyping is a key technique in the definition of IT requirements. A prototype is a partial representation or 'mock-up' of the final IT solution, showing the key features of the new systems, usually as a series of computer screens. Prototypes demonstrate the computer system's support for the new ways of working, and the "look and feel" of the interface.

Prototypes are used in three different situations (Figure 8.5):

1. To capture detailed information required for IS development. As noted above, process design teams are unlikely to have the depth and range of knowledge to supply sufficient detail about all of the information required. For every information item, additional parameters, such as allowable values, validation routines and permissible formats, have to be specified. In addition, the rules or controls that operate on information items during processing have to be captured. In this role the prototype is used as a focal point between the process designers, IT analysts and designers and the staff within the business who can supply the detailed knowledge about specific information items. Any three-way discussions of this type are driven by the process designers. The process designer

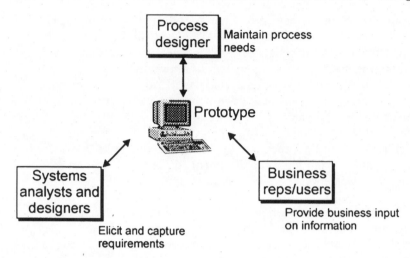

Figure 8.5 The role of prototyping

maintains the overall vision and direction of the process and must ensure that the information requirements distilled reflect the new ways of working in full, rather then minor "tweaks" or improvements to the existing methods.

2. For general validation purposes. The overall flow of the process end to end has to be validated against current business practices. Prototypes are used to show how the various elements of the IT systems connect from one step to another, primarily by demonstrating screen flows and the information captured and processed within those screens. By using a prototype, feedback is easily solicited and obtained at an early stage of design, as well as promoting buy-in through early involvement in the change activities.

3. To communicate and demonstrate the new processes. The new ways of working embodied in the processes have to be demonstrated frequently and clearly to the wider organisation to ensure their successful uptake. Given that a significant time lag often exists between design and roll-out (while development is undertaken), action has to be taken to maintain momentum in the organisation. In this context, the prototypes are used as demonstration systems, shown to staff who are not directly involved in the project, to give them a sight of the new ways of working. Often this is the first tangible evidence of the new ways of working that staff encounter after the process designs themselves. As such, the prototypes must be carefully targeted to ensure relevance and correctness, and used to begin "selling" the benefits of the new ways of working. Use of prototypes as a

representation of the new ways of working, rather than a comprehensive working system, has to be made clear; prototyping requires a delicate balance between illustrating what the new system will look like and representing it in full. Such demonstrations should be tested carefully before they are presented to the wider organisation.

Given the right development environment and tools, prototypes may be used further during IT development, for example through development into pilot systems.

RETURNING TO THE IT DEVELOPMENT LIFE CYCLE

At this stage, the development of IT capability links back into the more "traditional" IT life cycle, as shown in Figure 8.2. It is beyond the scope of this book to consider the activities of the life cycle in detail, given that they take place as in a typical IS development and are addressed much more comprehensively in other texts. Our focus is on where the remaining stages differ as a result of a process-led development.

Data Modelling

By this point, an understanding of the information required should be sufficient to enter the data modelling stage. Using the information identified in the detailed IT requirements analysis, this stage formally models the data required by the new processes and the relationships between various data items: entity modelling is the prime technique used. Data modelling is an essential step in ensuring corporate data integrity and preparing for the designing of databases and applications which follows. In addition, the valid values, validation routines, types and sizes of the data items will be captured. In reality, data modelling is likely to begin during the analysis of IT requirements, rather than waiting for it to finish, and to proceed in parallel with it.

Systems Design

The systems design stage determines how the requirements identified previously are to be satisfied by IT systems. Depending on the methodology being followed, this may be further subdivided into logical and physical design stages.

The logical design involves the design of the key applications and the definition of specific functions within them, which combine to meet the desired requirements. The starting point for defining functions is the task breakdown provided during specification, and the further analysis that has been carried out as part of analysing IT requirements. These functions establish the heart of the new computer systems support and how it operates; functions and the interactions between them form the basis for the construction of modules or programmes in the development stage which follows. The design stage typically includes logical database design (based on the data structures identified in the previous stage) and confirms the full set of screens or human–computer interfaces required. In addition, the requirement for any interfaces is confirmed. This includes interfaces to other technology (such as telecommunications or imaging facilities) as well as to other systems.

The physical design stage is concerned with identifying how the logical design will be implemented in reality on the particular hardware or IT infrastructure that the organisation has, or will choose to have, in place. A key part of this design is to consider alternative means of satisfying the logical systems design requirements. The options range from building the new capability from scratch to tailoring a packaged solution that already provides much of the functionality. Again, these are major steps in the IT life cycle in their own right, and appropriate evaluations and cost–benefit assessments need to be made that take into account factors such as development time scales, flexibility, support and the degree of customisation required. As part of the systems design, existing applications and systems and the files and databases within them need to be reviewed to consider to what degree (if any) they provide part of the capability required.

Rationalise IT Requirements

Throughout this book there has been an emphasis on developing the most appropriate infrastructure or capability to support new business processes. A process design is nothing until it is brought to life by the people, systems or other mechanisms that will carry out the various process steps. An essential step in the creation of this new capability is to design and select the most appropriate combination of supporting mechanisms. Depending on the process steps in question, and the objectives of the organisation, a different emphasis on the balance of, for example, human and technology elements may be necessary. In a high-service, high-value-added environment a more extensive level of HR support may be necessary to provide the personal touch. In a low-cost, high-throughput situation, a greater level of IT support to provide the maximum levels of automation is more likely.

With this in mind, the holistic, multidimensional nature of the process approach requires an additional stage to be added to the traditional IS life cycle—the rationalising of IT requirements. This stage is concerned with revisiting the IT requirements and reviewing them for suitability within the wider process perspective, for two reasons.

Firstly, to maximise commonality and suitability across the process(es): this ensures that an IT solution is developed which is appropriate and consistent across all processes. Although the process itself provides an end to end, cross-functional design, IT requirements are drawn from individual steps within it.

Consider the example of the process step "capture customer details", which occurs in the early stages of many processes involving customer contact, whether it be to sell to, service or administer the customer. The likelihood is that within these different processes a slightly different set of information, or slightly different presentation of it, will be required. In the "sales" situation the imperative will be on the collection of information quickly to provide a quotation or response; ideally, no information will be collected that is not required to undertake the quotation. The administration or service process, however, is likely to require more detail, and often in a slightly different format—full addresses rather than postcodes, telephone numbers and occupation, perhaps an alternative address or phone number. Similarly, different products may require their own slightly different subsets of information.

A frequent objective of process-led change is to eliminate hand-offs and delays by enabling one individual to perform many tasks. To do so, it is essential to maximise the commonality and consistency of different parts of IS systems which serve different parts of the process. Otherwise, the old problem returns that the operator has to become familiar with many different systems, interfaces and screen layouts for each different process or product.

To achieve this consistency, some compromise in IT requirements may be required within individual process areas or steps, so that the optimum overall solution can be reached. The objective is to maximise the consistency, or the "look and feel" of IT interfaces, across different processes. Wherever possible, information should be gathered and displayed using the same format and position and using the same conventions. This obviously requires a degree of rationalisation and tradeoff to achieve. In achieving the overall process orientation, it is rare for all those involved to be completely satisfied. Compromise is a key part of good process design, and making the IT tradeoffs is an important element of that compromise.

The second reason relates to the application of the 80:20 rule. Among those not closely involved with the complexities of IT development, there is often a conviction that IT is a panacea for all corporate ills. Where a particular task or requirement needs to be undertaken, the attitude towards IT tends to be "the system can do that". There is a belief, in short, that IT can be used to carry out any type of information processing required, whatever volume, speed or flexibility is required, and whatever the complexity and frequency of the transaction. In essence, this assumption is true. Given the time, processing power, analysis, design and programming skills, virtually any information processing activity can be captured, coded and computerised.

The reality is that time, money and other resources are all invariably limited in one way or another. Although it may be possible to computerise a particular process step, it is not always practical or sensible to do so. Consider IT development in the context of pareto analysis (the 80:20 rule), which states that for any activity 80% of the results are achieved by 20% of the effort. Conversely, 80% of the effort is needed to achieve the remaining 20% of the results. Within computer development, this basic principle is true, although frequently it is even more extreme, with probably the final 5% of transactions requiring the greatest part of development effort. It is relatively straightforward to computerise the standard, regular cases within any one set of transactions. They tend to fall within a consistent set of parameters, for which a set of distinct rules and routines can be defined quite easily, which will cope with the majority of situations. The problem arises in addressing the more complex or exceptional cases. In effect, the development effort required to cope with every exception rises dispro-portionately. In the worst cases, individual rules and lines of code are required to cope with each individual exception or anomaly. Worse still, the checking, validation and processing required to handle these exceptions sometimes has to be applied to the straightforward cases as well, with the outcome of an additional layer of complexity being added around every straightforward transaction.

Traditionally, there has been little alternative to this situation. Once it was decided that a particular aspect of a business was to be computerised, a complete, all-encompassing computer solution was expected. The result was that the delivery of a solution to cope with the vast majority of cases was often delayed by the development work to resolve individual complexities and anomalies.

A process-led development provides an alternative approach. Because process is a means of designing a business as well as a specification for running and operating it, it provides a way of seeking an alternative solution to the problem, where the computerisation of a particular step indicates that a vast amount of development effort is required. This can be achieved either by designing an alternative way of carrying out the task or process step, or by considering an alternative mechanism (for example, human or manual means, using procedures etc.).

Rationalising requirements and making the decisions about what constitutes the appropriate solution overall is an essential, ongoing responsibility of the process design team. They are the only group equipped with the knowledge to see the wider picture, and understand the impact of particular decisions across the whole process. At this stage, the process design is used to help make the tradeoffs and maintain the overall process view above the demands of individual process steps or functional areas.

Following rationalisation of requirements, the traditional IT development life cycle is entered once more.

Develop

This stage is concerned with developing or building the new IT capability in line with the requirements and designs established above. This is the real construction or "code-cutting" stage, during which programmes or modules are actually designed, created and tested. Success during development is highly dependent on the quality of the requirements and specification provided from previous stages. Where system design decisions have dictated using a package rather than a bespoke development, this stage may be more concerned with modifying and adapting a third-party solution rather than building new applications from scratch.

Depending on the exact design of the overall change programme architecture, development is likely to take place in a number of discrete "project" areas. This partitioning ensures that development of different components can be managed and controlled tightly to within time scales and budgets, before being integrated back into the bigger process picture with other systems, people, and tools and techniques capabilities.

Testing

Testing takes place at a number of levels following construction. In accordance with traditional methods each module or package of work is unit-tested to ensure that basic functionality is satisfactory. This takes place within the individual areas responsible for the production of particular parts of the new system. This is followed by link testing, which confirms the fit with other modules, and system testing, which validates the performance of the system as a whole. System testing typically includes some element of stress testing to ensure that the new applications can cope with the volume and throughput of transactions required to support the new ways of working. These stages all take place in accordance with a typical structured method.

The final stage of testing unique to the systems areas is that of user testing. This introduces the ultimate user to the system, and in doing so introduces a new level of rigour to the testing activity. User testing involves users themselves testing the system, but in isolation from any other aspects of the process. The final stage of testing is business testing, which validates the performance of the system with other elements of the process (people skills, procedures etc.). This is described in Chapter 10, on deployment.

Note that the specification, rationalisation and migration of data to new systems capability is a cornerstone of delivering new IT capability. This is covered in Chapter 10, under the heading "Stage 2: Preparation".

ADAPTING DEVELOPMENT METHODOLOGIES

Most organisations utilise a methodology for development of their IT systems. Such methods have arisen from the recognition that IT development is a long, costly undertaking, with numerous opportunities for error and delay, and, in the worst cases, failure along the way. A methodology adds rigour to the whole development life cycle, ensuring that certain key stages are followed, standards adhered to and essential tasks completed. Increasingly, these methods tend to incorporate some type of rapid application development (RAD) tools and techniques to shorten development time scales. A CASE (computer aided systems engineering) environment, which acts as a central repository from which to manage the whole development life cycle and, in particular, the definition, use of and changes to data items, is frequently also a part of such development approaches.

The presence of such established development methods is often seen as a major stumbling block in the adoption of the process-led approach. Arguments are advanced that the two are incompatible, with a process view of the world implying a complete change to the way systems are built, and requiring new development methods, resulting in a substantial waste of previous investment. The reality is somewhat different; the flexibility of the process approach actually facilitates the use of many alternative development environments. The main issue is adapting the method in use to the core attributes of the process approach. The key differences that have to be accommodated are:

- The process design rather than the existing business is the source of requirements.
- Development proceeds in close alignment and combination with other (especially HR) capabilities to ensure an integrated solution.
- Iteration is required between process designs and IT requirements, and between IT analysts, process designers and business representatives and users.
- There is an opportunity to redesign the process and find better solutions where IT meets a "brick wall".
- Parallel development occurs with other (people, manual) capabilities.

In summary, process-led change does not seek to replace existing IT methods. It merely changes the source of requirements and provides more dialogue with the other elements in the equation. Ultimately, the very nature of process-led change is likely to make the rigour and discipline of a formal development methodology essential.

MANAGING THE IT DEVELOPMENT

Much has been said and written in recent years about the art and science of successful IT development. It is beyond the scope of this chapter to revisit those issues in detail, because our concern is more with how traditional development life cycle methods can be successfully adapted to dovetail with a process view of the world. The single most important point is that the process designs drive IT needs. If IT is not built to support the new ways of working, then it will fail to deliver. When the IT department begin to look to the process specification, rather than review the existing business, then a key message is starting to get home.

Beyond this, there are a number of issues important to managing a process-led IT development.

Firstly, experienced managers who have been through the development cycle before are critical to success. Where the organisation does not have proven in-depth experience of major IT development, or appropriate exposure to the IT development methodology being used, then additional external resources should be used to supplement in-house capability. Successful development must then be underpinned by strong, structured project management techniques, which, again, must be tried and tested, with the individuals responsible able to demonstrate a proven track record. IT departments, like the rest of our organisations, tend to suffer from a tendency to promote people on the basis of service and experience in existing positions rather than on their ability for subsequent ones, which often results in inappropriate staff occupying project management positions. IT development is too critical—and strewn with too many tripwires—to allocate anyone but the best staff to key roles, and those driving the change programme must be ruthless in assigning the best staff to key IT and project management roles. Not to do so jeopardises the whole development activity.

But if the right IT staff are critical, so also is the way in which they deal with problems. IT development is fraught with difficulties, but the successful IT projects are those that have a way of consciously addressing failures, problems and changes to requirements rather than trying to avoid them. By tracking progress and identifying and tackling the issues that arise, it is possible to recover from setbacks and delays and keep a project on track. Problems must be surfaced rapidly and honestly, something that is harder to achieve in practice than it is to consider in theory, given that no one likes being the bearer of "bad news". An open, honest approach to acknowl-edging problems needs to be underpinned by an attitude of fairness. It is the job of management to encourage the type of non-judgemental culture which ensures that problems can be surfaced, examined and resolved. Such openness has to be encouraged by frequent, fairly informal meetings, providing an open floor for anyone to raise issues and areas of concern.

Cultural issues also have to be considered in the role that IT plays in the development as a whole. The emphasis in a process-led approach is to find the best process, not the best IT solution. A shift in perspective has to be made until IT is regarded as one of several possible ways of fulfilling a process requirement. If the proposed IT solution proves to be particularly cumbersome or difficult to develop, it may be more appropriate to seek an alternative process solution. The requirement is to develop the best process solution, not the best IT solution.

Such attitudes are nurtured and enforced by ongoing dialogue and contact beyond the walls of the IT department, especially with the process design team. No development proceeds without obstacles, and there are always occasions when subsequent analysis or development shows that the original solution is not feasible. In such situations the IT staff should convene further discussion with process teams (and possibly end users) rather than battling with their own solutions in an isolated corner. This ongoing dialogue with process owners and design teams is essential, and is often best achieved by co-locating the two skill areas of process design and IT development. As well as keeping a close eye on IT development, those with the knowledge of the process are available on the spot to answer questions and provide further detail when required.

☞ SIGNPOSTS FOR SUCCESS

Don't wait up

Of the three capabilities to be developed, IT undoubtedly takes the longest to complete in a workable format. IT automates the processing of information, and, by its nature, requires the specification and development of routines or programs to cope with every single data item, value and rule that may be encountered. Even in the smaller change programmes, such developments take many months to complete. In larger, cross-enterprise initiatives, final roll-out may take several years. Completion of IT support should not delay progress, and, wherever necessary, new processes should be introduced ahead of full IT support. This may limit the process to roll-out in only a partial form initially, but it ensures that the new processes begin to go in sooner, rather than later.

Consider outsourcing

More and more companies now consider the outsourcing option as a part of their IT provision, and it can be appropriate within process-led change, especially if IT support is required in areas where the organisation does not have appropriate skills or capability. This is particularly true in specialist areas such as telephone call centres and image processing, but is increasingly also an option for core applications of the whole business if a move to a new technology platform is being considered. The alternatives need to be evaluated carefully, especially if such moves leave the organisation without an internal resource or skill base for future development and maintenance.

Process designs are not data models

While those closely involved with process design know this, IT departments often jump to the wrong conclusion. Process designs are typically represented graphically as a series of interconnected boxes, with the transactions between processes shown by labelled lines. IT people have a tendency to treat such a design as a data model, which utilises several similar diagramming conventions. Such misunderstanding can easily set a project off on the wrong track from day one—IT staff expect the process design to set out the data required for development, and the full analysis of process designs is omitted, with all the serious consequences for development that this entails.

Education

With the above points in mind, a constant programme of education is necessary to reshape the thinking of IS people if they are to successfully grasp the concepts of process. IT staff often hold established, difficult to shift views on IS development and how it should be approached. Key messages have to be hammered home again and again. After "process provides the requirements", one of the most important is that IT is but one part of the final solution, and must be developed in close conjunction with the people and organisational issues.

Solutions to old problems

The traditional approach of IT has been to automate existing methods of work, or processes such as they existed, within the business. Often this has built in further complications as the complexities of the existing business were automated. Good process designs should eliminate the worst bottlenecks, replacing them with a simpler, straightforward solution, more easily supported by whatever combination of the supporting mechanisms is selected. Unfortunately, those with their heads buried in the sands of development tend to be inspired by solving problems as much as by avoiding them. During IT development a close watch has to be kept to ensure that capability is being built to support new process designs, rather than old problems still being tackled.

Beware of new toys

The development and launch of new products in the IT world, as in many other market-places, is driven aggressively by manufacturers, backed by the resources of powerful marketing operations. The result, amid a backdrop of intense competition and falling prices, is a vast and sometimes bewildering array of new products on the market, loaded with ever more features and facilities, all promising to solve an ever greater number of problems. While many of these products have their uses, the real need for them, as ever, has to be determined by the process requirements. If the new ways of working do not require a particular new technology, then a large question mark should be left hanging over it.

Dissect development bottlenecks

During development, certain parts of the process tend to prove more troublesome than others. Although many of these are only temporary obstacles, the worst cases require many iterations before resolution, during which time resources are diverted and other areas of the development are held back. Concentration of masses and masses of development resources into one area suggests that an alternative solution may be more appropriate. This can be achieved either by modifying the process design itself (removing the problem) or by seeking an alternative (human, manual) means of supporting the process. As ever, the focus must be on developing a practical rather than a perfect solution within the desired time scales.

Secure the opinion leaders

IT departments, just like any other, tend to have their peer groups and role models. Given that IT is a fast moving area, immersed in the latest innovations and developments, one or two people usually stand out as opinion leaders in the pack. Securing the backing and commitment of the IT department to process-led change is crucial. Often it is worth investing extra time and commitment to bring the opinion leaders on board, rather than trying to convince those in the lower ranks of the programming and code cutting shop, one by one, of the rationale for change.

Process drives IT requirements

To close, we return to where we began, with an emphasis on requirements, for this single principle simply cannot be overemphasised. Actively designing the way an organisation works is one of the most powerful aspects of process-led change—but it only works if the design itself, rather than a view of the existing business, is used to drive the development of the new capability. It is a message that needs driving home again and again, otherwise those developing the IT support merely meddle with the business as it is, in search of minor improvements, rather than adopting the new design. The message "analyse the process, not the business" has to be sent constantly to those in the IT department.

Chapter 9

Tools and Techniques

The third and final area in which capability has to be developed to support the new processes is that of tools and techniques (T&T). This encompasses any other mechanisms used to carry out a process or part of a process step other than HR and IT. This ranges from the more formal "tools" such as the plant and equipment that provide production and manufacturing capability through to the "techniques", which include less sophisticated but equally important mechanisms such as checklists and procedures.

As has been continually emphasised, process-led change seeks to design new processes—but transformation does not occur and improvements are not yielded until the appropriate combination of mechanisms brings that process to 'life'. During process-led change the development of HR and IT capability tends to take up the most significant part of development effort; tools and techniques are, however, an essential capability to complement these mechanisms and to ensure that the overall process is complete. In particular, they are important in ensuring that the "right" capability is implemented. Given that the most sophisticated solution is not always the best one (and rarely the cheapest), T&T can provide an alternative mechanism where IT and HR capabilities are not appropriate (Figure 9.1).

The design and subsequent development of desired T&T capability typically require less effort and resources than the two preceding areas, often leading to it being seen as something of a poor relation in comparison to HR and IT, being regarded as the "add-ons" used to wrap up the few parts of a process that IT and HR are unable to address. In practice, the reverse is often the case; the provision of T&T often proves to be the final piece in the process jigsaw, which ensures that an effective and efficient process capability is provided.

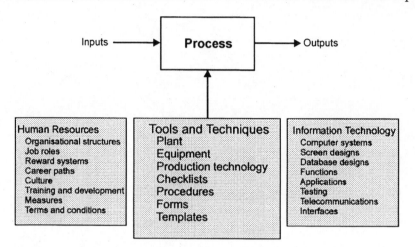

Figure 9.1 Components for process: tools and techniques

In addition, it should be noted that the less structured characteristics of T&T (in particular, techniques) are a key ingredient in the development of "quick wins" or early process implementation, because they facilitate the rapid development of *ad hoc* solutions. The development of T&T should therefore be afforded as much importance and attention during the change programme as the development of any HR and IT capabilities.

COMPLETING THE JIGSAW: TOOLS AND TECHNIQUES

A process is holistic or multidimensional, made up of a number of different mechanisms that actually undertake activities or process steps. T&T is the third of the three capabilities needed to turn design into practice, and ensure that a process design ultimately becomes reality. They are the mechanisms used to carry out any part of a process or process step not undertaken by people or IT.

The two groups are made up as follows (Figure 9.2):

• *Techniques.* "Techniques" incorporate the simplest mechanisms used to complete the make-up of a process. They are the basic, least sophisticated methods and techniques used to provide a simple alternative where a more complex IT or mechanistic solution is not necessary or cost effective. They include checklists, forms, prompt cards and procedures. Often they act as a bridge between technologies or people capabilities. They are particularly applicable where the volumes of transactions are low and do not justify development of more sophisticated capability because they provide a means of dealing with the cases or events that occur on a

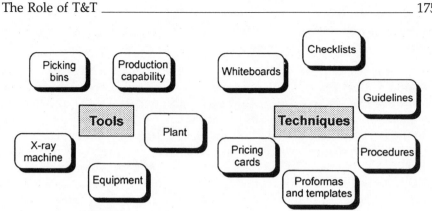

Figure 9.2 Tools and techniques

"one-off" or infrequent basis. Their importance is summed up in the phrase "fit for purpose". They ensure that the most appropriate solution can be used—a short checklist in preference to a detailed procedures manual, or a clutch of Post-it notes as a means of capturing and rearranging information.

- *Tools.* These are the "formal" mechanisms that produce. They consist of the machinery, tools and equipment used to make or transform goods and raw materials, processing physical things rather than information. In manufacturing they could be the production lines used to make and assemble goods. In distribution they could be the fleet of vehicles used, or in logistics the warehouses and picking bins. In healthcare they are the X-ray machines, testing facilities or operating equipment used in the diagnosis and treatment of patients.

In essence, these mechanisms may be thought of as the physical or "non-information" technology—the facilities used to carry out a process step, just as IT is used to process information. The use of the term "non-information technology", although perhaps more indicative, is avoided because of the obvious confusion this causes with information technology itself. The extent to which tools are required within the make-up of a process depends very much on the nature of the particular industry. Those industries with a high degree of information processing (such as the financial services sectors, including insurance and banking) typically have less requirement for such mechanisms.

THE ROLE OF T&T

T&T is the third and final component in the overall process framework, and is important in ensuring that the process solution is appropriate as well as comprehensive. There are three reasons for considering T&T capability during design and development:

1. *To complete the process infrastructure.* First and foremost, T&T embraces any additional mechanisms required to deliver the full process capability. It ensures that any parts of the process not undertaken by IT and HR are catered for. This in turn ensures that the overall infrastructure to make a process complete and bring it to life can be designed and built.
2. *To achieve optimum combination.* In practice, a good process is dependent on having the most appropriate combination of supporting mechanisms. Each (whether human, IT or other T&T) should be used to contribute its unique capability to the working of the process, often in combination with other mechanisms. By considering T&T, the most appropriate combination of mechanisms can be selected. Even if the required capability already exists (such as an X-ray machine or a production plant) and development is not required, including such mechanisms in the overall design ensures that their role and position within the process can be considered and combination with other mechanisms optimised.
3. *To complete the business model.* The addition of T&T provides the final capability in the process jigsaw. The business and its core processes can now be viewed in terms of people, organisation, IT and any other T&T that undertake the process, enabling the process design itself to serve as a business model. The process design is no longer just a means of managing the change programme; it is a rich and powerful representation of the workings of the business itself.

This use of informal "techniques" highlights an angle of the process approach that is vital, yet often missed. Remember—the overall aim of process-led change is to deliver a process that is effective and efficient at meeting business objectives. If a manual solution is more cost effective, practical and quicker to bring business benefits, then that is probably the one that should be used.

REQUIREMENTS FOR TECHNIQUES AND TOOLS

In common with the HR and IT components, the requirements for T&T are driven primarily by the process. It is the process specification, along with the design principles and measures, which will ultimately determine the supporting mechanisms required. The application of T&T is split into two distinct parts, discussed in the following subsections.

Techniques

The most important application of T&T is the design and development of more "informal" mechanisms or "techniques" where HR and IT alone are appropriate. This ensures that the most appropriate mechanism for the process step or activity can be selected, or to put it another way, avoids using a sledgehammer to crack a nut. T&T development may be as much about plugging a small gap so that the overall process works, rather than providing a major capability.

In this respect, designing and developing the most appropriate mechanism to undertake a process can be compared to selecting a brush to paint a wall. For the most part, it is easiest and most effective to paint the wall using a roller; it carries a large amount of paint, covers a large area at once, and achieves the desired levels of quality. There are some areas, however, where the roller is no longer appropriate, such as around doors and window frames; here, a small brush, with its ability to handle small spaces and fine lines, is the tool for the job.

Selecting the right mechanisms for process requires the same balance—the process itself is essentially the same, but different mechanisms may be used as appropriate to actually carry it out.

As ever, the main source of requirements is the process design, and the analysis that identifies HR and IS and requirements. During this review, certain aspects of the process surface that are not best served by either a human solution or an IT one. The most likely solution in this case is the development of a "manual" or checklist-based solution. A secondary source of requirements is the emergence of any consistent "sticking points" in the development of the IT infrastructure itself. Where extensive development effort appears to be required to address only one small, inconsequential part of the process, an alternative, manual means should be considered.

Such techniques help to acknowledge the realistic face of change. While a process that embraces every aspect of the businesses in a slick new design is fine in theory, it rarely works so well in practice. Multi-skilled operators using state-of-the-art IT systems that encompass every last single aspect of the business are a worthy objective, but unfortunately the real world doesn't work like that.

Exceptions occur and every business has its VIP customer or exceptional case that falls beyond the mainstream parameters laid down. T&T acknowledges the fact that the process will not always cope with one hundred per cent of business cases or transactions (be they insurance clients, patients, orders or fault reports). Rather than ignoring this reality, techniques provide a way of addressing it in a manner than can be managed and controlled rather than allowing such idiosyncrasies, exceptions and special cases to clog the arteries of the rest of the process. If it is understood, designed and addressed, it cannot become unmanageable.

The techniques that may be appropriate vary widely depending on the requirements of the process. Ultimately, the overriding rule is that whatever is appropriate for the process can be considered. The most common are:

- *Procedures.* Procedures are the documented descriptions or guides as to how particular process steps and activities are carried out. As well as defining how a particular process step is carried out, procedures may be used to clarify the correct combination of mechanisms during a process. Procedures refer to other mechanisms used (e.g. tools to use, computer systems, forms to fill in) within a process. Procedures are especially important for handling exceptions and one-offs because they are likely to cover those areas where users are unfamiliar with the exact course of action.
- *Guidelines.* Guidelines provide a framework for carrying out an activity or particular process step. Rather than specifying the work to be done task by task, they lay down certain parameters within which to work, and certain standards that have to be followed or results that have to be achieved. In addition, they provide guidance on particular aspects of the work—such as points to watch, common problem areas, likely exceptions etc. Guidelines are a key mechanism for enabling empowerment—they allow responsibility to be devolved, and the individuals concerned to determine how they will carry out the work, while helping to maintain appropriate standards, control and consistency.
- *Pro formas.* Pro formas are forms and templates designed to capture information. They are particularly useful for collecting unstructured information, capturing information from many people or capturing information rapidly to facilitate further analysis and structure at a later point. Examples are new product development (NPD) and organisational learning or brainstorming activities.
- *Card indexes.* Card indexes are used to provide access to reference information. They are particularly useful where structured (e.g. alphabetical) access or indexing is required. Examples include product information or features. Although such card indexes may be seen as a substitute for more sophisticated on-line reference information, they may be more effective in a manual means. In one organisation, albums with plastic sleeves, designed for storing photographs, were used for such material.
- *Whiteboards.* Whiteboards are an effective, highly visible, rough and ready means of providing information on matters such as scheduling, status, progress, work outstanding etc., especially where that information is irregular or unstructured. They can be updated rapidly and easily.

The important point with the application of any of the above techniques is less what they are than what they provide. If they fulfil the objectives of the process in the most effective manner, then they may be appropriate.

Tools

During the distillation of HR and IT requirements from the process, appropriate applications of tools are identified and documented. Usually this

One of the pioneering hospitals of process-led change in the NHS redesigned its outpatient process in a bid to reduce waiting lists and improve treatment times. Part of this involved the streamlining of appointment systems and the collapsing of examination activities. The overall effectiveness of the process depended on being able to facilitate rapid throughput of the patient at all stages, from examination and diagnosis through to testing. Analysis of part of the neurology outpatient process revealed that some patients spent significant time moving between the different locations that housed particular testing and diagnosis facilities such as those required for X-rays, blood and ECG testing. Because these testing facilities were not coordinated, further delays and opportunities for error occurred in the collation and analysis of results.

This was resolved by co-locating the most commonly used facilities, such as testing and X-ray. Patients were no longer forced to move to a different location every time that testing facility was required, and clinical staff were no longer required to coordinate results and information from several different sources.

The changes made helped to realize a significant improvement to the overall performance of the patient visit process, including reduced waiting times and elimination of unnecessary visits.

Figure 9.3   Reviewing boundaries and interfaces: redesigning processes in the NHS

is a straightforward activity, given that the main uses of tools will already be known. Familiar mechanisms, tools, equipment and plant, which are used to carry out particular steps within the process, usually exist already. In a hospital, for example, it is already clear where an X-ray machine is used to provide a particular capability; in a manufacturing plant, it is clear where a particular machine provides a particular cutting, stamping, shaping or assembly capability.

Given that the capability of such tools is already well established in an organisation, this stage acts as a check for completeness, the actual development required often being minimal. Two activities are required:

1. *Review boundaries and interfaces.* The way in which equipment, tools or plant interface with other parts of the process is reviewed to consider how process performance could be improved by changing the combinations or locations of particular tools, plant or equipment. For example, although the manufacturing capability provided by equipment may remain unchanged, it may be possible to reduce delays by physically relocating parts of the process (see Figure 9.3). Within a logistics process, where much of the time tends to be spent in walking (or driving) between different warehouses and picking bins, this might involve rearranging picking bins, so that the delays involved in moving between them are reduced.
2. *Review existing capability and identify any proposed changes.* A check is made on the existing capability to ensure that it meets the requirements of the process. Given that it is not usually the objective of process change to

make changes to an organisation's core "production" capability, any shortfalls are identified and proposed changes suggested. Process-led change would not, for example, expect to redesign the working of an X-ray machine or a chemical processing plant.

The incorporation of tools and techniques helps to ensure the completeness of the process view. Even if it does necessitate any changes, it can be used to incorporate any ongoing changes to tools beyond the scope of the process-led change programme. Where such new development and capability (for example, the installation of new plant or equipment) is not taking place as a direct result of the process-led change, its impact can be clarified and understood. Any modifications and changes can therefore be coordinated in line with other aspects of the change programme.

EARLY IMPLEMENTATION

One of the most important applications of T&T is in supporting the delivery of early process introduction or "quick wins'. This is covered in more detail in Chapter 10, but the essence is to implement the process in some partial form ahead of its full version; this is usually desirable because of the long development times required to provide full systems and IT capability. As well as delivering business benefit in terms of financial pay-back, early implementation is desirable because it familiarises the organisation with the shape and form of the new processes, and provides further testing and validation.

Given that much of a process orientation is about working across functions and completing transactions with fewer hand-offs, some of the objectives of the new processes can be achieved prior to developing the full-blown HR and IT capability. This is achieved by implementing the process in some partial form, with the main role of T&T being to "plug the gaps" where the full capability is not yet available.

Earlier, we compared the whole process-led transformation exercise to a major road-building programme. The route of a new three-lane motorway is like a new process, the bottlenecks of traffic lights and roundabouts replaced by uninterrupted progress, which allows faster throughput and the carriage of greater volumes. And in both cases the real work lies not in the design but in the development and implementation of the underlying infrastructure— be it the laying of tons of rock and earth or the development of new computer systems and retraining of staff.

But one final comparison can be made between the two, using that much cursed symbol of motoring delay, the humble traffic cone.

Not surprisingly, these draw the wrath of many drivers when they are used to divert and delay the flow of progress on existing highways. But

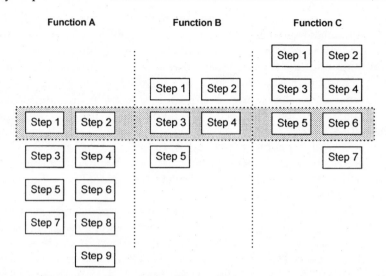

Figure 9.4 Procedures for early implementation

consider how such cones are deployed on new roads. They are used to bring about progress, not delay it. They are the tools used to achieve early implementation. Invariably such road-building programmes result in the completion of one half or section of the new highway first. And a strip of cones, setting out the demarcation and the temporary use of the new road (or process) enables an early taste of the final benefits to be achieved. The new highway is opened early, even if only in a partial format, and the benefits of better traffic flow and quicker journeys start to come on stream even while the rest of the highway is being completed.

Procedures, like traffic cones, enable the "quick wins" of process change. They allow the temporary, rough and ready solution to start bringing the benefits in as soon as possible. This can be achieved in two ways:

1. By providing some sort of a *manual* solution in preference to the final mechanism. This might be a paper form to complete rather than a computer screen to enter data into, or the implementation of controls by manual review rather than on-line validation. While obviously not as efficient as the final solution, such changes start to bring in the new ways of working.
2. By defining *procedures* that combine disparate parts of existing processes. By this means, the desired process perspective can be achieved in part by using different parts of current processes, whether human, manual or systems based. Again, this helps to move along the path to the new process orientation, even it is achieved from the existing working arrangements (see Figure 9.4).

By way of further example, consider the internal arrangements of a traditional financial services firm struggling to adopt a process orientation. Work organisation within such institutions has typically been set up by function, with additional walls often existing between products. The result was that a customer had to deal with several different departments or organisational units, depending on both the product in question, and the nature of the transaction. This occurred whether the customer was seeking a quotation for a new product or service, an adjustment to an existing policy, the completion of a payment or deposit, or the making of a claim. The divisions between functions were usually reinforced further by separate IT systems, which typically reflected a product or functional view rather than that of the customer.

A common response to such functionally based organisation is to create processes that work across products and, where possible, functions, so that the customer only has to deal with one member of staff. A single job role is therefore able to satisfy requirements across most of the process, such as quoting, setting up new policies or accounts and performing account administration.

The biggest obstacle to realising the new process vision is likely to be the development of new systems and IT capability. A cross-functional, cross-product set of applications is likely to take months, and more probably years, to develop. Existing systems have to be rationalised and new ones designed, built and tested in accordance with the process design.

But through the use of interim procedures, such as the definition of forms or checklists, it is possible to achieve a partial process perspective. If, for example, the customer phones for a quote but also wishes to notify a change of address it may be possible to capture this information manually, rather than pass the customer on to another member of staff, who will have to recommence the whole dialogue. This information can subsequently be used to update records, even if it cannot be achieved during the duration of the actual call. Alternatively, it may be possible to define procedures that guide a customer service clerk through several different systems, to extract or update the information required; this forms a stop-gap solution until the new computer application, allowing a more seamless transfer between different parts of the process, is provided.

FUTURE PROOFING

T&T provides the final capability in the process jigsaw. A comprehensive suite of people, organisational, information and non-information technologies and capabilities are now at hand to provide the infrastructure that brings the process to life. But as well as providing the mechanisms required actually to make the process work in the current environment, the combination of these three capabilities also plays a key role in ensuring the viability of an organisation's processes in the longer term.

Pressures to change, as we noted earlier, act ever more frequently and forcefully upon our businesses and organisations. The problem such enterprises face is how to balance the opposing needs of stability and change. On the one hand, there is clearly a requirement for rigour and discipline in processes. Quality has to be assured, standards have to be followed, and the integrity and validity of information has to be retained; a far from trivial task in a multi-user, cross-functional environment. But at the same time, there is a requirement for these organisations and processes to respond and reshape as customer pressures and market developments dictate. How, having developed a comprehensive and rigorous process infrastructure of people, systems, tools and equipment, is this flexibility and responsiveness to be achieved?

The completion of the new process infrastructure with the T&T mechanisms outlined in this chapter provides two characteristics essential for coping with change:

- *Completeness.* With the addition of T&T the process is now complete—not just in use but as a model of the operations of the very business itself. What is more, it provides this view of the business in terms that can be understood—people and systems, tools and procedures. The picture is a real-life description of the business in terms of tangible objects, rather than concepts. As such, it is a fundamental tool for change. Because it acts as a picture of the business's processes—how it works and operates at any one time—it provides a means of deciding what changes have to be made to that infrastructure to cope with new opportunities. Traditionally, this is not something that has been easily available to the manager seeking to making changes to the business. Knowledge about how the organisation works, how people, systems and procedures combine to produce particular outputs of the business, is usually buried away within functions and divisions. Managers are measured on whether they deliver what is expected from their function—and the means was traditionally not that important. Within process, ways of working, methods, cut across departments, functions and products—therefore, everyone has to know what is going on, and everyone affected has to understand the impact of change. The model of the business that process establishes provides a way of doing this, and thus a way of making controlled, planned changes.
- *Speed of response.* The second key capability that T&T provides for an organisation is that of rapid response. Opportunities emerge rapidly, within days and weeks, not months and years. But people take time to train and reorganise, and systems, however well they are designed with

corporate information needs in mind, still need enhancements and new releases. The provision of a manual and *ad hoc* capability within process ensures that a rapid (albeit often temporary) response can be made. Earlier, the notion of T&T as the sticking plaster of change was considered. But it also acts as a sticking plaster for future, incremental change. It can be put in place very rapidly, to achieve a desired result. It can be used to combine existing people capabilities and link diverse skills groups on a temporary basis. Tools and techniques may not be tidy or neat, but they are practical and functional, and allow time for something more comprehensive and effective to be created in the meantime.

Finally, the context of T&T within the overall process capability helps to ensure that such interim solutions are not forgotten. Such manual processes and "quick and dirty" solutions are not new to organisations—indeed, it is their very build-up over the years that has created the burden of inertia and complexity which makes so many organisations difficult to change. Quick fixes and manual procedures have been created, but then left to become a part of the organisation. The result is that standards, consistency and simplicity go out of the window, and complexity returns.

Managing change is about putting in place an *ad hoc* response initially so that opportunities can be snatched and openings can be taken. But the use of T&T within the process view must then realign the overall process design so that the process remains simple, effective and consistent rather than becoming gradually riddled with quick fixes and *ad hoc* practices.

☞ SIGNPOSTS FOR SUCCESS

Keep it simple

Use the most appropriate solution, not the most sophisticated one. IT is an incredibly powerful tool, invaluable for capturing, processing and storing structured information. There are times, however, where pen and paper solutions can be more effective, especially where the information being manipulated tends to be more unstructured and free flowing. In this situation, a formal IT mechanism can actually be a constraint. Process design itself is a good example of this, as, often, are the early stages of the product development process. Keep the emphasis firmly on "fit for purpose".

Keep it short

Documented procedures are an important part of underpinning quality and consistency within processes. But their viability depends on them being followed—procedures that document every single step of the process in infinite, unnecessary detail are unlikely to be effective because they are more likely to be skipped than followed. Procedures are most important when they provide the guidance and clarity where the steps taken are unfamiliar; where the steps are performed regularly and consistently, the actions to be followed should be instilled by training.

Be realistic

However good the process design or however ambitious the intentions, there are usually some parts of a business process that will prove the exception to the rule. A slick solution with manual methods may be more appropriate than a complex one with IT and extensive automation. Do not try to squeeze every last single object or transaction handled by the business into exactly the same process if in doing so it hinders the performance of the rest of the process.

Focus on improvement

Above all, change is about improving performance, not about producing all singing, all dancing processes. A process design has to be implemented and it can be implemented by people, by IT or by tools and techniques. It is the solution that brings about the overall improvement which is the appropriate one. Elaborate mechanisms are of little value if they do not bring about performance improvement, whether this is to the bottom line, the treatment of patients, better customer service or whatever.

Use process to manage change

The addition of T&T completes the overall process view of the business. This view should now be used to identify and direct future change to the enterprise by both identifying the changes needed to the process design and selecting the individual mechanisms that have to be modified. Change undertaken in this way can take place by design, and change undertaken by design can be carried out without unnecessary disruption to the existing operations.

_____ Part IV

Making Change Stick

The first three sections in this book have shown how to design and build the new capabilities required to bring about change within an enterprise. By clearly establishing a design, and then using that design to drive the creation of new mechanisms—be they people or IT, organisational or procedural—it is possible to bring about co-ordinated change.

This section shows how to bring those components together to realise the new ways of working in a 'live' environment. The backbone of this is concerned with deployment, (Chapter 10) which considers how to integrate and roll-out the new capabilities and make them work as one process in practice. Chapters 11 and 12 introduce concepts essential to the whole transformation activity—programme management, and communication.

Deployment or "Making it Stick"

The final stage within process-led change is the deployment of the new process capabilities into the operational environment. At first sight this may conjure up inspiring images of a "big bang" roll-out, complete with fanfare, fireworks and flashing lights as the curtain is drawn up on the new process capability. The reality, though, is likely to be altogether less dramatic.

Process change is about delivering business improvement, and the nature of the holistic approach, with the many component parts inherent in it, tends to imply that new process are rolled out bit by bit, rather than with a big bang. People change may precede systems roll-out, or procedural enhancement may put interim processes in place ahead of the full version. This chapter, therefore, comes with the warning that has accompanied several previously—the position of this subject in the book should not dictate the point at which these techniques should be used on the change programme. Issues of deployment have to be considered from a very early stage—deployment in some areas will happen before design and definition has even occurred in others.

But, more than anything, is it the use of early implementation or "quick wins" which ensures that the process is likely to be implemented incrementally rather than with a big bang. Early implementation is a key part of process-led change, and is covered in this chapter as a technique to provide early financial returns, but also for the commitment and buy-in it establishes. It is an essential approach to creating ownership, and ensures that the transition in thinking occurs from regarding new processes as something being provided by the project team to the adoption of "our" new ways of working.

In addition to the techniques of deployment, which may be applied at any point during a change programme, the second part of the chapter—making it stick—concentrates on approaches to ensure that the new ways of working become permanent.

EARLY IMPLEMENTATION: THE CONCEPT

Early process implementation (it may also be known by the terms "quick wins", "early benefits" or "interim roll-out") is a powerful technique for implementing change. It is based on implementing new processes in some partial form ahead of the final version. "Early" in this sense essentially means any manifestation of the process that is less than complete; this may mean that not all of the components or mechanisms are in place in their final form (perhaps the systems are not yet complete) or that the process is not complete in an end to end format (it might be possible to provide seven out of ten process steps within a process in advance of having the full process capability in place).

The main imperative for early implementation is to see some returns from the change programme. The time taken to rebuild systems, achieve cultural change or run-off old products and services may run into several years. Given that the pace of change is forced by pressures of competition, cost and customer need, frequently the business just cannot wait until all parts of the process are complete before rolling it out. In addition to financial reasons, early implementation also helps to trial and test the process and to communicate change to the organisation

These points alone provide a strong case for seeking early implementation. But arguably the most important of all reasons is that early implementation provides the opportunity to create ownership. Early implementation provides the opportunity to hand the process to the organisation and say "This is it. It's yours; help to make it work". This "ownership" is the most effective means of getting the roll-out and the ultimate manifestation of the process right because it shifts the onus from the project team to those responsible for staffing the new processes. The "us and them" mentality can thus be tackled before it becomes a black hole. Passing the ownership into the hands of staff also begins to foster the whole attitude of learning and improvement that is essential to keep processes viable in the face of future change. It begins to replace the sense of "that's no good but it's not my job to sort it" with an attitude of "how do we make it work?".

The second imperative is that early implementation can be used to create a demand for the new processes. By implementing the process in part, it should be possible to deliver at least a subset of the benefits of the new ways of working. By doing so, it is possible to create a taste for the benefits and improvements that will ultimately accrue. This, managed correctly, is an incredibly powerful lever for change. People begin to see the new ways of working as desirable, rather than an imposition, once they have seen what a partial implementation can provide. It turns one of the biggest problems of organisational change on its head—the difficulties raised by imposing solutions upon people are replaced by a demand for the new ways of working so that they replace the partial ones.

Selecting Processes for Early Implementation

The essence of early implementation is to identify processes or parts of processes that can be implemented in some form prior to the development of full capability. Typical means of achieving such changes are:

- Temporary IT solutions to make good gaps in the IT infrastructure. This includes menus to link disparate systems and "bridging" systems that capture data subsequently uploaded to main systems (e.g. PC to mainframe links).
- Team working, based on specialists from several areas being brought together as a team to provide all of the required expertise in one location until individuals become multi-skilled. One organisation made use of video conferencing technology to create this team virtually, rather than bringing them together geographically.
- Procedures that bring several disparate steps together into a sequence which represents the desired process. This may require pulling together activities that are currently the responsibility of several different functional areas. The analogy of procedures and checklists as the "sticking plaster" of change is again appropriate.

Early implementation of processes is initiated by reviewing process designs at an early stage (typically once the process architecture has been completed and the task of process specification is under way) and identifying places where the new process can be implemented in some partial form. Early implementation then proceeds in the following steps (see Figure 10.1):

- *Feasibility.* To review the feasibility of the proposed process changes in terms of practicality, time, cost, resource etc.
- *Benefits.* To review the benefits that will accrue from such changes, both financial and those that will foster ownership and buy-in.
- *Selection.* To choose those areas in which early implementation is to be carried out.

The progress of early implementation then mirrors the progress of the overall change programme, namely:

- *Planning* of the actions necessary to bring about early implementation.

As part of their process-led change efforts, a medium-sized financial services company redesigned the payment process by which customers paid for products. The company had a reputation for slowness in processing applications and payments for products, and errors and inaccuracies were commonplace. From a range of payment methods, which included postal orders and money orders as well as cheques and cash, they were moving the emphasis onto electronic methods of payment such as debit cards and credit cards, with all the benefits of bulk transfer these included.

Due to the massive systems rebuilding programme which was taking place to provide support for the new processes, full implementation of the processes was expected to take several years.

The company selected part of the payment process for early implementation. Using manual forms to collect payment details, they were able to offer debit card and credit card payment as an option long before the full on-line systems support was available. Because on-line validation was not available, procedures and guidelines were provided to guide customer service clerks through the form filling process and dialogue with customers. Rather than just encompassing the basic process itself, these procedures were structured so that the benefits (speed, convenience, no need to write a cheque) of using card payment were explained to the customer.

As well as the benefits of using debit cards and credit cards, this early implementation provided two further important examples of the leverage of process-led change. Firstly, by encouraging customers to move on to methods of card payment in preference to cheque payments, it was possible to reinforce the new customer-focused, state-of-the-art service image that the company were trying to create in the market-place. It also started to change the culture among the staff, as well as the customers.

Secondly, it shows how it is the combination of mechanisms which process-led change provides that is important. It was a combination of the forms themselves, the procedures governing the collection of payment card details and the incorporation of dialogue to convey the benefits to the customer that ensured the overall success of the process.

Figure 10.1 Early implementation: card payments in financial services

- *Definition* and *development* of the necessary capability (HR, IT, T&T) to bring early implementation about.
- *Deployment* of the new capability into the live environment.
- *Monitoring* of the changes to identify problem areas and make any refinements to optimise performance.

All manner of *ad hoc* mechanisms and Heath Robinson solutions are possible to achieve early implementation. It is important to bear in mind that it is the end result, and the overall performance of the new process, that is important—it might not look tidy, neat or slick, but it can still be effective.

However rough and ready such a solution may seem from the inside, it is possible to make it appear quite smooth from the perspective of the customer. So, for example, a team of staff, six different computer systems and several manual mechanisms could be used behind the scenes to provide a seamless service to the customer. The customer judges the end results, not the hotch-potch of *ad hoc* solutions that have been cobbled together behind the scenes.

The Fatal Distraction

The main caveat attached to such early implementation is in deciding just how much time and effort should be invested in it. Without strict control, the pursuit of early implementation can very rapidly become a fatal distraction from efforts to build the full capability. Nowhere is this more true than in the area or IT, where a "quick fix" estimated at a few dozen person-hours can rapidly become a diversion that swallows major resources. A ruthless watch has to be kept to prevent this happening.

The other risk, of course, is that attempts to achieve early implementation do not go as planned. The very strength of early implementation, that it is a highly visible and high-profile exercise, can also be its greatest downfall. Efforts for early implementation will be watched closely by staff, especially those more resistant to change, in search of a justification for why the new processes will not work.

Early implementation initiatives therefore need to be managed accordingly. In particular, it is important to manage expectations and not to oversell the expected benefits—there is no more sure fire way of losing staff commitment and enthusiasm than making great pronouncements and then failing to deliver. If these caveats are followed, early implementation can become a powerful technique by which to encourage the ownership of new processes and the generation of demand for the full roll-out.

DEPLOYMENT

The objective of deployment is to release the process into the operational or "live" environment so that it becomes the accepted, rather than the "new" way of working. As ever, the process design itself must guide the shape of the process in its final form. The process specification which was originally used to drive the requirements in individual capability areas is now used to guide the integration of component parts to form the whole process (Figure 10.2).

In reality, given that parts of the new process will already be in place, roll-out is rarely concerned with deploying the whole new process capability.

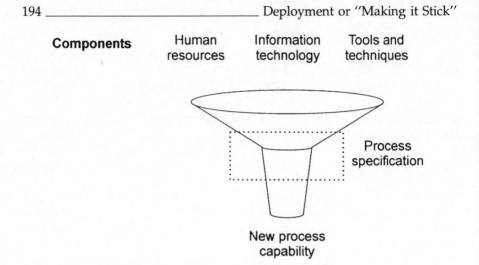

Figure 10.2   Deploying the New Process Capability

Often the people side of the process will already have started to take shape, along with improvisation to bring the new way of working about.

Although there is sometimes a perception that roll-out is the biggest stage of the change programme, this is rarely the case. The work done in building the components as described in previous chapters has been concerned with creating the capabilities themselves. Deployment is therefore more about bringing those capabilities together and making sure that they work in practice. A key part of this is managing risks; in particular, minimising disruption to the existing operational environment and maintaining customer service levels as new processes are rolled out. This includes selecting the appropriate time for roll-out or deployment, then making any refinements to the new ways of working once they are in place, and setting in place the mechanisms for continuous improvement.

Before proceeding, it is worth repeating the caveat about timing. Roll-out is likely to occur many times, rather than once, over the life of the programme, so these techniques should be considered and applied whenever they are required; they are not limited to use in the closing stages. Data migration, for example, may need to be initiated many months before roll-out. Deployment takes place in four stages:

- Testing
- Preparation
- Roll-out
- Refinement

Stage 1: Testing

The actual development of capability takes place in different project areas, and typically these capabilities will have been tested to the full in their individual project areas, quite extensively in the case of IT. This stage is concerned with ensuring that the appropriate capabilities to implement or "run" the new processes work in combination.

Although such capabilities can be tested theoretically—against design principles and by walk-through and review with the business staff—ultimately the best test is something that represents the actual business itself. This is best achieved by developing test cases or scenarios based on real-life situations similar to those used within process design. Coverage must include both the common "cases", which occur in high volumes, and the exceptional ones, to determine that there is a means of addressing them even if it is a slightly different process.

Such testing should take place in a discrete environment that mimics as far as possible the final manifestation of the live process. This includes setting up whatever infrastructure is required, such as furniture, plant, telecommunications and computers, as well as staff within appropriate organisational and management structures.

Stage 2: Preparation

The second stage of deployment puts in place any logistical or infrastructure changes necessary to make the new processes work. The exact set of actions will always depend on the environment and industry in which the changes are being implemented, but the following need to be considered:

- *Communications to customers.* Customers have to be advised of any changes to process, such as new phone numbers, new contact points, or changes to opening hours. Depending on the extent of the process change at the interface with the customer, distinct training and communication needs in their own right may be identified. This may be achieved by advising all customers in advance, or by having a mechanism in place to inform them in the course of their next contact.
- *Data migration.* The migration of data from existing or legacy systems onto new computer systems. The main considerations are "when?" and "from where?". Appropriate capture, validation and cleansing need to take place to ensure completeness and suitability. This may be from either physical (e.g. paper files) or electronic (other systems) sources. Data migration is usually a long, complex task requiring extensive resource. Depending on the data required and the quality and completeness of information held, it may be necessary to either validate existing information with customers or contact them to supply missing information. This may require significant

additional effort, resources and planning, either by carrying out such activities as a separate data migration project or by building them into contacts with the customer during the course of normal business activity.

- *Physical layout.* The creation or rearrangement of office or working space to accommodate process teams, new staffing arrangements etc. Office or premises moves may require significant additional planning and resource in their own right, depending on the size of the change.
- *New phone numbers.* As well as setting these up technically, new documentation or advertising may be necessary to enforce them and see them become the norm. This includes everything from updating adverts in directories to mail-shotting affected parties. A means of routing or redirecting calls received on old numbers needs to be established.
- *Documentation.* The preparation and delivery of any new documentation to support new ways of working, such as simplified product structures or new service or contractual agreements.
- *Publicise and advise.* The production and display of any signs and information needed to reinforce the new ways of working. This ranges from the everyday essentials such as new filing trays and the display of new departmental titles to new entries in internal phone directories. Publicity needs to advise other staff, departments and process areas within the organisation impacted by the changes of the new ways of working and any changes needed to accommodate them.

Stage 3: Roll-Out

The third stage of deployment, the actual roll-out, requires consideration of a number of issues. Again, these are dependent primarily on the extent of process change and the nature of the industry in question. For example, it may or may not be possible to limit roll-out to specific areas of the business, depending on whether the customer base can be partitioned. The following need to be considered:

- *Migration or cut-over options.* The manner in which the transition between new and existing processes is to be carried out. For example, is the whole portfolio of business to be transferred overnight *en masse*? Is it to be transferred on a case by case basis as the natural course of the business cycle brings a particular customer to the forefront? Is only a partial (perhaps lower risk) segment of the business to be migrated first to minimise risk? Are only new cases or customers as they enter the business to be serviced by the new ways of working? In the latter situation, a means has to be established of identifying on subsequent occasions whether the customer or case is a product of the new or the old process. These decisions depend on the make-up of the business, and the nature of any particular cycle inherent in it.

- *Timing*. The most appropriate timing for the roll-out to occur. Investigation usually reveals that there is no ideal time for roll-out—there will always be some other significant event in progress that threatens to overlap. However, factors that must be considered include seasonality (when does the business experience particular peaks and troughs in its workload), main holiday times (with the corresponding impacts on resources) and other events occurring in the business (new product launches, accountancy year ends etc.).

- *Existing service*. Maintaining existing levels of service to the customer is a number one priority. This may mean bringing in temporary, extra resource to cope while staff introduce new ways of working.

- *Resource*. Providing the necessary resource to roll-out the new processes. During initial use, when new ways of working are not yet second-nature, processes may be less than totally efficient, requiring some adjustment between the initial and final levels of staffing.

- *Fall back*. Contingency plans are needed that identify how to revert to previous processes if the roll-out does not go according to plan.

- *Run-down*. The procedures for "running-down" old processes. This may include phasing out old products or versions of products where rationalisation has occurred, closing down old computer systems once all cases have been transferred to new systems (including any necessary archiving), replacing existing contracts with new ones as they come up for renewal and using up or disposing of existing inventory no longer required. Where run-down proves to be a sizable activity in its own right, procedures to guide staff through the steps of the various transition or "run-down" activities have to be documented.

- *New measures*. The change over to new measures to monitor the performance of the new process. New reporting periods and "to and from" dates need to be set up. New MIS reports may have to be initiated.

- *Inspiration*. As we have stressed elsewhere, the hard, deliverable-based elements of process-led change must be complemented by the softer ones. Nowhere is this more true than at roll-out, when enthusiasm and commitment to the new ways of working will go a long way toward covering the gaps and the glitches that will inevitably occur. Staff have to be inspired and enthused to take on the new ways of working and run with them in the early days when teething problems arise.

- *Support*. The final aspect to consider is the provision of support and assistance to the new processes. This should include the process designers themselves as well as any necessary procedures, with specialists "on-call" to assist in any situations that may have been overlooked. In the longer term such support may be provided by a help line or help desk.

Stage 4: Refinement and Improvement

The final stage is to monitor the performance of the process and its component parts and perform any fine tuning or adjustment necessary. This is actually a two-step process. The first is to identify anything within the new process that is sub-optimal once the process is in an operationally live environment, and identify corrective action. Working with the process designers, it may be necessary to change the process design itself, or to carry out additional training, revise computer systems or make further refinements to procedures in the light of experience.

The second task is to embed this attitude of refinement and improvement into the activities of the organisation on an ongoing basis—the so-called "performance improvement" of which so much has been written, spoken and theorised in recent years. At the simplest level, this is made up of the following steps:

1. Monitoring performance and identifying where the process fails to come up to scratch.
2. Identifying the required improvements.
3. Making the required changes, without upsetting other parts of the processes in the organisation.

The final point is obviously the most important, but invariably also the most difficult to achieve. In this respect, the recent enthusiasm for "continuous improvement" although it initially appears to promise some radical new approach, does not in fact provide much new. The truth is that most organisations have battled long and hard to make refinements and improvements to their operations or processes. But usually the problem is less to do with the change itself than with the "knock-on" effects of change. Modern organisations are such a web of complexity that every change impacts some unseen aspect elsewhere. Improvement is one thing, but if it merely clogs up the process further down the line it may not be an overall improvement at all. To minimise any interference, the process design has to remain the sole source of both identifying changes and managing changes to the existing infrastructure.

Only then can change be made in a coordinated, controlled manner, which retains the integrity of the processes rather than allowing the individual idiosyncrasies and anomalies, which ultimately chock a process, to creep back in.

Embedding the attitudes necessary to make performance improvement happen in practice is not an easy task. Like process-led change itself, such improvements must ultimately come from within—to be carried out as responsibilities of the staff themselves. Targets and incentives for performance improvement must be built into both staff and management appraisals to help achieve this.

A Question of Timing

Successful transformation is ultimately dependent on getting the people of the organisation or enterprise behind the changes taking place. New processes will never be perfect first time, and it is the commitment of staff to making the new ways of working successful that ensures that teething troubles are ironed out and necessary modifications are made.

But building such commitment takes time. People are cynical about change and the introduction of new ways of working, often because of failures in the past. Attitudes towards change tend to be split between those who support change, those who oppose it and those who are ambivalent towards it, with the group who are ambivalent usually being by far the biggest. It is securing the commitment of the group who are ambivalent which is critical to making change work, but the time pressures to complete transformation usually mean that it is not possible to win over every single person in the organisation, one by one.

The comparison of change to pushing a huge boulder up a hill has been used before. It is a long, hard slog to inch the boulder to the top before it can be released down the other side. On many change programmes there comes a time, therefore, when the final heave to the top has to be made to really set change moving. This push is used to convince the laggards and those with a "wait and see" attitude and get them on board. By doing so, the boulder can be brought to the top of the hill and set rolling down the other side, so that the organisation can begin to reap some of the benefits of change.

The big push is about saying "we've come this far, now let's get together and make this work". Its timing and content need to be carefully judged. It may be appropriate after a successful pilot or when a new process needs to be rolled out operationally across a wide area. Too soon, and people will not be ready for the changes taking place and it will tend to backfire; too late, and new processes may not be rolled-out soon enough, resulting in a "nothing's happening" feeling among the organisation's staff. Judging the need and timing for such a push is very much a case of "look and feel", rather than being signposted by any concrete evidence. There have to be enough people who are familiar with the new ways of working and enough people with the attitude and influence to help carry the big push through and propagate it to the organisation.

MAKING IT STICK

The path toward putting a new infrastructure in place is now almost complete. Using process as a holistic means of design and implementation, it is possible to build the components required to create a new set of capabilities. And using effective programme management in conjunction with the stages of deployment outlined above, it is possible to integrate these new capabilities and bring the new processes to life.

But, as ever, attention to just the more structured parts of change is not enough. These stages need to be underpinned by the activities and approaches that address the softer, more subtle aspects of the organisation and wrap up the remaining problem areas, which otherwise fester away and prevent progress.

Tricks of the Trade: Golden Rules for Making it Stick

Rule 1: Letting Go of the Reins—The Secret of Acceptance

From the outset it has been clear that change, and enterprise-wide, process-led change in particular, is difficult. To address it, we have proposed various ways of coping—an integrated design that addresses all parts of the equation at once; the ability to specify and create the new capability in people, IT systems and T&T, and techniques that address the soft as well as the hard aspects of change. But, so much for the design, the specification and the creation; so much for the components. How do we make sure people embrace the new ways of working, and, what is more, stay with them, even if they are not completely right in the first initiation? Change is difficult—but making change stick is even harder.

One of the biggest barriers to change, besides a fear of the unknown, is a lack of ownership. People do not readily and actively embrace solutions handed to them. Usually this is because they are foisted upon them from above. The trick of acceptance is to make those whose way of work is being changed part of defining the solutions. Ultimately, if individuals feel that they are in control of their destiny, and in particular if they feel that they are improving the way they work, they will be more committed to the final solution. And if an individual, or a group of individuals, feels that they have contributed to solving the problems that have dogged the organisation for the past five, ten or twenty years, they are ten times more committed to making that change work in practice.

To do this requires that those responsible for process design let go of the reins—and let go even if this means a partial loss of control: the final solution enters into the hands of those who will undertake it, which may mean that its shape is not exactly as originally envisaged. If this means that the process finally selected and implemented is less than the ideal one, then so be it. A process that is implemented—and then evaluated for improvement—is far better than the perfect one which never makes it past the design and build stage.

Doing this requires a genuine letting go, which is often difficult. Those tasked with process design tend to develop an ownership and adherence to the design, which may be difficult to break. But let go they must. This letting go is not without its risks—risks that wrong directions will be taken and inconsistent solutions developed. It is essential that the framework in which the process is completed is clearly established and communicated. The parameters or ground rules to be satisfied have to be set down from the outset; if the implementation taken on by the organisation proves to be too impractical it can be reined in again in line with the parameter laid down. Where appropriate, this may necessitate defining what the finished result looks like or what standards it must comply with, rather than the detailed step by step tasks to achieving it.

Rule 2: Manage Resistance

Resistance to change is inevitable. However good the communication, the implicit buy-in and the underlying feel-good factor, resistance will still be out there. If it is not visible, then it will be there underground. Some may resist because they feel that their jobs are under threat; others will resist because they do not agree with the changes; still others will resist because they quite simply have an in-built aversion to doing whatever those in senior positions tell them to do.

Resistance will not go away, so it has to be managed, and managed so that its impact on progress is as small as possible. Often this resistance is not visible. The staff of organisations, weary of the change initiatives that have gone on over the past few years, have learned how to play the yes game; they have learned how to say "yes" with their lips when they really mean "no" with their hearts and minds.

The key to dealing with resistance is to address the root causes, not the symptoms; to deal with the concerns at heart, rather than the objections that are manifest on the surface. If people are concerned about the unknown then they need to be shown the way forward. If they fear for their job prospects, then they may need help in developing new skills.

Ultimately, of course, some sources of resistance cannot be brought around. Emotion and feelings and historical events may still be stronger than rationale and reason and explanation. Ultimately, sometimes the rocks have to be forcibly moved from the runway; whether they are nudged quietly aside or blasted apart with high explosive depends on the nature of the obstruction.

Rule 3: Peer Group Pressure is the Most Effective

It is a damning indictment on the failed "promises" of management that staff are so cynical about what they hear from the upper levels of organisations. "We've heard that before" is one favourite response; "I'll believe it when I see it" is another. Operating within such an environment of cynicism and suspended belief, encouraging people to change their ways sometimes begins to seem an impossible task.

But if the words of those driving and sponsoring change come to be regarded as "propaganda" one of the most effective forces for change lies in the opposite direction, in the peer group. Management and change leaders often spend months trying to send home messages of improved ways of working and better processes, but it is when a colleague who has been on the pilot team, or a representative from another region, speaks highly (and freely) of new ways of doing things that people tend to sit up and take notice. Get one individual from the group on board of his or her own accord, and typically you will get them all. One of the most effective ways of leveraging this is to use staff from a successful pilot to train and educate the staff on subsequent roll-out teams.

Rule 4: Look and Listen

Throughout this book, the importance of the "hard" and the "soft" aspects of change has been stressed. Change has been presented as a two-pronged stick—the ability to talk to people, tap the grapevine and sense the undercurrents being equally important to the production of deliverables. Now, more than ever, these softer aspects of change are critical. They are critical because the things most likely to cause a change programme to stumble or even fail at this point are those things that have been missed by every other mechanism—the things for which no response has been prepared or deliverable designed.

Looking and listening is the safety net of successful implementation. It is the last chance to identify anything missing or inappropriate and take the relevant action to address it. It requires that someone is deployed to sense the nuances, read the undercurrents and search out the unexpected, to find the problem areas and the sticking points so that the appropriate action to tackle them can be defined.

Rule 5: Prevent Reversion

Successful change is all about momentum. We have compared change to a huge boulder, which has to be pushed up a hillside, and only at the top, when it is released to race down the other side, do the changes really begin to take effect. The problem is that the hillside is slippery and every time the boulder is edged a few inches upwards resistance and hold-ups threaten to send it sliding backwards.

Change is difficult because it requires us to let go of the old as well as embrace the new. And even when we pay lip-service to change, most of us find it more comfortable (and, indeed, natural) to slip back into our old ways at the first opportunity. Remember how often after a training course, even when we know the new theory and the new techniques, we still tend to revert to our old, familiar ways, even if they are less effective.

To prevent this reversion, the backward slide must to be prevented. The boulder of change must be chocked up at every step. The process orientation must be created even if it is not yet possible to realise it in full. Measures must reward the new ways of working and penalise the old. Appointments, and the salaries commensurate with them, must demonstrate what the organisation regards as the new star roles to achieve the process orientation. These are the actions that show staff at all levels that management are committed to driving the changes through and getting it right, come hell or high water. These are the positive, concrete actions—not the lip-service—which underpin the progress of change. Gradually the hilltop is reached, and then the momentum for change can be released.

Rule 6: Tackle from Every Angle

We end, where we began, by stressing once more the importance of the holistic approach. Process allows it, because it embraces every angle of the organisation, and it must be used at every step to make change happen in practice. Lead with a design, inspire with a set of design principles, devolve ownership with early implementation, use prototypes to demonstrate new ways of working, reward with new compensation systems, enforce with procedures, show the significance by removing the roadblocks—for there is not one single course to making change happen, only multiple ones.

☞ SIGNPOSTS FOR SUCCESS

Hold your nerve

Ultimately, the success of new processes and ways of working will be judged on performance. Is the customer getting a better service? Are fault rates down? Have costs been reduced? These factors should be tracked by the measures established for the new processes during the design stage. But, by their very nature, the results of process changes may take some time to be reflected in the measures. This is the time of nail biting for the process design team and the test of character for the organisation—to stay with the new processes and wait for the results to pan through, even if it takes some time. This is particularly true where changes to the processes will only gradually affect the infrastructure or lifeblood at the very heart of an enterprise—be it a database of information, a network of telecommunications lines or an installed base of customers.

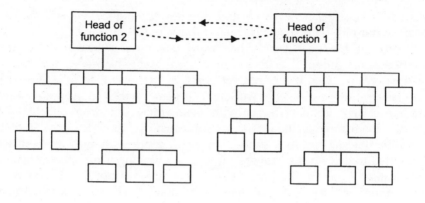

Function 1   Function 2

Figure 10.3   Shuffling the pack

Equip and encourage

Staff in many of our organisations are not yet ready for the new opportunities. Freeing people to do things themselves creates further problems if they are not equipped with the capabilities required to do the job. Few organisations possess the people capabilities to just abandon old habits and establish new roles overnight. Training has to be provided, new skills have to be developed and new abilities nurtured. Once new roles and ways of working have been adapted, the nurturing activity has to go on to fine tune, encourage and improve the new capabilities.

Measure the management

Managers as well as staff have to be seen to be measured (and preferably rewarded) on the basis of the new ways of doing things. As well as the effect this has on the performance of managers, it sends important signals to the rest of the organisation.

Shuffle the pack

Process change is often thwarted by those in positions of influence. They have all of the reasons why (and all of the reasons why *not*) changes should not be made. A simple yet effective means of breaking such stalemate is to exchange key people in the organisation for different roles. Typically this might be the heads of two or more functions or departments who have proven management skills. By swapping individuals between roles, each position becomes party to a much broader perspective and a whole new set of knowledge, as a result of their experience gained elsewhere. This is particularly effective in the early days of bringing about a process perspective, as the individuals understand the complication and constraints in the adjoining area. All of a sudden, the tables are turned and reasons for why it cannot work begin to be replaced with ideas for how it can (see Figure 10.3).

Acknowledge politics

However many times the claim is made, "non-political" enterprises just do not exist. As long as organisations are made up of one or more people, they will be political in some shape or form. Hidden agendas (and not so hidden ones) exist, and even the least political player has preferences and leanings that will affect the political make-up of an organisation. To pretend otherwise is a fallacy. Understand the power players, who holds the influence and what they are after—and act accordingly.

Create headroom

Do not let operational pressures swamp you. You need to be able to focus on the process and give the time—to everyone from the clerks to senior management. Ramp up resource to free people from their existing roles and responsibilities. This often requires a not insignificant budget commitment, but that is the way.

Chapter 11

Programme Management

THE SIZE OF THE TASK

Preceding chapters have concentrated on the design, definition and development of the new capabilities required to bring about change. The holistic nature of process ensures that these separate elements can be created in parallel and then brought together to create the new capability. But consider for a moment just what that means in practice. We talk glibly about a new IT infrastructure, but what this really means is 200 man-years of development effort in the IT department. We talk about reorganisation, but what we really mean is the training and reorganisation of staff just as existing operational workloads reach a new peak, and we talk about roll-out but this occurs just as the marketing department launch six new products.

Managing any major project presents a multitude of challenges and demands. What makes process-led change so difficult are the number and the type of elements involved. The changes are about developing the new and dismantling the old—but across a diverse range of disciplines—people, information technology, procedures, even culture. And all this has to be achieved with a particular set of resources, within a particular set of time scales, while coping along the way with whatever unplanned glitches and gremlins rear their heads.

Programme management is the means by which all of these disparate disciplines and activities can be managed, controlled and finally brought coherently together.

A Warning

Programme management has never had the most inspiring or glamorous of reputations. However much people try to tell you otherwise, it conjures up images of endless project plans, Gant charts and ticks in the boxes against progress. On peeking into the toolbox of programme management, many are tempted to close the lid and quietly pass it by.

But be warned. If these aspects of change appear to be a little dull after the excitement of redesign and the challenge of culture change, they are actually the bedrock of process-led change, the final strings in the bow, ensuring that transformation happens.

Process-led change works. It works because it provides a means of actively designing how an enterprise will work, and it provides a framework for the definition and creation of the various components that will bring it to life. But the pressures of competition, the requirements of legislation, and the expectations of shareholders demand that such changes are achieved sooner rather than later. Within it all the potential for complexity and chaos is overwhelming.

Process change is holistic, but without a means of controlling, coordinating, managing and ultimately integrating those components back together, even the best design and build initiatives will fall over. Programme management is essential to make process-led change work, nothing less.

PROGRAMME MANAGEMENT: THE ART OF JUGGLING

Programme management is the formal means by which the whole change programme is managed and controlled. Ultimately, it ensures that the changes intended will actually come about. It is concerned with ensuring that the desired results are achieved by monitoring and managing the hundreds of work packages and activities which have to be undertaken to put one or more parts of the new business infrastructure in place. Like the rest of the change programme, the process design itself is the key driver—it is used to determine the work that has to be carried out and to ensure that the parts under development can be brought together to form a coherent whole. Programme management does not actually produce anything (or very little) itself; it makes sure that those responsible produce their components.

But to see programme management as a discipline of project plans and version control is to miss the point. Programme management fulfils the role of the control tower at a major airport, and without it the new process orientation will never emerge. It is used to maintain control over the many different activities going on at once, each of which has to be managed and directed towards its proper destination. With it, many different variables can be managed to completion, in close proximity. Without it, chaos will soon ensue. Just as the air traffic controller can identify problems by looking at the bigger picture, so the programme manager can identify any parts of the programme where risks occur or problems arise and take the necessary avoiding action. It is the whole enabling mechanism, which allows process-led change to move forward in so many areas at once without chaos occurring. Programme management is concerned with:

- determining how the overall package of work will be undertaken
- monitoring progress and delivery of the required packages of work
- ensuring the availability of the required resources
- managing quality and standards
- ensuring acceptance by the organisation
- coordination of the different aspects under development and deployment
- managing risk and addressing problems that arise along the way

On the one hand, programme management is incredibly simple (work out what to do and then ensure someone does it); on the other hand, it is infinitely complex (because it involves doing everything along the way—working out actions, putting teams together, securing budgets, motivating staff, implementing pilots). By plotting the route between these two extremes programme management moves from requirements to delivery, from problems to solutions.

Managing by Deliverables

At the heart of programme management is the notion of the deliverable. A deliverable is the specific, tangible output (which may be electronic as well as physical) produced as a result of a particular phase of work.

Deliverables make even the biggest task achievable. They are the building blocks of change, which ensure that massive change programmes can be broken down into smaller areas of work, which can be specified, built, tested and managed to completion. Every deliverable, however large, can be broken down into component parts of its own.

Consider a process-led change programme that has resulted in the production of process designs across the whole of an organisation. The design has been drafted out, the change team has been selected and it is time to begin implementation. The processes point the way towards the creation of a major new capability—new information systems have to be built, people have to be retrained and management have to adopt new ways of managing. But how, the CEO might wonder, is it all to be achieved? Where do you begin? How are requirements to be conveyed to various disciplines? Who is

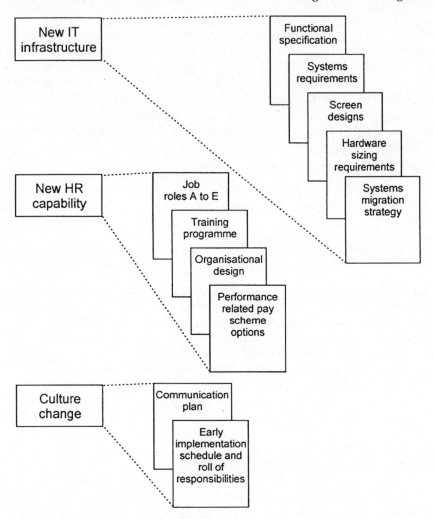

Figure 11.1 Managing by deliverables

to be responsible for the various areas of work, and how are they to be controlled and managed? Who decides what the various steps along the way are?

Deliverables enable such high-level requirements to be broken down, and ultimately created. Now consider Figure 11.1.

From the initial high-level wishlists, the building blocks emerge and specifics can be derived—the actual things that have to be produced, modified or dismantled can be identified. The deliverables listed in the figure are just a subset of those that might be required, and in turn they would have more deliverables within them. Large deliverables can be broken down into sub-deliverables, and with deliverables comes the capacity for control and coordination. Deliverables force the question "what do I have to produce that the next person in the development or deployment chain requires?".

The other key aspect of a deliverable is the word "specific". The notion of the deliverable forces a constant focus during the change activity on what is being designed or built or tested or implemented. Managing by deliverables ensures that work under way is closely focused on outputs— outputs that are directly derived from the overall requirements of the programme.

The size and complexity of major change projects tends to mean that diversions occur, distractions set in. People get sidetracked into vague activities such as research into customer needs or the endless modelling of existing processes. The deliverable-based approach brings with it one question, a ready test for relevance: "Which deliverable is this activity contributing to?". If the deliverable cannot be named, the activity should not be continued.

The final aspect of deliverables is that they can be governed and produced in line with standards; standards which set out certain requirements for the final "product" in terms of format, layout and content. Standards help to enforce quality, and enable parallel working by ensuring that even when many people are working on many deliverables they are still consistent with a defined standard.

Like design itself, much of the discipline attached to programme management and deliverables is not new, only new to organisational change. The engineering and construction trade has successfully carried out massive, multi-billion pound projects for years based on the concept of breaking massive tasks into smaller, manageable parts. The Channel Tunnel is a good example of the application of such techniques (and, indeed, of other aspects of the whole design-led change programme). The basic concept and design was quite simple, but the overall project quite immense, and it could only be managed by a number of sub-projects, addressing both engineering and non-engineering activities. Thus, some projects could be established to undertake the actual engineering work, including the tunnelling itself. Others could be established to address issues of appropriate routes at either side and the logistics of matching rolling stock from different countries. Enabling activities, such as maintaining financial support, could also be managed separately. No one individual could be responsible for completing all this work alone, but by allocating responsibilities into projects, the overall programme of work could be specified, coordinated and ultimately achieved.

Projects

The second key strand of programme management is the project. Projects allow work to be divided into discrete packages with the right team of skills and experience gathered to achieve one thing—the end result. When the work is complete, the project can be disbanded and the staff within it freed up for work elsewhere.

The project concept or "mindset", although it may be familiar to consultants and computer systems staff, is foreign to many people in organisations. It is a world far removed from much of operational, routine work, where the same tasks are performed day in, day out with the same people and the same unwavering formula. It depends on the culture of contribution necessary for change talked about in Chapter 3—requiring staff who can work out an approach rather than having to wait for step by step direction. In the project environment, problem solving and teamwork are the order of the day. Teams get together for a period and then disband, releasing staff back into the organisation again. Peer groups change and reporting lines may be turned on their heads; it is not uncommon on project teams for more junior staff to be challenging or facilitating much senior management.

Adopting such approaches requires a significant culture change. Project teams tend to overthrow traditional reporting lines and hierarchies. Witness the middle manager, 20 years with the organisation, who is co-opted onto a process review team expecting to have his experience and knowledge called upon. Instead, he finds the very control system that he instigated ten years ago now being challenged by one of his juniors in the light of a new process. In addition, there are logistical issues. Taking people in and out of the operational environment onto the project team causes disruption and upheaval; not least, there is the issue of continuity when individuals return to the organisation after a significant period on the project team. Where do their careers go next? Do they rejoin on the salary and grade at which they left, or at that which they have achieved while working on the project?

Together, the concepts of deliverables and projects make process-led change a realisable proposition. The complexities of process-led change mean that there may be many dozens, sometimes several hundreds, of people deployed on parts of the change programme. To track what they are all doing, on a day to day basis, and how it relates to what everyone else is doing, is almost impossible. But by devolving responsibility down to a series of projects and by tracking what they are producing, and how it relates to the other components of change, the task becomes realistic.

The analogy of air traffic control is relevant again—the air traffic controller does not need to know what is happening on each individual aircraft—just where it is going and the progress that is being made towards that destination. The business of actually getting it there is down to the individual pilot.

PROGRAMME DESIGN

Programme design is concerned with determining how the multitude of activities required to bring about the various aspects of change are to be partitioned, allocated and undertaken, and how the maximum amount of coordination between them can be achieved. It defines the highest level deliverables, the projects that will be established to carry them out, and outline time scales.

In programme design, as everywhere else, it is essential that the changes which are planned are driven from a design. The process specification is used to develop an understanding of the work to be undertaken using gap analysis, as introduced in Chapter 6. Using the process design itself as the main means of determining projects and project areas ensures that the change activities which go on are contributing towards a coordinated goal.

Programme design is concerned with establishing the high-level "shape" of the change programme: how the work is allocated into discrete packages or projects, which can be managed, monitored and controlled to ensure satisfactory delivery of their particular responsibilities. Usually, project areas will be defined by common areas of capabilities, rather than by processes. Systems development will be the responsibility of one area, for example, while telecommunications would be the responsibility of a different area, and testing yet another.

Once the overall shape of the programme and the areas within it are established, the focus moves on down to individual project areas. Project managers are assigned responsibility, and this will involve identifying the sub-deliverables and planning resources required. Ultimately there are likely to be hundreds of deliverables and sub-deliverables, and they do not all need to be viewed or managed from the top level. (On an enterprise-wide transformation programme there may be several thousand.)

Programme design (Figure 11.2) is undertaken at a very early stage in the programme but will be refined as progress brings out new requirements. The exact packages of work or project areas will change as the transformation programme progresses; packages of work identified at the outset (such as process design) will be completed and others will emerge in the course of time. Process design, for example, is likely to be completed well before roll-out (although process designers are likely to remain working with HR and IT development teams), and new areas of work (such as early implementation, product simplification or data migration) may have to be set up for a period of time during the life of the programme.

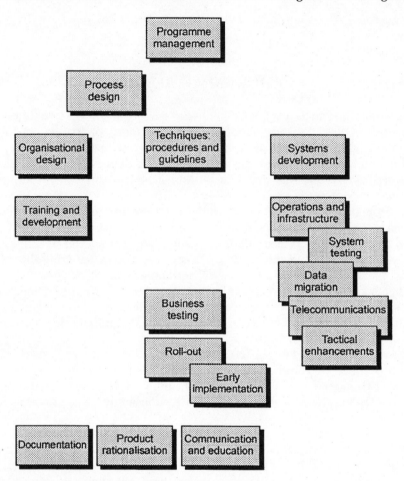

Figure 11.2 Projects Within Programmes

PROGRAMME MANAGED BUT PROCESS-LED

Programme management is about ensuring that new capabilities can be developed and put in place, but at all times the process specification itself has to act as the overall driving force behind the changes.

Process is holistic, and this ensures that a process specification can encompass all the components of the new infrastructure required to put a new process in place. But if these requirements are not correct, then everything that is subsequently produced will be incorrect. Garbage in, garbage out, as the computer programmers' phrase goes. The design, architecture and specification of processes set out in Chapters 4 and 5 establishes the requirements, and it is worth stressing again here that without getting those designs right, there will be no effective change.

But the holistic nature of process also ensures that it can be used as the basis for managing complexity and considering how other activities within the organisation fit into or impact the overall process perspective. Because the process view embraces technology, people and other manual methods, it can identify any other areas of change going on in the business. Even if such activities do not come within the scope of process-led change, it is still possible to identify them and manage any impact.

Programme management is an increasingly mature and sophisticated discipline to be applied during business transformation. Within it are a number of recognised techniques, as described below, which underpin the concepts of projects and deliverables. In addition, there are a number of "unwritten rules", which help to ensure its success.

PROGRAMME MANAGEMENT: THE WRITTEN RULES

Rule 1: Plan and Track

At the heart of programme management is a massive planning and tracking exercise. The work itself is devolved down to a series of projects, but the overall programme management umbrella has to ensure that the complete deliverables come back together at the right time.

Individual projects have the responsibility for planning their particular package of work, but these plans, and their key delivery dates, are then integrated back into the overall programme plan. Possible shortfalls can be identified and corrective action, such as the deployment of additional resource, can then be taken.

The planning and tracking activity needs to be underpinned by an environment that facilitates the free and open debate of problems, issues and risks. Project plans and progress can always be squeezed and manipulated to show the progress that is desired, but it is a culture of openness and a willingness to get problems resolved, rather than pointing the finger, that will guarantee real progress.

Rule 2: Maintain High-Level Commitment

High-level commitment and sponsorship have to be maintained throughout the life of the programme. At its centre is a programme steering committee or project board made up of a group of individuals appointed to oversee the change activities. Those appointed are drawn from high levels of the organisation, with at least one board director usually included, unless the change programme is relatively small in scope. If the transformation is organisation-wide then the CEO or managing director should be involved.

The role of the steering committee is to:

• Supervise and accept work being undertaken on the change programme
• Commit the resources necessary
• Make high-level decisions necessary for the change programme to progress

The supervisory and acceptance role ensures that the progress of the change programme can be considered in the light of other imperatives within the organisation. It provides an opportunity to keep the senior players in the organisation up to date with progress (both good and bad) and to consider the impact of changes on other areas of the business, both operationally and strategically.

But it is the decision making capability that is most important. Change must be driven from the highest point in an organisation, and the key decisions—whether they are about a commitment to a new client/server infrastructure or the restructuring of existing departments—must come from the top. The biggest problems with steering committees, given that they are invariably made up of high-level representatives of the company, is in making them a forum that is open enough to bring in bad news. Nobody likes admitting problems, but try doing this in front of the chairman, the CEO, the programme manager and the IT director. The danger is that progress appears to be good, while problems fester away beneath the floorboards.

As this book has constantly emphasised, successful change requires attending to both the hard and the soft issues. Formal phase reviews and deliverable sign-offs therefore need to be accompanied by a willingness to probe the design, development and build being carried out "on the ground", by talking to those tasked with creating the new capabilities. Management by Walking About still has its place.

Rule 3: Set Standards

Documented standards define the criteria to which any particular deliverable must conform. By laying out certain requirements to which deliverables must adhere, standards ensure that deliverables of a particular type will be consistent in content and layout. Standards are a basis for ensuring quality, and provide a means of testing and reviewing deliverables. In addition, they facilitate parallelism by allowing different people to work on deliverables, with a shared understanding of the shape of the final product or outcome. So, for example, if there is a standard for the layout of computer screens across every process a certain common look and feel is guaranteed at the end, even if there are many different developers undertaking the work.

Standards typically set out requirements in one or more of the following areas:

- *Type*: the nature of the deliverable (design, plan, new organisational structure)
- *Format*: what form the deliverable takes (electronic, paper, physical)
- *Content*: the main components of the deliverable
- *Method*: how the deliverable is to be produced
- *Derivation*: the key source of requirements
- *Acceptance criteria*: the minimum criteria that the deliverable must fulfil to be accepted

By providing an understanding of what has to be produced, standards guide the development and production of a deliverable to its final conclusion. Standards may include guidelines on the preferred method of production.

Rule 4: Monitor Risks

Risks are those things that threaten to disrupt the progress of the change programme (or the wider business) and prevent final objectives from being reached. They range from the obvious and visible (that it might not be possible for the organisation to achieve the desired culture change, or the new computer systems capability cannot be delivered on time) to the more intangible and unexpected (the programme manager suddenly leaves for another job).

Like changes, risks cannot be eliminated altogether so the requirement is to identify them and minimise their impact through pre-emptive action. This involves four stages of risk management:

- identifying risks (risks arise from many sources; internally and externally, technically, politically, accidentally or deliberately from individuals opposed to changes and through over-ambitious scope)
- analysing their impact (which part of the programme they would effect) and their potential severity
- determining an appropriate response to address them
- tracking the risk

Risk management takes place as an ongoing monitoring and tracking activity. This is usually achieved through a risk register. Existing risks are reviewed on a regular basis, and the project as a whole has to be polled for any new risks arising.

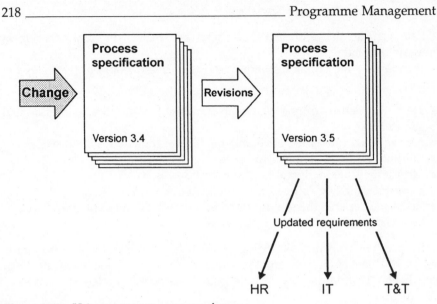

Figure 11.3 Using process to manage change

Rule 5: Change Control—Hitting a Moving Target

High levels of changes to requirements often threaten to bring projects to their knees. The reality is that, however high the quality of the initial requirements and specifications, change will occur. To pretend otherwise is foolhardy. The important message is not to try to prevent change, but to control it.

The design-led approach facilitates change control in two ways. Firstly, the breadth and detail of the description, in particular the process specification, ensures that all aspects being changed are specified together. It is thus possible to identify what impact a change in one area will have on another, rather than making changes in isolation without an understanding of any knock-on effects. Secondly, because the design-led approach is top-down, any changes made can be "rolled-down" to whatever subsequent areas of the change programme are affected. Thus, if a process requirement itself is changed, the change can be rolled-down through IT requirements analysis again to identify any revisions to the IT requirements (Figure 11.3).

Change control itself is achieved by a using formal change management procedure, which has to include as a minimum the stages of change request, impact analysis, a decision that either rejects or accepts the change, and any updating of requirements consequently necessary. Individual projects within the programme are the main mechanism for raising, reviewing and change requests and actioning any resultant changes.

Effective change control is a key mechanism for process-led change. Parallelism, by its nature, will ensure that sometimes it is necessary to move forward even before all requirements are complete: change control therefore ensures that the gaps can be filled at a later date.

Rule 5: Scope Tightly

Tight scoping is essential to minimise the impact caused by ambiguous or unexpected changes to requirements. Scoping process-led change is particularly difficult because processes, by their nature, cut across products, departments, functions and layers of the organisation.

It is therefore essential that scoping is tightly defined at all possible points—stating both what is included and what is excluded. This should be carried out initially within any particular process or process design, and subsequently within individual deliverables.

Process change begets complexity—and without very clear scoping it rapidly becomes impossible to identify whether particular components of the new infrastructure have or have not been specified and are being delivered. This is not to say that areas of the enterprise initially excluded must always be excluded; merely that their inclusion or exclusion is clearly known at any point in time.

PROGRAMME MANAGEMENT: THE UNWRITTEN RULES

Rule 1: Document and Define

It is a frequent complaint of process-led change programmes that they generate vast amounts of paper—documents, reports, process designs, specifications. The age of IT has, it seems, created an expectation that the electronic media which surround us will swallow every communication and eliminate paper for ever.

The reality, alas, is one of practicality rather than sophistication. Process-led change creates change in every last corner of the organisation, and, as we have noted before, such a multidimensional approach to change, which amends people structures at the same time as procedural and technical ones, leaves the organisation at times on a finely balanced tightrope between control and chaos. Documentation—whether electronic or physical—helps to ensure the integrity of two key areas in this environment:

- *Requirements.* Change puts innumerable ideas, suggestions, possibilities and options onto the table. But it is only when an issue, requirement, problem or concern has been documented that it can be controlled, managed, pursued and ultimately made someone's responsibility to resolve or complete. Design principles and process diagrams are fine, but unless they are turned into a set of requirements, which someone can refer back to and cross-reference in the months ahead, they will probably disappear into the ether.

- *Changes to requirements.* Capturing a requirement ensures that it can be updated or changed. The speed, scope and nature of process-led change leads to a not insignificant level of change to requirements and specifications. If a requirement has never been documented, it cannot be changed.

Rule 2: Force the Sign-Off

The basis of change is the deliverable, but deliverables, ultimately, are of little value unless they are accepted by those who will use, manage and deploy them. During change, especially during the early stages, there is a risk that deliverables are accepted with tacit agreement but without real commitment; such superficial commitment to change then rebounds months later, when managers and those responsible come to understand the full extent of the changes. Sign-offs help to smooth and accelerate this acceptance process.

A sign-off is quite literally what the phrase implies—a signature by a relevant representative of the business (say, the process manager or the HR director) to indicate acceptance of a particular deliverable. Change, inevitably, is not welcomed in every corner of an organisation, and enforcing the sign-off or acceptance of deliverables helps to bring such resistance to the surface. Rather than hiding away in the far corners, such sticking points can be surfaced at an earlier stage.

But sign-offs are effective for more than the physical signature; namely:

- *Focus.* They force those who will ultimately be responsible for managing or implementing a particular deliverable or requirement to give it their proper attention. The modern organisation is such that everyone has many calls on their time, and this is especially true higher up the organisational tree. During major change it is often difficult to secure sufficient senior management commitment to the real detail of changes. Nothing is guaranteed to bring focus and attention more rapidly than the requirement for a signature of acceptance.
- *Mandate.* The sign-off of a deliverable—whether it is a design principle, a process design or a new organisational structure—acts as a rubber stamp. It sets a seal of approval and ensures that the deliverable can be used as a mandate for change, put in front of the most obstinate, feet-dragging individuals in the business as an example of what senior management has accepted and is committed to driving forward.
- *Pace.* The sign-off is used to force and maintain the pace of change. By setting a date by which a particular deliverable must be accepted, it helps

to ensure that work is focused and directed on specific outcomes with specific deadlines, rather than being allowed to meander along on a day by day basis.

Rule 3: Clarify Terminology—The Programme Glossary

The variation in language and terminology within an organisation has sometimes to be seen (or heard and documented) to be believed. It is a variance that can cause untold confusion if not tied down and clarified at the earliest opportunity. Consider the following examples. "System" is to some the word associated with a computer system, where IT is used to carry out automatically a set of tasks, yet to others it merely implies a regular, ordered way of doing things, whether manual or automated. It is daunting, considering that it is at the heart of the whole change programme, how many different meanings may be attached to the word "process". To some it represents the way in which the activities within an organisation combine to produce the end result; to those of a computing background, it is often associated with the execution of a predefined computing routine in much the same way as a function. Another example is the word "customers"—does it include past and potential as well as current customers, and is it synonymous with the words "clients" and "consumers"?

The matter becomes crucial with the importance of the process specification as a documented set of requirements at the heart of process-led change. Terminology that is ambiguous can rapidly result in confusion and misunderstanding, which continues all the way down the route to implementation.

The answer to such confusion lies in the simple mechanism of a glossary. The glossary defines the use of key words and terms within the change programme and is used for arbitration in points of dispute. It should be initiated on the programme from day one, and incorporate key terms (e.g. system requirements, process) and acronyms as well as individual words.

Rule 4: Keep Control—Managing the Satellite Project

There sometimes seems to be an expectation, no doubt encouraged by the "process is the answer to all our ills" type attitude, that once work begins on a process-led change programme, everything else in an organisation will fall into step behind it.

The reality, of course, is that the change programme, whether enterprise-wide, or confined to a single process within one operating division, is unlikely to be the only change initiative or project in progress. Programme management must therefore look around the organisation and identify other projects under way that may overlap or conflict with the process-led change initiative. One (medium sized) company described how this ferreting around uncovered over 70 projects in progress in various parts of the organisation at the same time. Another set up a database to list all projects under way, on which project managers and sponsors had to register their projects before beginning.

Either way, an awareness of such peripheral projects and activities has to be developed and maintained. By its nature, process-led change tends to impact many elements in the equation, therefore parallel projects may be impacted, or may interfere with change activities. These range from everything such as IT systems projects, quality initiatives and training programmes through to new product launches and changes necessitated by external legislation or regulation.

Again, it is the breadth of the process model—extending to people and organisational as well as technology issues—that provides the strength in dealing with such peripheral issues; because the full spectrum of the business can be included in the process specification, the impact of any changes or peripheral projects—whatever their remit—can be understood. The action to be taken depends on the size of the initiative in question. If the process-led change programme is extensive in scope it may be possible to bring smaller projects within its jurisdiction (and sometimes this is necessary to prevent overlap and duplication). If the change programme is smaller in scale it may be sufficient to be aware of the existence and objectives of other projects, and to monitor the main changes planned. In either case, communication is paramount—project managers have to be advised of key changes and activities so that any implications can be identified.

Rule 5: Manage the Sponsor

The importance of sponsorship has been highlighted by the post mortem of almost every major change initiative over the past few years. Having a high-profile, influential figure as a champion for the changes taking place is essential to bring transformation about.

But sponsorship has to be more than the occasional nodding visit by the chief executive. It has to be an active involvement, based on a real understanding of the changes taking place. Too many sponsors merely see their role to be the odd half day chatting to the members of the change team or sitting in on the occasional workshop. Such activities make no real contribution to actually making change happen.

The effectiveness of sponsorship is dependent on bringing credibility to the changes and "clout" to the decisions being made; doing so requires a fundamental understanding of the changes taking place. The reality is that the sponsor has to be in a position to get behind the unpopular decisions as well as the popular ones to help carry the changes through. To this end, the sponsor needs to be managed to ensure that the greatest impact can be leveraged from his or her position, including being:

- exposed to the complex realities of change, not just the dramatic ground-breaking aspects
- used to drive the sensitive issues such as changes to pay and remuneration and job roles
- pointed towards the problem areas as well as the successful ones
- used as one of the key mouthpieces to the organisation to explain why the changes are necessary

Those managing and driving the change have enough to occupy their time without having to justify every change to the wider organisation, or continue to petition the board for more resource and ongoing commitment. The sponsor has to be closely involved so that he or she can take on more of the "enabling" work to shift the roadblocks and clear the way forward. Too many organisations see sponsorship as merely a figurehead role. The risk is that in doing so the commitment to change will remain only skin deep.

Rule 6: Lead by Example—The Change Team

Having considered the size of the change task in some detail, it can be seen that the responsibility for actually making change happen is an onerous one. The change team—the core group of process designers, managers, and project and process managers who design and drive the change—are the key bearers of this responsibility. But as well as delivering results, the change team have to act as a focal point for change itself, leading and even inspiring the rest of the organisation by example and action.

Given that much of the overall framework within which process-led change takes place is new, an important part of this is in demonstrating understanding and confidence in the overall approach to change. This has to be underpinned by a professionalism and attitude that reassures the wider organisation and the various supporting functions which will be involved (IT development, marketing, personnel etc.) in making the changes happen.

But, in addition, every contact with the rest of the organisation should be used as an opportunity to spread the word of change. The change team have to act as ambassadors for change, with every action and involvement with the wider organisation used to seed the confidence and enthusiasm for the changes taking place. As well as the specifics of the approach, this should be used to instil the desired solution-orientated culture. Staff will always be cynical about change, and the impact of seeing their own colleagues talking, leading and driving the change in practice is a much more powerful lever for change than yet another management homily. Contact with the change team should send those involved away with a whole new sense of energy to help make the change happen.

Staff co-opted onto the core change team for shorter periods of time should also be seen as a channel for change, when they return to their normal operational duties. One member of staff enthusing about the changes taking place from his or her own involvement and experience of the change activities will be a far more effective way of spreading commitment at the grassroots level than any formal communication can be.

THE PROGRAMME MANAGEMENT FUNCTION

This chapter has talked about the disciplines and responsibilities of programme management, and its role in enabling the whole programme of change to come about.

In reality, the activity of programme management is likely to form a project in its own right, just as systems development or HR design or training might. As well as architecting and coordinating the activities of other project areas, the programme management function or project is likely to have the following responsibilities:

- to architect the programme design, allocating deliverables and responsibilities for those deliverables to different projects
- to assist individual project managers in the identification of deliverables and planning of their sub-projects
- to plan and coordinate the overall production of the various deliverables so that the change programme can be completed by the given date. This includes updating programme plans in line with project plans
- to monitor the progress of deliverables and ensure they are delivered by the due date
- to review and adjust the allocation of resources to project areas
- to monitor the quality of deliverables and ensure their acceptance and sign off
- to take any necessary recovery action where problems and delays occur
- to monitor risks and dependencies and take any necessary further action
- to be the guardian of standards, versions and revision to deliverables
- to initiate, coordinate and implement change management
- to work closely with the communications project to identify communication and education needs and audiences

Earlier, the analogy of the control tower was used to explain programme management. It may also be seen as a role of coordination and clearing house, which ensures that all of the pieces in the process jigsaw will ultimately fit into place so that the new infrastructure can be created.

☞ SIGNPOSTS FOR SUCCESS

Avoid perfectionism

In these days, when the enthusiasm for quality runs so strong, it may seem like the voice of a heretic to suggest seeking anything other than the perfect solution. The truth, though, is that a quality solution can usually be achieved long before a perfect one.

In a project environment, where so much work is interconnected—the systems analyst relies on the process designers, plans for the testing team rely on the system design team, next year's budgets rest on the new organisational design—an attitude of perfectionism has to be avoided. Nobody likes to release a piece of work before it is complete, but sometimes the emphasis has to be on fit for purpose, rather than fit for a king. Dotting is and crossing ts does not always add any further value, and the most sophisticated solution is not always the most effective. The focus has to be firmly on the improvement of the overall processes—measured either quantitatively or qualitatively—and often the flow of benefits will begin to dry up long before a perfect solution is implemented.

Delegate as far as you dare

One message that should be clear by now is the amount of work that process-led change is likely to entail and the diversity of areas of the enterprise in which it has to take place.

The result is that no matter how good the programme manager or how innovative the process design team, everyday people in everyday jobs and project teams have to be called on to bring about the implementation. Not only is this the only way to ensure that all of the changes can be undertaken, it is the only way to ensure their acceptance—ultimately change works through involvement and ownership, not imposition.

Deliverables and projects allow the work that must be undertaken to be handed down to the people of an organisation so that they can help to make it work. With the appropriate standards in place, the work can be coordinated and controlled. Delegation, then, has to go as far as you dare.

Push the pace

By its nature, major change requires activity in many areas of the business at once, and invariably these changes have to be implemented within a framework of tight time scales. Add to this the interdependency of many areas of work—new processes require new IS support, new IS support needs new hardware platforms, new systems need retrained staff—and the pressures to get the job done become ever greater. Often the interdependent nature of the work can mean that one person's (or one project's) delay can be a bottleneck for other design, development and deployment activities.

To this end, it is necessary to instil and maintain a vigorous and ambitious pace of change within the transformation programme. Major change cannot take place at a dawdle, yet there are still many organisations where the attitude is one of working to fill the hours in the day rather than to get a particular piece of work completed. The project "mindset" has to be firmly established with its focus on getting results delivered, and this needs to be underpinned by the setting of ambitious goals, ensuring that people are continuously stretched to ensure that the multitude of change activities can actually be achieved in the time allowed.

Refresh the team

The points above have highlighted both the fundamental importance of the change team in bringing about change, and the pressures and responsibilities upon them. In turn, this means that staff within the team have to be well looked after, to ensure that they do not run out of steam and energy before the changes have been implemented. On the one hand, this has to be carried out by motivating and sustaining those actually carrying out change—something that is often forgotten in the relentless push for deadlines, deliverables and implementation. Now and again it is important to sit back and ensure appropriate credit (and, where appropriate, reward) is given to those involved.

Secondly, it is important that the team who manage and deliver change are from time to time refreshed with new blood, by regularly cycling in new team members from the wider organisation. As well as the renewed energy and drive this provides, it allows those members of the team who are replaced to return to the wider organisation. Besides allowing them to return to continue their careers and jobs beyond the project, this provides an opportunity to spread the message of change at a grassroots level in their operational capacity.

Create ownership

One of the biggest dangers of project working is that it allows a gap to open up between those developing new capabilities and those who will ultimately be responsible for staffing and managing the new ways of working. The "them and us" attitude is perpetuated, ultimately detracting from the success of the new ways of working when they are implemented.

This gap has to be filled by creating a real sense of ownership of the products of the change programme—whether they are deliverables or new ways of working, new measures or new skills and competencies—from the earliest point possible. This is encouraged by involving staff and managers from within the organisation at all points of the design, development and deployment process. The sooner an attitude of "we're in this together" is created, the more readily acceptable the changes are likely to be. It has to be made clear from an early stage that the change activities are not a package that is suddenly handed over after two years, rather that "we're all in this together". Such involvement and ownership is particularly crucial if there is any significant involvement of external consultants in the change programme, which tends to foster the "not invented here" type of response, in a further attempt to shrug off ownership. Early implementation of processes in a partial format, by facilitating a gradual takeover rather than a big bang approach, is also key to creating ownership.

Chapter 12

Education and Communication

A genuine understanding of the importance of communication has dawned late in the day in major change programmes. For years, survey after survey and textbook after textbook have highlighted the importance of communication. In the early 1990s companies battled with downsizing, re-engineering and BPR initiatives, some enjoying more success than others. After them came the post mortems and the inquests, and these too documented almost religiously the importance of communication.

But although its importance was acknowledged, a real understanding of communication has continued to elude most organisations. Some lessons pointed to structured communication programmes and closely targeted audience segments, while others pushed the burden away in the direction of training and development. But there were no real disciplines put in place. Communication tended to remain an add-on, a technique to announce a training programme or introduce the project steering committee.

To pitch communication in such a limited role is to miss the point. Communication and education are the linchpins of successful change, the very lubricants which oil the wheels of progress. Change of any kind is upsetting. It takes away all that is familiar and comfortable, and replaces it with turmoil and fluidity. It creates uncertainty and cynicism and often resistance. For change to be successful people need answers and explanations; they have to be shown how working methods will change and what their new jobs will look like. But, most of all, they need reassurance; reassurance that has to be provided by communication if they are to have confidence in the journey they are making.

Furthermore, the process-led approach brings its own additional demands for education and communication. Making the transition to a process-structured organisation is right and is essential, but it is a radically different view, a view that requires new concepts, development methods and ways of managing, and people get it wrong again and again. In taking up such an orientation a whole programme of education is required to ensure that the organisation can grasp the process mindset.

Communication is critical to process-led change, but it can no longer be treated as just another technique in the change toolbox to be sprinkled around just before roll-out. It has to be comprehensive—delivered from the centre so that it underpins every amendment made and every alteration implemented. It has to be core to the whole change programme.

COMMUNICATING WHAT? GETTING TO GRIPS WITH THE SUBJECT

The chapters preceding this one have dissected the change programme down to its lower levels of detail. In doing so, they have illustrated the vast amount of work to be undertaken—whether in design or definition, development or deployment. Embedded in the fabric of these changes are innumerable implications for communications—both implicit and explicit.

The significance of the change task makes the scope of communication far broader than was ever realised. It is about far more than just telling staff about new ways of working; it is essential to the whole change programme—a means of tackling resistance, changing culture and ensuring buy-in. Education and communication needs break down into five areas (Figure 12.1):

- *Process.* Process is a new way of viewing, managing and operating a business. It requires a fundamental reorientation in the way work is done and managed. It comes with its own terminology and conventions. Worse still, it is not a subject that is easily grasped first time. People think they understand process when they don't. You only have to ask for a definition of process to show how widespread the confusion is. The whole concept of process takes a long time, and many repetitions, to sink home. It requires a comprehensive and ongoing education programme to ensure that the process mindset takes root. (For most of the organisation a higher level understanding about the need to reorganise around processes is enough. For some, such as process managers and those concerned with measuring and monitoring processes, a more in-depth grasp is needed.)
- *The method.* Communication and education about the method of change are frequently overlooked. Those managing a change programme have a clear understanding of their approach to change, and all too often assume that it exists in those co-opted or recruited to assist them. In reality, if process is one new concept to grasp, process-led change is something quite different again. The approach has to be clearly articulated to those tasked

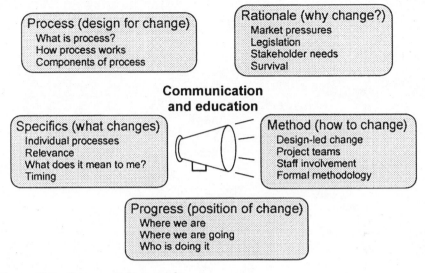

Figure 12.1 Communication needs

with delivering it. New ways of working, such as parallelism and iteration, have to be communicated, and new cultures of contribution and team working nurtured. Chapter 3 outlined these fundamentals of process-led change.

- *The rationale.* It is the most basic messages that so often are missing from a change programme. These are the messages about the rationale for change, the very reasons for all the upheaval and discomfort. Senior management are so close to the pressures they face that they take them as read, but further down the organisation such knowledge is much less widespread. Understanding these issues helps smooth the path of change; when staff can see why change is necessary, rather than having it thrust upon them, commitment and buy-in come much easier. Expecting people to accept change with no real understanding of the rationale is like expecting a patient to happily enter the operating theatre with no clue about what illness is about to be treated.

- *Progress.* People need to be kept aware of the direction, status and progress of various parts of the change programme. Exact communications will depend on the stage of the project; in the early days the focus will be on overall aims and approach; in time, it will move on to the work being carried out in particular project areas. These progress updates include the main deliverables of an area (appropriately interpreted for understanding) and the key players and their relation to other aspects of the programme, and relevance is key. Staff relate far more closely to specific dates when

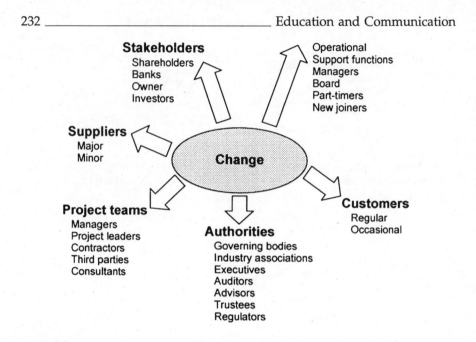

Figure 12.2 The audience

they are likely to see some tangible changes than a description of what code is being cut in the development shop.

- *The changes.* Finally, and most obviously, communication has to be made about the changes themselves. These are the specifics about how working methods change, jobs have to be redesigned, departments reorganised and systems re-coded. These are the essentials of change, which people are waiting to hear about. But they are far from the only ones.

Looking at the subject matter reveals just how big the task is. It is one of education as much as communication. People do not learn about process-led change from a few newsletters.

KNOWING YOUR AUDIENCE

Communication and education have to encompass far more players than immediate employees (Figure 12.2). Everyone from CEO to filing clerk and once-a-year customer to main supplier may have to be informed of the changes under way at some point, and advised of the impact these will have on their particular area. In some areas this will merely be a point of courtesy, advising those affected of a change to procedures or operating methods; in others it will require a more fundamental shift in working methods, and a more vigorous "selling" exercise or education programme to ensure that new ways are accepted.

Reverence for Relevance

For communication and education to be successful, each message or explanation must be tailored to the appropriate audience. Early on in the project this means identifying segments, and determining the messages that must be conveyed to those segments or groups. Later, when the final details and specific changes to individual job roles and organisational structures emerge, it means tailoring messages ever further; ultimately, it means sitting down with individuals on a one to one basis to clarify the implications for their particular role.

This in turn demands that those driving and leading the change are able to communicate many different messages, to many different audiences. On the one hand, they may have to explain the impact of changes to stakeholders and shareholders. Later, they may interpret the changes from the point of view of front-line employees, sharing a vision of the way in which they will be interacting with customers and with each other; yet again, they will have to send messages to middle managers, showing how their role changes from one of delegator and hands-on specialist to one of coach and facilitator.

The following rules of thumb help to ensure that messages are adequately focused:

- *Set the context.* An understanding of the end to end process that is being changed has to be fostered so that individual staff are aware of their role as part of a bigger picture. At the same time concepts have to be converted into specifics and designs into reality.
- *Interpret.* The early stages of a change programme focus on design activities and the development of new capabilities, without delivering much new to the organisation itself. Process designs, which are conceptual, have to be interpreted to show what the "brave new world" in theory will actually look like in practice. This can be achieved using "scenarios", which show how current business situations and events are handled by the new processes.
- *"What does it mean to me?"* Ultimately, this should be the guiding force behind every communication. People get out of bed and come to work to perform a particular job role; at the end of the day they are interested in how their job changes, not the overall migration of the organisation into a new shape. Change might be happening at an organisational, national (and even global) level but, realistically, individuals are rarely interested in every aspect of it. They are interested in how it affects them. Sooner or later every communication has to get down to the level of answering "What does it mean for me?".

- *Roll-down measures.* CEOs and board directors understand the need for change because they are close to the figures that drive an organisation's performance. Whether it be the need for a 5% cut in costs or the opportunity for 11% growth, their proximity to the "drivers" ensures that they understand the imperatives for change. But further down the organisation these measures have less bearing on performance. Tapping data into a keyboard or assembling goods on a production line, it is difficult to see what relevance "11% growth" has. The work you do will be the same tomorrow and the day after, regardless of that. To see the point and relevance of such change the measures or performance drivers that a business navigates have to be clearly visible. This is achieved by rolling down high-level figures and targets to operational, process and unit level, through mechanisms such as the balanced scorecard, until they can be seen in the light of day to day work and changes. In one organisation this involved distributing a list of over 70 "structured objectives" to business units to make the changes relevant.
- *Terminology and language.* Different audiences have different vocabularies, so communications have to be couched in terms that people understand. Endless talk about "process", for example, is not meaningful—changes have to be explained in terms of their impact on functions and day to day transactions that people understand. Jargon and buzzwords have to be rigorously slain. "Pressures on the business" have to be translated into the actions that competitors are taking and the legislation that the government has announced.

COMMUNICATION AND EDUCATION: FROM CONCEPT TO DISCIPLINE

Communication has remained a nebulous subject for too long. While there has been general agreement that it is important, and that it encompasses concepts and ideas which have to be tackled, it has remained an indistinct discipline lacking specific actions to be completed or steps to follow. The result at the end of the day is that communication has all too often been limited to a few glossy project newsletters and a forgotten suggestions box. Communication is essential for change, everyone has agreed. But nobody seems to know what to do.

To play its part, communication has to grow up. It has to be refined from a few wishlists and ideas to a discipline that can be designed, planned, managed and measured as an active part of the change programme. It has to become a whole portfolio of well-thought-out techniques and approaches, which can identify communication needs and design messages across the

	Process owner	IT department	HR department	Wider organisation	Stakeholders	Customers
Process (theory)	Detail	Detail plus IT specifics	Detail plus HR specifics	Key concepts	Overview	None
Method and approach	Detail	Detail	Detail	None	Overview	None
Rationale for change	Overview	Overview	Overview	Detail	Overview, possible detail depending on who	Relevant parts of high level overview
Specifics of process change	Detail (via process specification)	Detail (via process specification)	Detail (via process specification)	Detail in specific areas	Overview	Detail in specific areas
Progress	Detail, all areas	Detail, own areas; overview others	Detail, own areas; overview others	General overview, more detail in specific areas	Overview	Where it affects or is about to affect them

Figure 12.3 Communication and education plan

whole programme rather than just send out the odd flyer about demonstration systems and training seminars.

To achieve this, the role of communication in the whole change programme has to be assigned a new status. Communication is rarely given the weight and attention it needs on a project; frequently it is treated as a poor relation, perhaps assigned a place in the marketing or internal communications department. Ideally, communication should become an area of its own on the project, which is managed, resourced and aligned with other areas of work that are under way.

A Communications and Education Plan

Like much at the heart of process-led change, communication has been clouded by hype and confusing claims. But the basis of communication is simple. It is about considering:

- *what has to be communicated*
- *who it has to be communicated to*
- *how the communication (or message) is to be delivered*

The first stage is to establish an outline of communication and education needs across the whole programme. This is done by considering the areas in which communications are needed, and the people or audiences to which they must be made (Figure 12.3). As ever, the changes as specified in the process designs must be the source of requirements.

These communications reflect requirements at one particular point in time, in the case of Figure 12.3, a relatively early stage in the project. But communication needs do not remain static. Just as a consumer market matures and needs different messages, so too do the people within an organisation as a change programme progresses. Usually, this shift is reflected in a move from generalities to specifics, with concepts such as processes being replaced by the specifics of new job roles and computer systems, new management structures and performance measures.

Channels

The matrix in Figure 12.3 is used to establish the overall requirements for communication; in particular, it answers the "who" and the "what" questions. The next stage is to consider the most appropriate channels (or mechanisms) by which these communications are to be delivered. Sending (and reinforcing) communications by a number of different channels is essential to success, as any dyed in the wool member of the marketing or advertising trade will confirm.

Different channels obviously have different characteristics in terms of their suitability and effectiveness, some being more suited to relatively straightforward, simple messages being sent to a mass audience, and others more suited to smaller groupings or segments. One of the key differences is whether a channel is two-way or not. Typically, the channel shown in Figure 12.4 may be used.

Selecting the most appropriate channel depends on the subject being communicated, the audience, the level of existing knowledge and the need for any two-way dialogue. During launch, a simple booklet or overview of the change programme may be used to repeat key messages given at the launch event. When demonstrating with customers the new format for products or services, a seminar or workshop may be more effective; when explaining to individuals their new job roles and responsibilities, a one to one, face to face meeting is likely to be the most appropriate.

The Message

The design and preparation of the message is concerned with the "shape" or content of the message and any adaptation needed to address the audience or suit the channel itself. Obviously, the content of the message must be based on any experience of previous communications and knowledge of the audience, such as their understanding of and receptiveness to the messages.

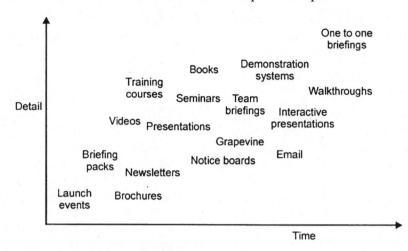

Figure 12.4 Channels of communication

The overriding essential, though, is that of relevance. This relates to both the destination of the message itself (is it going to the right audience?) and the actual content of the message. Often those close to development make the mistake of trying to communicate the features of new processes and systems to staff in the organisation. The result is that staff are told about new databases and increased processing power or new organisational structures. These, in the main, are irrelevant. The real benefits and advantages to users (ease of use, consistency, validation etc.), rather than features, need to be picked out and communicated.

Message design and preparation is a skilled task and a critical role. One of the key roles of those responsible for communications is to assist other people in the organisation in the design and preparation of the key messages in their communications, given that those who are the source of subjects to be communicated (e.g. process owner or IT designer) are rarely the best suited to designing the message because they are too close to the subject matter. Messages should be tested wherever possible, even if at a most basic level they are simply "walked-through" other people on the project team before being released.

The role requires someone with the skills to interpret subjects and design messages but also able to develop a grasp of the whole breadth of the project. It is a role that must be undertaken by appropriately skilled staff, not merely assigned to whoever is left over on the project team.

Prepare for Delivery

The final stage is the delivery of the message or communication itself. This is mainly concerned with the logistics of ensuring that the message is delivered, such as booking rooms, preparing handouts, printing and distributing materials—or simply ensuring that the CEO gets to the podium at the briefing centre on time.

Measure

The final step in communication (or the last link in the circle before starting again) is to measure the effectiveness of the communications made to ensure that gaps and inadequacies in the communication programme can be identified and appropriate action taken to address them. Measurement is undertaken in two ways. Firstly, this is done formally by means of surveys, questionnaires, feedback forms etc. to test the water and determine whether communications are getting through. Secondly, and equally importantly, these methods have to be supplemented by informal, more qualitative means, which determine the level of understanding and comprehension "on the ground". Whatever methods are most appropriate have to be used, from asking managers to gauge levels of understanding in their staff to tapping into the informal fabric of the organisation's grapevine.

THE STICKING POINTS

The areas outlined in Figure 12.3 are all primarily a top-down attempt to root out communications needs. Like every area of change management, the specifics of deliverables and project plans have to be complemented by a safety net of more informal activities.

One of the most important sources of communication needs is the sticking points—the areas of the project where messages are not hitting the mark, whether they fail to arrive, are misinterpreted or are ignored entirely. These problem areas have to be assimilated formally (through measuring the success of communications campaigns) but also informally through channels of casual gossip, the organisation's grapevine and the off-hand opinions and instincts of appropriate individuals. Issues are key to identifying the areas where problems are arising. As well as seeking out the problems that arise through poorly designed or delivered messages, such informal "listening and sensing" activities help to identify the areas of resistance. In either case, appropriate messages then have to be designed, depending on the nature of the problem (Figure 12.5).

Communication that merely bombards people with information about launch events or training programmes fails to address the real issues of change. It is the ability to address the underlying concerns and worries that marks the difference between reasonable communication and acceptance of change. Communication and education should envelop the people and

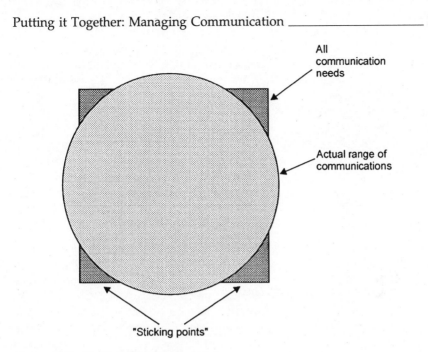

All
communication
needs

Actual range of
communications

"Sticking points"

Figure 12.5 Finding the sticking points

stakeholders of an organisation in a cloak of information so specific and so relevant to their individual concerns that they are swept along.

PUTTING IT TOGETHER: MANAGING COMMUNICATION

Communication and education can no longer be an afterthought to a major change programme. The extent of subjects and variety of audiences demand that a comprehensive approach to communication is established at day one (and, indeed, often it precedes day one of the real activity on the project). There is a need actively to solicit communication needs from areas of the project, then to plan and monitor the delivery of appropriate messages and education programmes. Communication, in all but the smallest projects, therefore needs to exist as a project area in its own right, providing a key resource that can be called upon by other areas of the transformation programme.

Not least, this demands a serious budget commitment so that (typically full-time) staff can be assigned to the communications role. There will be those who claim that this is overkill, and a more basic communications programme can be carried out with less resource. But such an economy is a false one, which leaves too many gaps unplugged. Those working within project areas are just not able to give the time and attention necessary to ensure good communication; they are too wrapped up in the subject matter itself to give adequate attention to how best to communicate it to specific audiences. The responsibility for communication therefore needs to lie with a dedicated team.

The overriding responsibility of this team is one of facilitator playing the role of broker or agency, just as agencies in the advertising or marketing industry advise clients on how best to get their messages across to the market. The communications team are therefore a resource to every other area of the change programme, to assist in the identification, packaging, coordination and delivery of messages. Their prime roles are to:

- Actively seek out the subject areas where communication needs arise, and consider the audiences they have to be propagated to. This requires an overall knowledge of what is being undertaken in different project areas as well as an ability to delve into detail where necessary.
- To work with those in individual project areas to determine the communications needs. This involves providing the service and advice necessary to put the message or communication together—assisting in the selection of channels, media, content etc. The role is one of facilitation and organisation as much as actual communication.
- To coordinate messages and their timing. During the long months of a change programme, many hundreds of messages have to be communicated—some organisation-wide, some to individuals; some contentious and some straightforward. Coordination is required to avoid conflict and confusion, and to maximise impact. For example, it may be important to begin demonstrating new computer prototypes at the same time as internal recruitment to staff a pilot team is launched. The team must also coordinate messages with wider organisational communications.
- To develop communications and education programmes in such a way that consistency and reusability are maximised. Where necessary, education needs may be handed over to Training for delivery.

Overall, the role is a difficult but crucial one, requiring a unique mix of skills. Those responsible need to be able to understand messages, and the requirements of those messages, without becoming so close to the detail that they become lost in it. Yet, as with other aspects of transformation, it is the ability to back up the structured, deliverable-based aspects of change with the subtle, qualitative techniques and "feelers" that is the key to success. The ability to sense the nuances and read the undercurrents of an organisation's people is as important as the ability to manage the delivery of a presentation. The concerns and worries of staff must be fed into the communications package, as well as the dates of new systems delivery. The role may involve chivvying senior management about what to say and how to say it as much as sending out project newsletters. Like the hidden speech writer and PR agent of the politician, it is a background and seldom seem role, but a critical one nevertheless.

CRUXES OF COMMUNICATION

The stages described above outline an approach to developing a comprehensive communications and education programme during process-led change. In addition, a number of rules for good communication underpin the more mechanistic, structured steps:

- *Listen.* Amid the mass of messages that have to be transmitted, it is often forgotten that communication is a two-way process. On the one hand, this means ensuring that presentations, seminars and awareness workshops have plenty of time for questioning built in. Staff should be encouraged and allowed to raise their concerns and issues. On the other, it means from time to time it is necessary to actively poll those in the organisation for their concerns—to go to staff, management and those on the project team merely to listen, to ask what problems there are, to solicit concerns and to identify worries. This should be done with a completely open agenda, not to take views on particular subjects. Most resistance and obstruction to change grows out of small concerns, often because those concerns are the ones that have been overlooked in the overall communications programme. However good the communications plan outline is, it will inevitably prove to be inadequate in certain areas. Listening helps to identify the concerns, and identifying the concerns allows the missing areas to be targeted.
- *Multiple messages, multiple channels.*Communication is not just about sending messages. For communication to be effective, it must change levels of understanding and ultimately alter behaviour. The reality of life is, of course, that even if the message is good, it will not always "hit the spot" first time. Sometimes the audience is not listening or more pressing concerns distract. And even when the message or communication gets through, it usually needs reinforcing several times, from several different sources, before it sticks. Communicating the concept of process itself is a classic example—it may appear to have been absorbed but it takes many passes before people really come to understand the underlying fabric of it, and can apply it in a way that actually allows working methods to be changed.
- *Hearts and minds.* Communication cannot be restricted merely to the things that can be touched and felt. Communication is as much about overcoming fears and worries as it is about telling people what the new

organisational structure will look like or when the next version of the customer database will be released. Change requires people to let go of old ways and embrace new ones—but the transition between the two is littered with a thousand and one doubts and fears about the unknown, many of them personal and emotional rather than logical and rational. It is these very personal feelings and concerns that have to be addressed by communication—whether through a corporate-wide campaign, or in a one to one briefing by a manager. It may be blindingly obvious to the CEO or the programme manager that competitive pressures mean that the nature of the job has to be changed, but try telling that to the hourly paid worked who has pulled the same levers and completed the same tasks day in, day out for the past 15 years. The concerns that exist may not seem rational, sensible or logical when viewed from the context of a new process design. But exist they do, none the less, and so they have to be addressed. If staff feel nervous about taking on a wider job role, then they have to be reassured about how new skills and capabilities can be developed; if they fear for the future security of their jobs, then they need to be told the realities; and if they are dragging their feet because they fear a drop in overtime, then these concerns have to be faced head on.

- *Don't underestimate the audience.* Most organisations are much smarter than their senior management give them credit for. This is particularly true when it comes to filtering management "propaganda". Staff can determine, often before managers, when things are going wrong; the organisational grapevine which operates in the canteen, the smoking room and the bar still disseminates information far more effectively than any e-mail system. People need to be given the facts—the good and the bad, the encouraging and the worrying—to have faith in what they are being told. Attempting to pull the wool over corporate eyes fools no one—staff have seen change initiatives before and they know that failures will occur and some promises not be delivered. Far better, then, to admit this and deliver the truth than to send out some perfectionist propaganda, which attempts to convince the organisation that every project plan is on target and every project under budget.

- *Illustrate and interpret.* Many communications fail to be effective because they remain too theoretical and abstract. Messages communicated have to be interwoven with examples and anecdotes to make them relevant and memorable. Talk about the specific services provided by competitors that customers are defecting to—not just the fact that competition requires the business to change. Phrases like "process improvement" are just so much hot air to the man on the production line—it is the restrictions that make his job harder eliminated by the new process designs which will make him sit up and take notice. Role play a customer transaction to show how it changes step by step, rather than just talking about new ways of working.

Share the corporate budgets, cost schedules and profit targets with staff, rather than just talking about the need to be more effective.

● *Harness the side effects.* It is an over-used cliché, but nevertheless a true one, that actions speak louder than words. A feature of the process-led approach is the number of changes that are happening at once and this is a key strength when it comes to communication. Seeing is believing, and when staff see that a process perspective is being rewarded, or can experience demonstration of new computer screens at the same time as they hear of new ways of working, behaving and managing, much more notice is taken. Actively harnessing other areas of the change—and coordinating communications with their appearance and roll-out—helps to ensure the maximum impact of communications, and the most effective uptake of messages.

WHO'S ROLE IS IT ANYWAY? THE LINK TO TRAINING AND CULTURE CHANGE

Throughout this book there has been an unflagging emphasis on the importance of a holistic approach to change. An enterprise and the capabilities within it are so diverse that to attempt to bring about change with one rather than several elements will never succeed.

Similarly, there are many different areas of capability development, some of which will inevitably overlap. So it is with communication, education and development. Confusion often arises when a communication requirement becomes so detailed that it appears to be verging on a training requirement. The rule of thumb is that once education and communication needs become substantial enough to require more than half a day's effort to be invested, they are best treated as a training requirement.

The important point, though, as much as demarcation, is one of identification. Where a need is perceived—whether it is called training or development or education—it has to be identified so that it can become a properly managed responsibility. This ensures that it will be undertaken. Whether it is ultimately carried out by those responsible for training or those responsible for communication is of lesser importance.

☞ SIGNPOSTS FOR SUCCESS

Be honest and open

At the end of the day, this is the overriding principle of communication. Emphasise the good, successful projects, but be honest about the failures and problems rather than trying to brush them off or disguise them. Staff within organisations have seen too many changes and too many half truths to have the wool pulled over the eyes any more. They understand that things go wrong; to pretend otherwise, and always preach "good news", only encourages cynicism about the reliability of the communication.

Take care with HR

The most sensitive messages tend to be those within the remit of human resources, in particular those relating to terms, conditions, salary and performance. If necessary, test the message first, because the most seemingly insignificant aspect of such communications tends to be picked up and misconstrued.

Seek reusability

Wherever possible, design communications materials so that they can be reused. Communications have to be made to suppliers, stakeholders, sponsors and customers so the continual rewriting and designing of such messages must be avoided. Most messages have to be sent and re-sent—key points and concepts should be structured and stored in a modular form so that they can readily be extracted and used in other contexts. Communications should be studied for their impact and the most effective methods, channels and materials. Particular texts and explanatory documents (e.g. induction packs, and set texts which explain about processes) should be retained for frequent use.

Test and measure

Test communications in trial areas before they are released organisation-wide. This restricts any misunderstandings or confusions to local rather than organisation-wide impact. Measure the results of communications to determine effectiveness, and identify further areas of need and misunderstanding that have to be addressed.

Copy the pros

Professional advertisers and marketeers are paid vast amounts of money to market and sell images, brands, concepts and products successfully. Mimic the techniques of the pros, which include segmentation, multiple reinforcement, and the selling of benefits while paying attention to timing and packaging.

Communicate constantly

Many organisations make the mistake of believing that communication is about telling staff something. It's not. It is about telling them something in as many different ways as it takes until they understand it and moderate their behaviour accordingly. One manager described this as the drive to get people to a point where they "think nothing else but process, rather than always trying to get the message across". Communication about key points has to go on almost until people are bored with it.

Problems as well as solutions

It is important to remind people of the pressures for changes as well as the solutions being created and rolled out. Getting staff to understand the business imperatives is a key part of building commitment. If a shared understanding of the problems can be nurtured, then a shared commitment to implementing the solution is more likely to follow. Use whatever mechanisms it takes to do this so that the rationale for change is not too distant—the Balanced Scorecard, competitor analysis, measures broken down to a process or business unit level.

Look out

Do not forget those beyond the organisation's boundaries. Customers, suppliers, stakeholders, regulatory bodies and associations, unions and industry watchdogs may all have to be involved in the project at some point. The clarity of the message (and the relevance of the benefits) ensures that these groups are brought behind the change effort rather than resisting or obstructing it.

Refresh the team

Those who manage and deliver communications have to be refreshed with new blood and ideas to avoid getting stale. New ideas and feedback should be sought from the grassroots of the organisation to ensure that communications reflect the current state of understanding and knowledge.

Tap the grapevine

The informal grapevine or "gossip" within an organisation gives a fascinating insight into the temperature, feelings and emotion of an organisation. Whatever formal or managed means exist for two-way communication, feedback and upward appraisal, the grapevine will always remain a more ready indicator of the way the people in an organisation think and feel. For one, the grapevine enjoys a feeling of freedom and excitement (in part, at least, because it is something not controlled by management) which positively encourages people to participate. Rather like the Internet, it works, and works effectively, because people get a buzz out of it through expressing whatever they want across its wires. Secondly, the grapevine is powerful because people speak freely. Because management does not control it, people express the opinions they really feel, rather than the ones they believe management want to hear. In an age of job insecurity and increasingly frayed bonds of loyalty, the disenfranchised worker has become ever more skilful at telling the boss what he wants to hear or "making the right noises".

Induct

Finally, it is important to remember that, just as the audience as a whole matures, so it also changes in parts. Newcomers to the organisation have to be brought up to speed with the direction of the change programme, so key messages and education (process, project teams etc.) have to be incorporated into induction materials and initiation for the new joiners.

Index